Child Abduction

Child Abduction

Prevention, Investigation, and Recovery

ROBERT L. SNOW

Westport, Connecticut
London

Library of Congress Cataloging-in-Publication Data

Snow, Robert L.
  Child abduction : prevention, investigation, and recovery / Robert L. Snow.
    p. cm.
  Includes bibliographical references and index.
  ISBN 978–0–313–34786–3 (alk. paper)
1. Abduction. 2. Abduction—United States. 3. Children—Crimes against—Prevention. I.
Title.
HV6571.S65   2008
364.15'4083—dc22   2008020461

British Library Cataloguing in Publication Data is available.

Library of Congress Catalog Card Number: 2008020461
ISBN: 978–0–313–34786–3

First published in 2008

Praeger Publishers, 88 Post Road West, Westport, CT 06881
An imprint of Greenwood Publishing Group, Inc.
www.praeger.com

Printed in the United States of America

The paper used in this book complies with the
Permanent Paper Standard issued by the National
Information Standards Organization (Z39.48–1984).

10 9 8 7 6 5 4 3 2 1

This book is dedicated to my old Air Force buddy, Ed Kawasaki.

Remembering all of our escapades, and for over 40 years of friendship.

Contents

Child Abductions in the United States

It was every parent's worst nightmare. Steve Groene's eight-year-old daughter Shasta, nine-year-old son Dylan, and 13-year-old son Slade lived with his ex-wife Brenda and her boyfriend Mark McKenzie. Early in the morning of May 16, 2005, someone broke into his ex-wife's house in Coeur d'Alene, Idaho, and killed her, Mark, and Slade. The intruder, police detectives later told the father, then likely abducted Shasta and Dylan. For Steve Groene, it was unbelievable. Things like that just didn't happen in Coeur d'Alene. People living around there felt so safe they didn't have deadbolts, and often didn't even use the regular locks.

The detectives assigned to the case, even though believing the children had been abducted, had no idea where the murderer had taken them, or even if the children were still alive. Abductors of children often kill their victims within hours of the abduction. Hundreds of searchers, some on foot, some on horses, and others driving all-terrain vehicles, combed the heavy woods around the crime scene, looking for the missing children. In the hope of increasing their chances of success, the police also brought in a helicopter and even cadaver-sniffing dogs.

"We're looking for anything right now, whether it be the children, the children's bodies or evidence—a scrap of clothing, anything like that," said Kootenia County Sheriff's Captain Ben Wolfinger.[1]

For Steve Groene, though, the brutal and bewildering uncertainty about the welfare of his children was nearly unbearable. Were they still alive? Were they being raped, tortured? What was happening to them? Unfortunately, he would be forced to live with this heart-crushing anxiety for over six weeks before finally learning the fate of his two children.

Although the police didn't find out for many weeks afterward what had happened to the Groene children, later investigation would show that in the early morning hours of May 16, 2005, Shasta and Dylan had been awakened by their mother calling for them to get out of bed and come into the living room. When the two sleepy-eyed children walked into the living room, they both stopped abruptly when they saw a stranger standing there holding a shotgun. The children's mother, her boyfriend, and their brother Slade had been bound with zip ties and duct tape. The police would later identify the man holding the shotgun as 42-year-old Joseph Edward Duncan, III, a registered sex offender.

None of the obviously terrified people in the living room that morning knew it, but Duncan was at that time on the run from Minnesota, where he had skipped bail on child molestation charges. Even though Duncan had been listed in Minnesota as a high-risk sex offender, diagnosed in his youth as an antisocial personality and sexual deviant, a judge had released him on only $15,000 bail following his arrest for the sexual assault of a six-year-old boy on a playground. Before skipping the state, though, Duncan had stopped at a discount store and purchased the equipment he would use in Idaho: a shotgun, a video recorder, and night vision goggles.

Prior though to his most recent arrest in Minnesota, Duncan had spent much of his life in prison for other sex crimes against children. Because during his youth he had demonstrated an aggressive sexual attraction to children, Duncan, before finally being sent to prison, had first been ordered to attend a sex offender treatment program. Regardless, however, of the judge's threat of what would happen if he didn't successfully complete this program, Duncan wouldn't cooperate with those running it, and the judge consequently sent him to prison. Duncan spent 14 years there, and then, after being paroled for a short time, a judge sent him back to prison for three more years because Duncan continuously violated the conditions of his release.

That morning in Idaho, though, Duncan was free and doing what he had done for most of his life: preying on innocent people. Duncan quickly tied up Shasta and Dylan and carried them outside and set them down in the yard. He then went back into the house and beat the three bound victims to death with a hammer. Shasta and Dylan, lying bound and terrified in the yard, could hear Mark McKensie screaming, and even saw their brother Slade, drenched with blood, stumble out the front door. Shasta and Dylan yelled for Slade to come over and untie them, but Slade was mortally wounded and apparently couldn't comprehend what they were saying. The Groene home, situated far away from any neighbors, made it an ideal spot for what

Duncan had planned, and consequently no one heard or reported the noise of the brutal and bloody murders.

Duncan, after murdering the three people, put the two children into a red Jeep Grand Cherokee he had rented in Minnesota (but not returned, and consequently was reported stolen) and then drove them to several remote campsites in Montana. At these campsites, he repeatedly sexually assaulted both Shasta and Dylan. He even reportedly videotaped the assaults for his later viewing and enjoyment.

Later in the morning of the murder, some hours after Duncan had left with the children, a neighbor, who stopped by the Groene home to pay Slade for mowing his lawn, discovered the three mutilated bodies and immediately called the police. Detectives summoned to the house walked in and discovered a grotesque murder scene with huge spatters of blood all over the living room. Although the detectives doubted it at first, after processing the crime scene they realized that there was a chance Shasta and Dylan might still be alive, because none of the blood at the murder scene, the crime lab reported, belonged to them. Consequently, the police put out an Amber Alert for the missing children. An Amber Alert, which we will talk about in detail later, is a multimedia announcement, using radio, television, and electronic road signs, that informs viewers and listeners about the abduction of a child, with the hope that someone seeing or hearing the announcement will spot the child, the abductor, or perhaps the vehicle used in the abduction.

To assist them further in the investigation, the local police in Idaho also established two telephone lines specifically for tips about the abduction of Shasta and Dylan. In the following weeks, the police received hundreds of calls. In addition, many of the local citizens, wanting to get involved, assisted the police by posting thousands of flyers with the children's pictures on them all around the area. The FBI, also eventually joining in the search, and hoping to spur the public's cooperation, announced a $100,000 reward for information about Shasta and Dylan, or about their abductor.

A distraught and desperate Steve Groene, willing to do anything to save his children, went on national television and pleaded for the safe return of Shasta and Dylan. "Please, please release my children safely," he begged their abductor. "They had nothing to do with any of this. Release them in a safe area where law enforcement can find them."[2]

Duncan, however, paying no attention to this plea, and in an effort to avoid being caught, moved continuously between various remote campsites. It would be more than six weeks before the police would finally get a break in the case and catch up with him.

At around 2:00 a.m., on July 2, 2005, a man and a little girl walked into the Denny's restaurant in Coeur d'Alene. Amber Deahn, a waitress there, thought the little girl looked a lot like the little girl on all of the flyers. She called the police and then stalled the milkshake the little girl had ordered until the officers could arrive. When the man accompanying the girl saw all of the police cars pulling into the restaurant parking lot, he grabbed the little girl and told the waitress he needed his check right away. But it was too late. The police detained Duncan and then spoke with the little girl, who told them that her name was Shasta Groene.

For better than six weeks there had been considerable speculation in both the community and the news media about the reason behind the murders and abductions, with talk of revenge, drug debts, and motorcycle gangs. When the police finally spoke with Shasta however, they discovered Duncan's real motive.

"He told her he was out driving around looking for children to kidnap," Kootenai County Sheriff's detective Brad Maskell said during a probable cause hearing. "He...saw her playing in the yard with her brother and wearing a bathing suit. At that point he chose them as possible kidnap victims."[3] Court documents also stated that Duncan told Shasta about how he had studied the family's habits, often using the night vision goggles, and about how he had peered into their home several times to learn its layout.

Following Duncan's arrest, the police recovered the stolen red Jeep he had used, and also found a shotgun and an empty zip tie bag. In her statement to the police, Shasta told them that Duncan had shown her and her brother the hammer he had used to kill their family members, and had told them in great detail how he had done it. Shasta described the hammer precisely to the police, down to the brand name. Detectives also recovered the videotape Duncan had taken of the children.

During their investigation following Duncan's arrest, detectives discovered that before his crimes in Idaho, Duncan had kept a blog on the Internet. In it, he talked about his sexual desires for children. "God has shown me the right choice, but my demons have tied me to a spit and the fire has already been lit," he said in an entry on April 24, 2005, soon after he had fled bail in Minnesota.[4] The police also found that Duncan had complained anonymously online to the Fargo, North Dakota, police chief about the unfairness of North Dakota's sex offender registry laws. That state, like Minnesota, had issued a warrant for Duncan's arrest, this one for failing to follow the conditions of his release from prison.

What happened to nine-year-old Dylan Groene? Apparently, Duncan shot him to death and then tried to burn his body at a remote campsite in Montana. Shasta related to investigators that Duncan had told her that before killing Dylan he had both sexually assaulted and tortured him with a lit cigarette. According to an affidavit filed by the police, "Shasta and Dylan were repeatedly molested. Shasta saw Mr. Duncan molest Dylan."[5] On July 10, 2005, the crime laboratory positively identified charred human remains found at a campsite in Montana to be those of Dylan Groene.

On October 16, 2006, in order to avoid the death penalty, Duncan pled guilty to the murders and kidnappings that occurred at the Groene home.

A judge sentenced him to multiple life sentences. However, federal authorities have stated that they also plan to try Duncan in the case, for Dylan's murder, and have said that they intend to seek the death penalty. They have charged Duncan with kidnapping resulting in death, sexual abuse, and several other crimes.

The story doesn't end there, however. In January 2007, the police said Duncan also confessed to the 1997 abduction and murder of 10-year-old Anthony Martinez in California. The police found one of Duncan's fingerprints on duct tape used to bind the victim. Duncan additionally confessed to the police that, while being in Washington state in 1996, he abducted and killed nine-year-old Carmen Cubias and her half-sister, 11-year-old Sammiejo White.

****

While the story of Duncan's life is a horror movie come true, readers may wonder if it is just an aberration. Does this sort of thing happen so seldom that parents needn't fear it? Unfortunately, no. As a police captain who headed the Indianapolis Police Department's Homicide Branch for six years, I can attest that the abduction of children in our country for the purpose of sexual assault occurs much more often and in higher numbers than most of the public would ever imagine.

The problem, however, with deciding just exactly how big of a concern this crime is becomes an even bigger problem because no national agency keeps reliable statistics about child abductions. No one keeps records of how many children are abducted every year in our country for the purpose of sexual assault, by mentally deranged individuals, in order to gain custody of a child awarded by a court to another parent, or for any other reason.

Interestingly, every year the FBI publishes a very detailed report, hundreds of pages long, titled *Crime in the United States*. In this document, the FBI, relying on reports sent to them by almost every police agency in the country, details how many murders occurred during the year, how many robberies, how many burglaries, how many vehicles were stolen, etc. However, for some unexplained reason, kidnapping isn't one of the crimes the FBI collects reports on, and so consequently the document doesn't include how many children were abducted.

Researchers who study child abductions are naturally appalled by this dearth of data collection by the federal government. David Finkelhor, professor of sociology at the University of New Hampshire, who coauthored a study on child abductions, had this to say about the lack of reliable statistics concerning this crime, "You only have to think about a comparable situation in public health. If there were some disease killing even a few hundred kids a year, and parents were anxious, you know the Centers for Disease Control would have good statistics."[6]

Because of this lack of national data collection, the best estimate we have at this time concerning the number of child abductions every year comes from a study titled *National Incidence Studies of Missing, Abducted, Runaway, and Throwaway Children*. This study, although published by the U.S. Department of Justice, was conducted by nongovernment researchers. It provides us with some startling facts about the problem of child abduction in the United States.

The researchers of this study reported their findings in two papers, one titled "Children Abducted by Family Members: National Estimates and Characteristics" and the other titled "Nonfamily Abducted Children: National Estimates and Characteristics." In these reports, researchers, gathering statistics from police departments across the United States, estimated that in 1999 there were 262,100 child abductions nationally, 203,900 by family members and 58,200 by nonfamily members.[7] Looking at reports through 2007, I can find no reason to believe that these numbers have decreased any since 1999, but have more likely increased. Newer studies believe the number of child abductions in the United States now to be closer to 350,000 yearly.[8] Also, keep in mind that many missing children (hundreds of thousands a year) are often labeled simply as "runaways," and no one really knows how many of these might actually be abduction victims whose bodies were never found.

The National Incidence Study also uncovered some other very interesting statistics. According to the research, in child abductions by family members, 44 percent of the children abducted are under the age of six. Also, researchers found, 53 percent of family abductors are the biological fathers and 25 percent are the biological mothers (other studies, however, show the rates of mothers and fathers to be closer to even). As to the racial/ethnic makeup of abducted children, the study said, "The racial/ethnic distribution of family abducted children corresponds to the distribution of children in the general population. This indicates that family abductions do not occur disproportionately in any one racial/ethnic group." The study also showed that 73 percent of the children abducted by family members are abducted from a home or a yard.

Interestingly, in nonfamily abductions of children, the study found that older children are a more popular target, likely because many abductors commit the crime for the purpose of sexual assault. For this same reason, girls are more than twice as likely as boys to be the victims of nonfamily abductions. And though much of the focus of child safety programs targets "stranger danger," this study found that someone known to the child committed 53 percent of the nonfamily abductions.

In contrast to family abductions, though, in which a yard or home was the most common site of the abduction, this occurred in only 23 percent of the nonfamily abduction cases. Much more likely spots were public streets, parks, and wooded areas. Sexual assault, as we talked about above, figures very heavily as the motive for nonfamily abductions, and so, not surprisingly, the study found that it occurred in 46 percent of the estimated 58,200 cases. And, as also might be expected, weapons often figured prominently in nonfamily abductions, with abductors in over 40 percent of the sexual assault cases brandishing a gun or knife.[9]

While, as shown above, family members commit the majority of child abductions every year in this country, that doesn't mean there isn't any danger to the children involved. These children, just as children taken by strangers, can be the victims of physical and sexual abuse, and even murder. And yet, while the over a quarter-million child abductions that occur every year in our country represent a huge problem, the cases, of course, that grab the public's attention are the ones in which child abduction victims, usually after being sexually assaulted, become murder victims. Few people haven't heard about the Polly Klaas or Adam Walsh cases, two young abducted children who were brutally murdered. However, because the national crime statistics gathered each year by the FBI don't separate these cases from other murders, until recently very little was known about them nationally.

Fortunately, the State Attorney General's Office for the State of Washington conducted two in-depth studies of child abductions that resulted in murder. In the first study, released in 1997, the researchers examined over 600 child abduction murder cases from across the country. In the second study, released in May 2006, the researchers added an additional 175 cases to the study base.

Although the numbers of these murders are small when compared to the overall homicide figures (averaging 20,000 a year in the United States), the victims in these cases are much different than in the majority of homicide cases. When I headed the Indianapolis Police Department's Homicide Branch, I found that in at least 90 percent of the murders we investigated the victim had in some way contributed to the murder: by engaging in a violent lifestyle, by closely associating with people prone to violence, or by becoming involved in lifestyle choices that greatly increased the likelihood of violence.

Child abduction victims, on the other hand, are usually totally innocent, with no contribution to the crime. I often found that whenever I went to give a talk at a neighborhood meeting, the people attending didn't really care about drug dealers and drug users killing each other. But they did care, and cared deeply, if someone killed a child. The value most people place on children makes a child abduction/murder one of the most heinous crimes imaginable.

In the study conducted by the Washington State Attorney General's Office, the researchers uncovered some disturbing facts. They found, for instance, that in cases of murder during a child abduction the chances were equal that the abductor/murderer would be someone known to the child as opposed to a stranger. And not surprisingly, with the motive of many child abductions being sexual assault, in 74 percent of the abduction/murder cases studied the victim was a female, whose average age was 11.[10]

"While 'stranger danger' continues to be a threat to children, this new study reveals that nearly an equal number of killers are known to their victims," said Washington State Attorney General Rob McKenna. "Based on the results of this study, parents need to warn their children not just to avoid getting into cars with strangers, but to not even approach a car, whether the occupant is a stranger or not—no matter what they tell them."[11]

The studies also found that almost two-thirds of the killers in child abduction cases had previous arrests for violent crimes, with half of them having a record of violent crimes against children. In 76 percent of the cases, the researchers found, the child had been murdered within three hours of the abduction, and in 88.5 percent of the cases murdered within 24 hours, usually after being sexually assaulted. In the majority of these cases, contact between the child and the killer took place within three blocks of the child's home.

However, one of the most interesting findings of this study was that the typical victim in these cases was a normal child from a good neighborhood. The typical victim was a member of very stable, normal family, hardly the type considered to be most at risk for abduction.

As for the abductor/murderer, the studies found that it was typically a male (98.5 percent of the time), average age of 27, unmarried, living alone or with his parents, and employed in unskilled or semiskilled labor. In two-thirds of the cases, the abductor was in the area of the abduction for some legitimate reason, such as work, social activities, or living in the area. And contrary to a very common belief, only 14 percent of the abductors said that they chose a child for any specific reason. Most were simply victims of opportunity, with the primary reason for the abduction being sexual assault.[12]

Interestingly, other research has shown that the race of child abductors who murder closely matches that of society at large. But still, these individuals are different. According to one study on child abductors who murder, "They can be characterized as *social marginals:* They are not active, successful participants in mainstream, conventional social life, but, rather, they occupy a position in society that is, indeed, on the 'edge, brink, border, precipice, or margin.'"[13]

A group of abducted children who unfortunately receive much less attention than the ones we have just talked about are those abducted children who are never found. Since no body turns up, as the weeks, months, and years pass, people tend to forget about them. For example, on June 3, 1988, seven-year-old Amber Swartz of Pinole, California, went out into her front yard to jump rope. A few minutes later, when her mother went to check on her, Amber had disappeared. A police search of the area turned up nothing. Amber's mother, suffering desperately through the 20 years since Amber's disappearance, has never given up hope of seeing her daughter again.

"I don't know which is worse—losing a child to death by accident or illness or losing a child to a mysterious disappearance," said radio commentator Barbara Simpson. "Actually, I do know. While either is a soul-wrenching tragedy, at least in the case of accident or sickness, there is an end, no matter how painful."[14]

And yet, while the abducted children are certainly the major victims of this crime, they are by no means the only ones who suffer because of child abduction. Experience has shown that parents who are forced to live through the hellish nightmare of a child abduction, sometimes for months or even years, often find that their emotional and physical health seems to diminish daily.

"Kidnapping is a multiple crime," said Simpson. "The kidnapper doesn't just 'steal' a child; he profoundly abuses that young life and destroys the spirit and lives of entire families."[15]

Still, as bad as this is, there are also other negative consequences of child abduction. A study published by the federal government, for example, reported that child abductions can also drain a parent's financial health. This study revealed, for instance, that in order to return a child abducted across international borders, parents spent, on the average, a full year's salary. Many though spend much more than this.[16]

So what can be done about this national problem, just the thought of which sends an icicle slashing into every parent's heart? Can anything at all be done to lessen the chances that a child will be an abduction victim, or to help speed the rescue of a child who has been abducted? Yes, much can be done. Parents are not totally helpless against child abductors.

But first, parents need to be aware of just how prevalent and dangerous child abduction is. Actually, every member of society needs to know about this threat. Recently, *The Today Show* staged a mock child abduction on a city street to see what witnesses to it would do. A seven-year-old girl was grabbed and dragged by a man. The girl would yell, "You're not my father!" Sadly, almost no one intervened. Almost no one believed that what he or she was seeing could be true.[17] The public obviously needs to be made much more aware of the reality of this crime.

Therefore, before I get into what steps can be taken to lessen the chances, or the length, of a child abduction, readers need to be aware, as we will discuss in the following chapters, of the prevalence and dangers of the various types of child abduction. This is important because each one will require a different prevention strategy, since, as children get older, they become targets for different types of abductors. As an article in the *FBI Law Enforcement Bulletin* stated, "As [children] age, their attributes, vulnerabilities, and accessibility change, and they gain exposure to and become desired by different types of abductors who exploit them for different reasons."[18]

We will first look at child abduction for the purpose of sexual molestation. As we will see, this type of abduction holds a large amount of danger for its victims, with sexual assault an almost certainty, and murder as a real possibility.

Sex Offender Abductions

For most of the afternoon of March 8, 2007, six-year-old Christopher Michael Barrios had been playing on the swing set of a neighborhood friend in Brunswick, Georgia. At around 6:15 p.m., however, Christopher knew it was time to go home. So he started the short walk to his grandmother's house. He never made it.

When Christopher didn't return home, his grandmother naturally became concerned. After looking unsuccessfully for him, she called the police.

Responding police officers scoured the area and eventually discovered Christopher's Star Wars light saber in the front yard of the home of David and Peggy Edenfield, who lived across the street from Christopher's grandmother. The Edenfield's son, 31-year-old George Edenfield, also lived there.

The police, during their investigation, discovered that George was a registered sex offender who had been arrested for crimes involving young boys, and so naturally they focused their investigation on him. After a bit of questioning, George finally admitted to abducting, molesting, killing, and then, with the help of friend Donald Dale, burying Christopher.

For the next four days the Edenfields and Dale led the police from spot to spot, claiming they had buried Christopher first here and then there. The police, though digging in the spots where the individuals claimed to have buried the six-year-old, didn't find anything.

"The father and his friend basically confessed to burying little Christopher," said Brunswick police captain Jim Nazzrie. "They took us to the area, several areas...for some reason they want to lie about it, they can't remember where they buried the body, or if they did bury the body." [1]

The police quickly realized the unreliability of the Edenfields and Dale, and began their own search for Christopher. They used cadaver-sniffing dogs, handheld infrared devices, and aircraft with ground search radar, which can be used to detect recently disturbed soil. Finally, a week after Christopher's abduction, a state park ranger discovered the six-year-old's body. The ranger found Christopher wrapped in a black trash bag and dumped along a road about three miles from where the police believe George had abducted him.

Reconstructing what they think happened, the police believe that George had watched Christopher for some time, since the Edenfields lived across the street from where Christopher lived. Christopher's grandmother, Sue Rodriquez, said of George Edenfield, "From what I've seen, the man just sits on the porch and watches all the kids out here."[2]

In a strange twist because of state law, George had recently moved with his parents to the address near where Christopher lived because the authorities had forced him to vacate his previous address, since, as a registered sex offender, he lived too close to a playground. Interestingly, even though ordered to, George had still at first refused to relocate, until the police finally arrested him. Then, after entering into a plea agreement with the court, George moved with his parents to the new address near Christopher, an area where dozens of children lived.

"This blood is on their hands," said Sue Rodriquez, blaming a flawed legal system for George's recent relocation.[3]

The police believe that on March 8, 2007, George apparently spotted Christopher walking alone and saw his chance. He abducted the boy and then took him into his parent's trailer, where he and his father reportedly took turns sexually assaulting him. According to the indictments against the Edenfields, George and his father sodomized Christopher and then forced him to perform oral sex, while George's mother looked on and masturbated.

Following the sexual assault, George allegedly strangled Christopher to death. In an affidavit filed by the police, officers say George told them that the devil had ordered him to kill Christopher.[4] Still, George's mother reportedly tried to use soap and water in an attempt to wash George's fingerprints off of Christopher's neck, afterward putting the six-year-old's body in a trash bag. The family then, according to the affidavit, had a friend, Donald Dale, help them dispose of the body.

A grand jury, on March 21, 2007, charged George Edenfield with murder and aggravated child molestation. The same grand jury charged George's father, 58-year-old David Edenfield, whose criminal history includes a conviction for incest (reportedly with a daughter), also with murder and aggravated child molestation, as they did George's mother, 57-year-old Peggy Edenfield. The prosecutor charged Donald Dale with concealing the death of another, obstruction of justice, and providing false information.

Stephen D. Kelley, the local district attorney, stated that he planned to seek the death penalty against all three of the Edenfields. "This is one of the most horrific crimes that I've seen in 21 years of prosecutions," Kelley said.[5]

Christopher's father, Mike Barrios, added, "They deserve the worst, for them to torture my son like that, every last one of them."[6]

****

Sexual assault, such as what happened in the Christopher Barrios case above, is the main motivation for those who abduct children not related to them. According to the "Nonfamily Abducted Children: National Estimates and Characteristics" section of the *National Incidence Studies of Missing, Abducted, Runaway, and Thrownaway Children,* "Girls were the predominant victims of nonfamily abductions overall and of stereotypical kidnappings as well (65 percent and 69 percent, respectively), reflecting the frequency of sexual assault as a motive for many nonfamily abductions." The report goes on to say, "Criminal assaults were a motive in most of the nonfamily abductions. Close to half of all nonfamily abduction victims and stereotypical kidnapping victims [58,200 in the study year] were sexually assaulted."[7]

The investigation by the Attorney General of the State of Washington, talked about in the last chapter, stated, "Sexually motivated abductions represent the most common type of nonfamily abduction and classically pose the highest risk of victim mortality."[8] An article in the *FBI Law Enforcement Bulletin* also stated, "In school-age children, sex represents the overwhelming reason for abductions."[9]

Most of the perpetrators who commit these types of abductions are what are known as pedophiles, individuals whose sexual urges are most satisfied through engaging in sexual activity with children. According to the *Diagnostic and Statistical Manual of Mental Disorders,* "Pedophilia is a paraphilia that involves an abnormal interest in children. A paraphilia is a disorder that is characterized by recurrent intense sexual urges and sexually arousing fantasies...Pedophilia is also a psychosexual disorder in which the fantasy or actual act of engaging in sexual activity with prepubertal children is the preferred or exclusive means of achieving sexual excitement and gratification. It may be directed toward children of the same sex or children of the other sex. Some pedophiles are attracted to both boys and girls."[10]

Unfortunately, pedophilia is very common in our country, and can include both men and women (as demonstrated by the many female teachers in the news recently who have been arrested for engaging in sex with under-aged male students). Pedophilia also includes individuals from all levels and classes of society. Pedophiles can be homeless people, assembly line workers, teachers, doctors, industry CEOs, religious leaders, and police officers.

Often, experts find, and parents need to be aware, pedophiles who abduct children for the purpose of sexual assault know the children they abduct. The U.S. Department of Justice, Office of Juvenile Justice and Delinquency Prevention, in cooperation with the FBI and the University of Pennsylvania School of Nursing, conducted a study of both abducting and nonabducting child molesters. Interestingly, they found that 58 percent of the molesters who abducted children were an acquaintance of their victims.[11]

So how do these molesters find their victims? One way is that pedophiles will often work themselves into jobs and positions that allow them unchaperoned access to children, who they then molest. For example, there are probably very few people in the country who haven't heard of the child molesting scandal in the Catholic Church. But such illegal behavior can occur in practically any setting in which a pedophile is allowed to be alone with children. For example, on July 25, 2007, a judge in San Diego sentenced former respiratory therapist Wayne Albert Bleyle to 45 years in prison. For 10 years, Bleyle had been sexually molesting and taking pornographic photographs of the children he cared for. The authorities said he specifically selected children who were comatose, brain-damaged, or too disabled to talk. Bleyle told the authorities that he had molested at least half of the children he treated in his ten years at the Rady Children's Hospital in San Diego.

In addition, pedophiles will also often volunteer for positions in athletic coaching, Scouting, civic and religious groups, etc. This is why it is important, as we will talk about in a later chapter, to check the leaders of these groups against the national sex offender registry database before allowing your children to participate in any such group. In addition to this, pedophiles now often use the Internet in order to find their victims. For example, in July 2007, MySpace.com, the extremely popular social networking Web site for young people, reported that they had found more than 29,000 registered sex offenders with profiles on their Web site.[12]

So how many pedophiles are there in America? No one knows for sure, but the number is likely to be very large. The huge market for child pornography in our country and around the world suggests that pedophilia is much more widespread than most people would suspect. And unfortunately, until they are caught, many pedophiles can masquerade as just ordinary people, and occasionally even as pillars of the community. And just as unfortunate, individuals who are pedophiles seldom voluntarily seek help for their condition, that is, until they are caught.

Not surprisingly, the police many times find that pedophiles who abduct children for the purpose of sexual assault also have a strong interest in child pornography. The report from the Attorney General of the State of Washington about child abductors who murder their victims, discussed in Chapter 1, had this to say about the differences in their 2006 report from the earlier

1997 version, "Another significant change is the increase in the use of pornography by killers as a trigger. This should not be surprising, given the overwhelming sexual motivation of killers in these cases."[13] Readers should keep in mind that a likely reason for this change is that the huge growth of the Internet between the times of these two reports has made child pornography now much easier to access and own.

Unfortunately, other than total abstinence and the avoidance of any contact at all with children, there is no truly effective treatment for pedophilia. A number of the mental health experts I have spoken with have commented that only when they die do most pedophiles stop having sexual urges involving children, as the following incident reveals.

****

On the evening of July 4, 2007, the father of 12-year-old Zina Linnik sent his daughter up the street from their home in Tacoma, Washington, to retrieve several of her siblings, who had wandered away while watching some 4th of July fireworks. Soon after he did this, Zina's father heard his daughter scream, and so he ran outside. He got out the door just in time to see a man jump into a gray van and speed away. The father, finding one of Zina's flip flops on the ground, managed to obtain a partial license plate number of the gray van, which he gave to the police.

Detectives investigating the disappearance of Zina used the partial license plate number to lead them to a convicted sex offender named Terapon Dang Adhahn, who they took into custody for the unconnected charge of failure to register as a sex offender. In 1990, the police had charged Terapon with the violent rape of his under-aged half-sister. In a plea bargain with the court, Terapon agreed to plead guilty to first-degree incest and undergo five years of sexual deviancy treatment.

At the completion of this treatment, Terapon's therapist wrote, "[Terapon] is aware that he will need to use what he has learned through the treatment process on a daily basis in order to remain offense free. As long as Terapon chooses to use these skills and techniques on a daily basis, his potential to recidivate vastly diminishes."[14]

Unfortunately, while Terapon had been able to convince his therapist that he had changed and improved, he actually hadn't changed at all. Once Terapon became a person of interest in the Zina Linnik case, police detectives discovered that he had reportedly abducted and raped an 11-year-old girl soon after he had completed the treatment program, and that he had also been continuously raping an under-aged girl who lived with him.

However, in the Zina Linnik case the police were in a quandary. Although Terapon had abducted and committed sex crimes against minors in the past, he had never murdered any of them. Eight days had passed since Zina's disappearance, and the authorities hoped that Zina might still be alive, perhaps lying injured somewhere or maybe locked up and starving. So the local prosecutor made a deal. If Terapon would lead the police to Zina, the state wouldn't seek the death penalty against him.

Terapon agreed and, on July 12, 2007, he and his attorney led the police to Zina's body in rural Eatonville, about 35 miles south of Tacoma. Terapon had hidden Zina under some brush.

"It is with great regret and sorrow that I am informing our community that we have located the body of Zina Linnik," Tacoma Police Chief Don Ramsdell later said at a press conference.[15]

The coroner's examination would determine that Zina had died from blunt force trauma to the head. Consequently, the police, along with charging Terapon with the rape and abduction of the 11-year-old soon after his therapy, and the rape of the young girl living with him, also charged Terapon with the rape, kidnapping, and murder of Zina. He is being held on $7 million bail.

****

As a result of their inability to overcome their strong sexual attraction to children, criminal pedophiles frequently have a very high rate of recidivism, as Terapon Dang Adhahn demonstrated. Prison terms, while keeping pedophiles out of society, seldom diminish the intensity of their pedophilia, and many of these individuals begin preying again on children, or making plans to do so, just as soon as they are released from custody.

For many pedophiles, the police find, the urge to engage in sexual activity with children can be so intense as to be almost overpowering. It can be so intense that these individuals will often disregard the high risk and engage in activities that they know will very likely end in their arrest and exposure. For example, in the Christopher Barrios case, George Edenfield wanted to have sex so badly and so intensely with Christopher that he apparently didn't think to take the time to clean up the evidence that would lead the police to him. Consequently, in his drive to get Christopher inside his parent's trailer so he could sexually assault him, George didn't take the few moments it would need to get rid of the Star Wars light saber that Christopher had dropped when George abducted him.

As another example of pedophiles involving themselves in extremely risky behavior that will likely end in their arrest and exposure, the *Dateline* television program did a series of shows in which they wired a house for video and sound, and then recorded dozens of pedophiles who came there hoping to have sex with an under-aged child. Many of these individuals had high social status and everything to lose. Several of these individuals even later said that they suspected it might be a setup. Yet still, they couldn't stop themselves from coming there with the hope of having sex with a child.

The ultimate example, however, of the high level of risk-taking a pedophile will engage in occurred in November 2006, when a judge sentenced former deputy press secretary for the Department of Homeland Security, Brian Doyle, to five years in prison for sending sexually explicit e-mails to what he believed was an under-aged girl. In his e-mails, Doyle said he had to be very, very careful because, "Law enforcement is very good at this. I have sooooo much to lose."[16]

He was right. As it turned out, he was sending the e-mails to a police officer pretending to be an under-aged girl.

Many pedophiles, in order to have sex with under-aged children, don't have to resort to abduction and sexual assault. Instead, they con their victims into having sex. They use a complex set of behaviors that, through bribes, affection, attention, and other things many young children crave and often can't get from their parents, break down a child's resistance to intimacy.

However, there are also many pedophiles who lack these social skills. Many pedophiles don't know how to interact with children or how to persuade them to have sex willingly. In order for these individuals to satisfy their intense urges, they must sexually assault their young victims, usually after abducting them.

The above quoted article from the *FBI Law Enforcement Bulletin* had this to say about sexually motivated child abductors, "They usually display poor social skills and work habits, and frequently are deemed 'socially incompetent.' Their inability to interact effectively with others may cause them to obtain victims by abduction."[17]

So far, all of the sexually motivated child abductions we have talked about in this chapter, the ones that usually grab the largest amount of media attention, have involved preteen victims. The *Diagnostic and Statistical Manual of Mental Disorders,* quoted above, defines pedophilia as a sexual interest in children 13 and younger. However, as the incident below illustrates, older children can also become the victims of sexually motivated abductions.

****

On August 1, 2002, in Lancaster, California, just north of Los Angeles, 37-year-old Roy Ratliff abducted two girls, ages 16 and 17. He took them at gunpoint after binding their dates with duct tape.

"He just kept telling her to stay down," said the date of one of the girls, who Ratliff duct taped to a pole, "keep her head down, don't look at him."[18]

Ratliff had a long arrest record, including theft, burglary, and drugs. At the time of the abduction he was wanted for sexually assaulting his 19-year-old stepdaughter. A judge had issued a warrant for rape and had set Ratliff's bail at $3 million.

After duct taping the two young men, Ratliff bound both girls and forced them into a Ford Bronco that belonged to one of the girl's dates, then sped off, leaving behind a car he had stolen earlier in Las Vegas. One of the young men quickly freed himself and then used his cell phone to call for help. An intense police manhunt quickly began, which included over 300 law enforcement officers and eight aircraft. However, before the police could locate the abduction victims, Ratliff reportedly raped both girls.

As a part of their investigation, the police issued an AMBER Alert. "And a good part of it is [with] this AMBER Alert system that we're able to disseminate all the information to every single law enforcement agency in the state, put it out to the media, put it out on the road signs, the electric road signs on the freeways," Los Angeles County Assistant Sheriff Larry Waldie told TV host Larry King. "We literally had four or five million people looking for this car, this individual."[19]

Twelve hours later, acting on a tip, the police spotted the Bronco near Lake Isabella, over 100 miles from the abduction site. Officers pursued the vehicle at high speeds until Ratliff eventually crashed the car. Police officers then shot and killed Ratliff when he pulled a gun on them.

The quickly responding officers, investigators later found, likely saved the two girls' lives. Kern County Sheriff Carl Sparks told TV host Larry King, "He was hunting for a place to kill them and bury them. We probably saved them by 10 minutes. He was parked. He had found the spot when the deputies rolled up."[20]

The two young abduction victims later related to the authorities that Ratliff had told them he was going to kill them, and then began a countdown. Fortunately for the two girls, the sheriff's deputies killed Ratliff first.

* * * *

While sexually motivated child abductions can be one of the most frightening, heart-wrenching things that can happen to the victims and their parents, another type of child abduction can be just as terrorizing. This, as we will see in the next chapter, is infant abduction, the kidnapping of society's most fragile and innocent victims.

Infant Abductions

On March 10, 2007, at Covenant Lakeside Medical Center in Lubbock, Texas, a woman dressed in blue, flowered hospital scrubs, and claiming to be a nurse, came into the room of newborn infant Mychael Darthard-Dawodu. The woman had been in the room several times before to check on the baby. Mychael weighed six pounds and had jaundice, a common condition that wouldn't be dangerous as long as she remained in the hospital.

According to police reports, the woman came into the baby's hospital room and "told the family they needed to take the baby for some tests and left the room."[1] The baby's mother watched anxiously as the woman left with Mychael.

After about 15 minutes, the mother became concerned and inquired about her baby girl. Hospital personnel soon realized that the woman was not a nurse, but rather an imposter, and that an infant had been abducted. They immediately locked down the hospital. But it was too late. Security cameras would later show the imposter, carrying a large purse in which they believe she had hidden the infant, leave the hospital and get into a red, Dodge pickup truck. Although Mychael had been wearing a security bracelet, the police later found it in a trash can. The authorities had members of Mychael's family view the video, but no one recognized the woman.

Hospital officials worried that Mychael's medical condition would worsen without proper care. They also worried about the baby's nutrition. "The biggest problem is that babies, within the first three days, need either mother's milk or an electrolyte solution," said Dr. Marc Siegel of the New York University Medical School. "They can't have cow's milk."[2]

The authorities quickly put out a description of the suspect and the abducted infant, and calls soon began coming in. One caller, from Clovis, New Mexico, about 100 miles northwest of Lubbock, told the police about a woman with a new baby. The caller didn't believe the woman had really been pregnant. Local police officers, acting on this tip, confronted 21-year-old Rayshaun Parson, and would soon find Mychael at a nearby home. The infant appeared to be in good condition.

Rayshaun, the police learned, had had brushes with the law before. In May 2004, a boyfriend had gotten a protective order against her. In January 2005, the police charged her with fraud, though they later dropped the charges.

Family members of Rayshaun told the authorities that she had recently suffered her second miscarriage, and that having a baby had been a dream of hers for a long time. Her strong desire for a baby had even brought on a bout of pseudocyesis, or false pregnancy, in which a woman, though not pregnant, still experiences many of its symptoms.

"Rayshaun wanted the baby so bad that she got the symptoms," said the mother of Rayshaun's boyfriend. "She was the perfect vision of a pregnant woman."[3]

****

It isn't only at hospitals, however, where infants are in danger of abduction. In June 2006, also in Lubbock, Texas, a new mother had a woman dressed in hospital scrubs, and who identified herself as a nurse, stop in her hospital room several times to check on her and her new infant. The woman asked the new mother for her address because she said she had some baby clothes and a swing she wanted to give her.

Two days after the new mother had been discharged from the hospital, this same counterfeit nurse came to the new mother's house. She said she wanted to show the baby to some relatives who lived nearby. The mother said okay and that she would accompany her, but then, when another child momentarily distracted the mother, the phony nurse abducted the infant.

"My son ran ahead of me so I tried to reach over and grab him and when I did that, I turned around," said the infant's mother. "Just like that, my baby was gone."[4]

The authorities, upon being notified of the baby's abduction, discovered that the abductor didn't actually work at the hospital. "It appears that she established something of a relationship—went to the hospital, presented herself as a nurse, checked on the status of the baby, and that kind of stuff," said Lubbock, Texas, police lieutenant Roy Bassett.[5]

The police soon began receiving tips. One of these tips led them to 33-year-old Stephanie Lynn Jones. Stephanie had recently been telling people where she lived that she had had a baby, but several of them didn't believe that she had really been pregnant, and called the authorities. When Stephanie found out that the police were looking for her, she reportedly abandoned the baby in a car that was sitting in 104-degree temperature. Fortunately, the police rescued the baby before it suffered any harm. Officers quickly arrested Stephanie and charged her with kidnapping.

"The doctors wanted to check her and I didn't want to let her go," said the mother upon having her infant returned to her. "I didn't want to stop hugging and kissing her."[6]

In another case of infant abduction, this one in August 2002, Margarita Chavez of Abilene, Texas, had just fastened her one-month-old daughter, Crystal, into the infant car seat of the family minivan. She then walked 10–12 feet away to put her shopping cart into the cart corral at the local Wal-Mart. When she turned around she saw that a woman had snatched Crystal and was putting her into her own car. Although Margarita tried valiantly to rescue her child, suffering numerous injuries as the abductor's car dragged her nearly 40 feet across the parking lot, the abductor managed to get away with Crystal.

Fortunately, store security video cameras recorded the entire incident. It showed the abductor's car circling the parking lot numerous times, apparently looking for an opportunity to snatch an infant.

"The surveillance video shows the woman circling around the parking lot," said Sergeant Kim Vickers of the Abilene Police Department. "We counted at least five to seven times. She had been looking for an opportunity and when it afforded itself, she seized it."[7]

After putting out the information about the infant abduction to the news media, the police soon began receiving tips. One tip led them to Quanah, Texas, a small town about 100 miles north of Abilene. A woman there had taken an infant to a nursing home to show it off to her mother's coworkers. Employees there, however, seeing the infant's healed navel, knew it couldn't be one-day-old, as the woman claimed, and they contacted the police.

The police in Quanah stopped a car matching the description of the car used in the abduction. In the vehicle they found 24-year-old Paula Lynn Roach, a former corrections officer, her mother (who apparently truly believed the baby was her granddaughter), and an infant. Upon questioning by the officers, Paula insisted that the baby was hers and that the officers were just harassing her. However, upon further questioning, Paula eventually gave the infant to the officers. A check of the baby's footprints showed it to be Crystal Chavez. The police returned Crystal, unharmed, to her mother.

The authorities arrested Paula and charged her with kidnapping. In May 2003, Paula pled guilty to kidnapping Crystal and a judge sentenced her to 10 years in prison.

****

As the above incidents demonstrate, the police many times solve infant abductions through tips from the public. Infant abduction is such a frightening crime that hearing about it can often quickly motivate the public to come forward. It is for this reason, as we will talk about in a later chapter, that the Amber Alert Program is so valuable and helpful in these cases. Putting out an Amber Alert can instantly make millions of people aware of the abduction and who and what to look for.

"These cases are usually solved through the use of extensive media coverage and publication of the likely profile of the abductor," former FBI agent Dan L. Vogel, who took part in the FBI's National Infant Abduction Research Project, told me.[8]

* * * *

However, it's not just strangers who abduct infants. It can occasionally be the infant's own parents, who have for some reason lost custody of the child. For example, in December 2006, in Moreno Valley, California, two women abducted an infant from the Riverside County Regional Medical Center. The child, born on December 23, 2006, had been found to have methamphetamines in its system. Because of this, local child welfare workers had a protective order issued that prohibited the mother, 36-year-old Audrey Arriola, a homeless woman, from removing the baby from the hospital.

The police, after receiving a tip and recovering the baby from a family the mother had left it with, found Audrey hiding in an abandoned trailer and arrested her. The police also arrested 46-year-old Debra Harrell for assisting in the abduction. The police charged both women with kidnapping and child endangerment.

In another case, this one in Houston, Texas, the police had to use a Taser (a device that delivers an incapacitating, but nonlethal, electric shock) to stop a father from abducting his two-day-old daughter from the hospital. The police said they were forced to use the Taser because the father had told them it would become a hostage situation if they didn't let him leave with the child.

According to Captain Dwayne Ready of the Houston Police Department, several weeks before the infant's birth, the mother had called the police and "stated that her unborn child's father called her and made threats on her and the child's life."[9] The police charged the father with child endangerment.

In a final case, in Lynwood, California, a father came to the St. Francis Medical Center and snatched a two-hour-old baby from its mother's room. The mother, after contacting the police, reached the infant's father on his cell phone and persuaded him to bring the baby back. The police charged him with kidnapping and child endangerment.

"Basically, mom's in the hospital. Dad comes in and walks out with the kid and goes for a joyride somewhere," said Sergeant Dana Ellison of the Los Angeles County Sheriff's Department.[10]

****

As these incidents demonstrate, perpetrators of infant abduction can many times be desperate individuals. They can occasionally be unfit parents who abduct their own children, but much more often they are strangers who want an infant so badly that they are willing to steal someone else's baby and claim it as their own. Knowing this can only make infant abduction that much more frightening for new parents.

"So many women go into the hospital and are terrified of this," said Ernie Allen, CEO and president of the National Center for Missing and Exploited Children. "The numbers are not in the thousands, but when it happens, it is just as traumatic as anything you can imagine. To have had a newborn in your arms, and then it is gone."[11]

An article in the *FBI Law Enforcement Bulletin* stated, "Compared to the number of annual births over the past 12 years, the number of abductions is, statistically at least, insignificant. However, the act of stealing a vulnerable baby rises above statistical significance."[12]

In the case of stranger infant abduction, many of the abductors (almost exclusively women), along with being desperate, also many times suffer from severe emotional problems and often are in a failing relationship with a man. These women hope that a baby will keep the man in the relationship. Many of these women have even faked a pregnancy in order to keep the man from leaving, and, after nine months, must now produce a baby.

"My experience with these abductors is that they are emotionally imma-ture and trying to replace a loss in their own lives by abducting a child," Dan L. Vogel told me. "They don't seem to care or realize that they could serve time in state or federal prison if caught. Their primary motivation is to obtain a child."[13]

Some of these women want a baby so desperately, as demonstrated in one of the incidents above, that they even develop pseudocyesis, or a false preg-nancy. "It's like those who want to be pregnant so badly they develop the physical symptoms of pregnancy—they even lactate," said Dr. Margaret Spinelli, director of maternal mental health programs at the New York State Psychiatric Institute at Columbia University. "It's hard to know what's going on in these women's brains. How do they think they can get away with it? My gut feeling is it is like a psychosis and there must be some sort of depression."[14]

Researchers who have studied hundreds of infant abductions have come up with a profile of the typical infant abductor. This person typically will be as follows:

1. Is an overweight female, with an average age of 28. Interestingly, a 2001 study by the National Center for Missing and Exploited Children found that African-American and Hispanic women were heavily overrepresented as infant abductors, with African-Americans accounting for 46 percent of the abductions and Hispanic women accounting for 31 percent, though they only account for 12.7 and 11.2 percent of the population, respectively.[15]

2. Has often carefully planned the abduction by learning the security measures at hospitals, obtaining hospital garb, and making several "dry runs" before actually committing the abduction.

3. Will usually visit several hospitals before finding the one that she thinks will give her the best chance of success.

4. Will usually make herself known to the infant's mother and other family members. By doing this, she hopes to not arouse any suspicion when she actually carries out the abduction.

5. Will often have been faking a pregnancy. Interestingly, most of these women are able to convince both family and friends of their pregnancy (one woman even gaining 60 pounds to make others believe she was pregnant). One study on infant abductions had this to say about these faked pregnancies, "It is interesting to note that nearly all investigative notes commented on the genuine ignorance of the significant other, family, and friends of the offender."[16]

6. Is married to a man or living with one, but the relationship is strained or failing. Consequently, the abductor, desperate to save the relationship, will produce a baby, supposedly fathered by her husband or companion. According to an article in the *FBI Law Enforcement Bulletin*, "[T]he infant abductor frequently attempts to prevent her husband or boyfriend from deserting her or tries to win back his affection by claiming pregnancy and, later, the birth of a child."[17] In addition, the woman many times becomes accustomed to the extra attention and resources she receives while her significant other thinks she is pregnant, and so now, after nine months, she must produce a baby in order to keep the attention and resources coming.

    Because of the abductor's need to convince a man that he has fathered a child, the baby has to match the supposed father's race and coloring. In an analysis of infant abductions by the National Center for Missing and Exploited Children, the researchers found that, "The abductor will take an infant whose skin color 'matches' her significant other's to ensure he will accept the infant presented to him as 'his baby.'"[18] Studies have also found that boy and girl infants are at equal risk of abduction.

7. Will be emotionally immature, have low self-esteem, and will have used manipulative behavior her whole life.

8. Will occasionally have a criminal record, which will usually involve nonviolent crimes such as fraud or forgery.

9. Will be unable to have a baby and/or will have suffered through several miscarriages.

10. Will often act alone. A 2001 study by the National Center for Missing and Exploited Children found that in the cases they studied, 79 percent of the abductors were females working alone, 12 percent were females with male

accomplices, 4 percent were females with female accomplices, and 2 percent were males working alone. In the other cases, researchers could not ascertain whether or not the abductor had accomplices.[19]

Even though many infant abductions take place in hospital maternity wards or nurseries, since abductors know that at these locations they will have a number of babies to choose from, and, as noted above, they want one that matches close enough to their significant other that he will accept the child as his, infant abductions can occur anywhere. As a matter of fact, statistics show that as hospitals have begun to incorporate more and more sophisticated security measures, infant abductions at these locations have begun to decline.

According to a 1995 study conducted by the National Center for Missing and Exploited Children, "Recent cases indicate that due to the success of the security measures implemented by hospitals, a larger proportion of infant abductions are now occurring from the victim's home or at public locations such as malls, supermarkets, or bus stops."[20] A 2001 follow-up study confirmed that this is still true.

In another study, this one in 2005, also by the National Center for Missing and Exploited Children, researchers found that of all the infant abductions they studied, 50 percent took place in a healthcare facility, 38 percent in the infant's home, and the remainder in other locations, such as malls, parking lots, etc.[21] This finding is important because other studies have shown that the likelihood of injury to the parent or caretaker increases significantly when an infant abduction takes place in the home. One study showed that one-third of all home infant abductions involved physical violence.[22]

A number of other studies about infant abductions have uncovered some more interesting facts about them:

1. Infant abductions generally occur during the daytime, with one study showing that 72 percent of them occurred between 9:00 a.m. and 6:00 p.m.
2. In abductions from healthcare facilities, the abduction site is usually the mother's room, the nursery, or a pediatric unit.
3. Few residence abductions involved forced entry. Most abductors instead figured out some way to con the victim's parent or caretaker into letting them into the house.
4. While the risk to the infant during an abduction is usually small, the risk to the parent or caretaker is not.
5. Although infant abductors often carefully plan their abductions, many of them do not have any specific baby as a target, but will abduct the most available baby that matches their needs.

In addition to the above, Dan L. Vogel also told me, "The abductor usually lives in the community where the abduction takes place, and frequently visits nursery and maternity units at local hospitals and asks questions about procedures and the maternity floor layout. They may also attempt an abduction in a home setting and usually plan the abduction, but don't necessarily target a specific child, but seize any opportunity present."[23]

Many people may believe that the resolution of an infant abduction is totally successful if the media reports that the police returned the baby to its mother unharmed, but this isn't always so. Abducted infants can often suffer emotional harm. For example, a study by the National Center for Missing and Exploited Children, completed in 2003, found that the mothers of abducted infants often report that their children demonstrate emotional problems long after the abduction, such as sleep problems, nightmares, and exaggerated startle response.[24]

While having an infant abducted can be a terrifying experience for the parents, another type of child abduction can be just as frightening, and this is an abduction by a psychotic person. As we will see in the next chapter, the parents of these victims can often suffer terribly because they have no idea why the psychotic person abducted their child or what horrible things the psychotic person may be doing.

Psychotic Abductions

In November 2001, Lois Smart of Salt Lake City met a panhandler, 49-year-old Brian David Mitchell, on the street and, feeling sorry for him, offered him a job. As a result of this meeting, Mitchell worked five hours at the Smart home repairing the roof, for which Lois Smart paid him a fair wage. Lois and her husband, Ed, often hired those down on their luck to do odd jobs around their house. While this may seem like a charitable, Christian thing to do, these type of people, as the Smarts found out, can occasionally be less than stable in their character, and sometimes even dangerous.

In this case, the man the Smarts hired suffered from severe psychosis and was often delusional. Mitchell believed that he was an angel sent to Earth to preach and minister to the homeless. He also believed that he had been sent by God to correct the Mormon Church by restoring its fundamental values. As a part of his delusion, Mitchell wrote a rambling 27-page manifesto, *The Book of Immanuel David Isaiah,* which he handed out copies of to anyone who would take them.

Mitchell, the authorities would later discover, had had a very troubled past. His father had allegedly exposed him to pornography very early in his life, and also reportedly once, when Mitchell was 12, had dropped him off in a strange part of town and told him to find his way home. At age 16, the authorities sent Mitchell to a juvenile facility because he had exposed himself to a young child. Soon after his release from this facility, Mitchell went to live with his grandmother. Once there, he quickly became involved with drugs and alcohol.

At age 19, Mitchell married a 16-year-old girl after getting her pregnant. The two had a stormy marriage, with their two children going back and forth between them after they divorced.

In 1980, one of Mitchell's brothers returned from a religious mission, and convinced Mitchell to clean up his life. Mitchell gave up the drugs and alcohol, and became active in the Mormon Church. Soon after this, he married his second wife, with whom he had two more children. Several years later, this marriage also fell apart and the couple divorced.

The day his second divorce became final, Mitchell married Wanda Ilene Barzee, who was eight years his senior. At that time Barzee had six children, which she left with her ex-husband after marrying Mitchell. One night, Mitchell and Barzee claimed, angels visited them, and told them that they were also angels. Mitchell's mission on Earth, the angels told them, was to preach to the homeless and to correct the Mormon Church. After this, Mitchell began calling himself "Emmanuel" and Barzee became known as "God Adorneth." From that day on, the two of them held firmly to the delusion of being angels. This is a relatively rare condition called "folie à deux," in which two or more people share the same psychotic delusion. Because of this delusion and Mitchell's consequent bizarre behavior, the Mormon Church eventually excommunicated him.

On June 5, 2002, Mitchell, just months after being hired to fix the Smart's roof, put a chair under a window and cut a screen at the Smart's 6,600 square-foot home on Kristianna Circle, an upscale neighborhood in Salt Lake City. He then slipped into the bedroom of 14-year-old Elizabeth Smart and pressed a knife against her, warning her to be quiet and to come with him. Elizabeth's sister, nine-year-old Mary Katherine, also slept in the room. Terrified at what was happening, Mary Katherine pretended to be asleep as the abduction took place. After the abductor had left with Elizabeth, Mary Katherine ran to tell her parents, who immediately called the police. The abduction, along with becoming a huge police investigation, also became an instant media event.

"I was awakened with the helicopters coming over," a neighbor of the Smarts recalls about the morning of Elizabeth's abduction. "The street was jammed with media cars and trucks and so forth," recalls another neighbor. "I remember the traffic and the police and the FBI," said yet another resident of the block.[1]

Although at the time no one knew the motive for Elizabeth's abduction, part of Mitchell's manifesto involved his belief that the Mormon Church needed to return to its fundamental values, one of these being their earlier belief in polygamy, which Mitchell called a "lost blessing." Elizabeth, there-fore, was to become Mitchell's second of seven wives. He was at that time still married to Wanda Ilene Barzee.

Mitchell and Barzee took Elizabeth and wandered the Wasatch Range around Salt Lake City, often sleeping under bridges and begging on the street. On July 24, 2002, Mitchell, apparently wanting to procure his third wife, put a chair under a window and cut a screen at the home of Elizabeth's cousin, Jessica Wright. However, alert family members scared Mitchell away before he could get into the house.

Eventually, Mitchell, Barzee, and Elizabeth took a bus to San Diego and spent several months there. Back in Salt Lake City, the months passed, and the police investigation stalled because detectives felt certain that another man who had done handyman work at the Smart home, 48-year-old Richard Ricci, had been Elizabeth's abductor. Ricci would die in prison, steadfastly denying any involvement in Elizabeth's disappearance.

Finally, many months after Elizabeth's abduction, Mary Katherine would suddenly remember where she had seen the abductor—it was the man who had fixed their roof! The family was elated at this break and, at the request of the Smart family, Mitchell's stepson produced a photograph of Mitchell, which the Smarts then gave to the police. However, the police, still believing Ricci to be their man, brushed aside the information about Mitchell. Many members of Elizabeth's family became frustrated at the narrow view the police held about the case.

"They should have caught [Mitchell] by now," said Tom Smart, Elizabeth's uncle. "The police are too vested in Ricci."[2]

This is, unfortunately, a problem common in law enforcement, and a problem that I saw occasionally as commander of the Indianapolis Police Department's Homicide Branch. Detectives can sometimes be blind to, or simply ignore, evidence that points to anyone else if they are certain they already have the right suspect.

"At the time, I thought I was making the best choice, but now in hindsight I wasn't," said retired police detective Corey Lyman about his belief that Ricci was the abductor. "And so, absolutely, I have regrets."[3]

After spending several months near San Diego, Mitchell, Barzee, and Elizabeth returned to the Salt Lake City area. Most people in America by this time, including me and many other police officers, felt certain that Elizabeth had been killed, and her body likely dumped in some remote area.

However, only hours after the trio returned to Utah, a person who saw them on the street in Sandy, Utah, a suburb of Salt Lake City, recalled seeing a photo of Mitchell as a suspect in the Elizabeth Smart abduction, and, recognizing him, called the police. Interestingly, when spotted, the trio was just passing a billboard with Elizabeth's picture on it. Officers responding to the call stopped and questioned an older couple and a young girl. The young girl wore a wig, a blue overcoat, and a veil. After a bit of questioning, the police found that the young girl was indeed Elizabeth Smart, and they took Mitchell and Barzee into custody. Soon afterward, the police charged Mitchell and Barzee with aggravated burglary, aggravated kidnapping, and aggravated sexual assault.

Following Elizabeth's recovery, her father said, "You know, there were certainly times when I had doubts. I mean, statistically, everyone said that she was dead...The not knowing was so horrible. I think that sometimes not knowing is worse than knowing."[4]

The Smart family reunion, as might be expected, was very emotional, with Elizabeth and family members hugging and crying. In Salt Lake City, people honked their horns and shouted to others on the street, "Have you heard? They found Elizabeth!"[5] In addition to this, soon after Elizabeth's recovery, several thousand Salt Lake City residents held a candle light vigil to celebrate Elizabeth Smart's safe return.

The courts, in 2003, sent both Mitchell and Barzee to be evaluated for mental competency. Psychiatrists found both of them mentally incompetent to stand trial. In December 2006, a court again had Mitchell evaluated for mental competency. The judge, after listening to the psychiatrist's report, once again declared Mitchell mentally unfit to stand trial. Consequently, he had Mitchell returned to the Utah State [Mental] Hospital in Provo, where authorities also held Barzee.

Naturally, Elizabeth's family was ecstatic at her return and, in the years since the abduction, Elizabeth appears to have recovered very well from the ordeal of her captivity. In May 2005, Elizabeth Smart and her parents watched President Bush sign a child protection bill into law. In July 2006, Elizabeth championed a bill in Congress that would set up a nationwide sex offender registry. The bill passed and President Bush signed it into law. Elizabeth and her family also attended this bill signing.

In July 2006, Elizabeth Smart told *People* magazine, "It will never be the same as it used to be, but it's good. I have a wonderful family, good friends... I have a lot to look forward to."[6]

When asked on a national talk show whether he still hired down-on-their-luck individuals to work around his house, Ed Smart, Elizabeth's father, said, "No, we no longer hire homeless people. After something like this we're paranoid."[7]

****

While seldom becoming as huge a media event as when a psychotic stranger abducts a child, occasionally the psychotic person who does the abducting can be one of the child's own parents. For example, at 3:00 a.m., on June 30, 2003, in Miramar, Florida, a community about 15 miles north of Miami, a car backed at high speed through the rear siding glass door of a home there. When the car came to a stop inside the house, two people jumped out, a man wearing camouflage clothing and a ski mask, and a woman later identified as Nora Montano. The two intruders grabbed Nora's children, three-year-old Lorena Montano and two-year-old Moises Montano.

The home belonged to Nora Montano's mother, Nora Sarria, who had custody of the children. The children's aunt, Karla Sarria, tried to stop the abduction, but got knocked to the ground.

"I jumped on his back, and I was grabbing and pulling him away from the children," said Karla. "He hit me with a forearm across the face."[8]

Nora Sarria added, "My daughter was not in her right state of mind. It was like she was doing some kind of military mission."[9] At the time of the abduction, Nora Montano actually was in the U.S. Army, stationed at Fort Sam Houston in San Antonio, Texas.

The police, responding to the call of a home invasion, immediately put out a be-on-the-lookout bulletin for Nora Montano and the two toddlers. Nora, the police soon learned, had a long history of mental problems, and, as a consequence, the children had been taken away from her and given to the custody of her mother.

Nora Montano had been diagnosed with bipolar disorder, a mental illness in which a person's moods can quickly swing from euphoric excitement to the deepest depression. Unfortunately, while medication exists that can effectively treat bipolar disorder, Nora Montano wouldn't take hers, and instead refused to believe that she had any type of mental problems.

"In the most severe cases," said Dr. Sanjay Gupta (a CNN medical correspondent) about bipolar disorder, "people can actually become psychotic. And what that specifically means is they have delusions where they see things that aren't there, or delusions where they may think that they're the president or that they can fly or something like that."[10]

Detectives assigned to the case quickly began following a trail of credit card purchases by Nora Montano, which soon led them to a motel in Bonifay, Florida, a small town about 50 miles north of Panama City. The police believed that Nora was headed with the children back to the Army base in Texas, where she was stationed. The vehicle they were using, officers also found, had Texas plates on it.

In order to safely recover the two abducted children, the police had the manager of the motel call Nora Montano to the office on a pretext, where police officers arrested her. At the same time, other officers quietly made their way to Nora's room, where they discovered the two toddlers safe. Also in the room, the police found Jose Montano, the father of the children, and Nora's accomplice in the abduction.

The police charged Nora Montano with two counts of parental kidnapping, armed burglary, and criminal mischief. Jose faced similar charges.

Upon hearing of the children's safe recovery, the grandmother immediately drove from southern to northwest Florida in order to bring the children home. She told the authorities she was glad the children were safe and that she was getting them back, but felt badly about the situation her daughter's mental condition had gotten her into.

****

While it is a frightening enough thing to have a child abducted, it can be even more terrifying to know that a person suffering from some type of psychosis has abducted your child. Who knows how in this person's delusions he or she sees your child, or what bizarre plans he or she has for the child. This is true even if the abductor is a relative. Individuals suffering from psychosis can see and do very bizarre, and occasionally even violent, things.

Psychosis is a mental disorder in which individuals lose contact with reality. They may hear voices telling them to do things, often bizarre, and occasionally violent, things. They may suffer from hallucinations in which they believe they are visited by God, the devil, angels, or spirits. Or they may see events happening that really aren't there. In addition, psychotic individuals may also suffer from delusions, making them believe they are someone they really aren't, such as royalty or perhaps the spouse of a rock star. Also, these delusions may give them false beliefs about events that are taking place, such as seeing a threat when there really isn't one.

The National Institute of Health, on their Web site, states that psychosis can be caused by many things, including alcohol and drugs, bipolar disorder, brain tumors, epilepsy, psychotic depression, schizophrenia, dementia, and stroke. Some of the symptoms of psychosis, according to the National Institute of Health, can be a loss of touch with reality; false beliefs (delusions); unfounded fear or suspicion; disorganized thought and/or speech; and seeing, hearing, feeling, or otherwise perceiving things that are not there (hallucinations). The Institute also says that certain antipsychotic drugs can be used to control these delusions and hallucinations.[11] Unfortunately however, many people with mental disorders, like Nora Montano in the incident above, will often refuse to take this medication.

How many people in our country suffer from psychosis and other serious mental disorders? Although there is no firm count, experts agree the number is likely in the millions. While not all of these individuals become involved in serious crimes such as abduction, some do. A booklet from the U.S. Department of Justice, Office of Juvenile Justice and Delinquency Prevention, for example, states that one of the early identifying risk factors for parental abduction is when a parent is delusional.[12]

Even though many individuals with psychosis don't become involved in serious crimes, still, since their behavior is many times unusual or bizarre, the public will often call the police because of incidents involving them. And while police officers must deal with these individuals, the officers really don't know what these people are experiencing. Yet, being able to know this would be extremely helpful. And so, to assist in correcting this lack of information, a Belgium pharmaceutical company has invented a virtual hallucination machine. This device allows individuals to experience what a person with psychosis experiences. This could prove extremely helpful for detectives investigating abductions involving psychotic individuals.

A person using the machine dons goggles and earphones, and then all at once seemingly normal activities take on the feeling of delusion and hallucination. Individuals using the machine may find that what starts out as a perfectly normal conversation can suddenly become threatening, that "voices" begin speaking to them, or perhaps the face of the person they are talking to will suddenly become horribly distorted. As stated above, this kind of insight could prove invaluable in a police investigation involving a psychotic person.

"The neurons are firing images in random order. Like being awake but dreaming," said Officer Paul Tieszen of the Des Moines (Iowa) Police Department, who tried out the virtual hallucination machine. "Like a lot of jumbled thoughts. Like being trapped in a nightmare but you are awake."[13]

After reading all of the information in this and preceding chapters, some readers may believe that anyone who would kidnap, sexually assault, and then murder a young child must be psychotic. However, this is not necessarily so. While many of the people who do this may have mental problems, they are often not suffering from psychosis. Instead, many of these individuals are sociopaths, borderline personalities, antisocial personalities, and so forth.

The defining difference between these types of individuals and those suffering from psychosis is that sociopaths, etc. know that what they are doing is wrong, and they will usually kill the child in an attempt to cover up their crimes. Unlike those with psychosis, sociopathic individuals, etc. usually have a good grasp on reality. They may be narcissistic, totally self-centered, and have absolutely no conscience, but they are grounded in the real world. Individuals with psychosis, on the other hand, often can't tell the difference between their delusions and reality, and many times don't realize that what they are doing is a crime. In their delusions, their actions are totally right and justifiable. The difference between psychotic individuals and sociopaths, etc. is extremely important because truly psychotic individuals usually can't be prosecuted, while sociopaths, etc. can be.

Although the types of child abduction we have talked about in this and the previous chapters are terrifying events for parents, they are not the most common types of child abduction that take place. As we will see in the next chapter, family abduction, and particularly noncustodial parental abduction, is more common than all of the other types of child abduction combined. Yet, it too can hold distinct dangers for its victims.

Family Abductions

On January 20, 2007, around 2:00 a.m., 30-year-old Jerry D. White, a man with a long criminal history and who had spent a considerable amount of time in prison, forced his way into the northern Indiana apartment of 31-year-old Kimberley Walker. Kimberley was an ex-girlfriend of White's, and the mother of his four children, Jaylan, Justin, Kyara, and Kayla. White had reportedly been harassing Kimberley for several days, and so her sister and her sister's boyfriend, Lathie Turnage, had agreed to stay with her.

White, upon breaking into the apartment, shot Turnage twice, once in the head and once in the chest, and then took his girlfriend, Turnage, Kimberley's sister, and his four children, ages nine to 16 months, hostage. He kept them at gunpoint in the apartment for over nine hours before finally, at 11:30 a.m., forcing Kimberley and the four children into a car and driving away. The oldest child, Jaylan, suffered from severe asthma, and needed to regularly use a ventilator, so, once called to the scene, and after sending Turnage to the hospital (doctors soon listed Turnage as in critical but stable condition), the police began an intensive manhunt for White and his five hostages.

In the opinion of the police, Jaylan's fragile health, and the fact that White had already shot one person, put the hostages in extreme danger. So quickly finding them became imperative. The police figured that White and his hostages might be headed for Chicago, as White and Kimberley had lived there and White had family there.

Yet, despite an intense police effort, several days passed without any news of White and his hostages, and the concern for their safety heightened. An Amber Alert had already been issued, and though the police received a number of tips, none of them proved helpful.

Finally, on January 24, 2007, after discovering that White had made several calls from a telephone located across the street from the Sleepy Hollow Motel in Elkhart, Indiana, the police moved in. After questioning the motel manager, the authorities found that a family answering the description of the Walkers was indeed staying at the motel. Officers knocked on the door, and a crying, trembling Kimberly Walker answered it. The police quickly got her and her four children out of the room, and then arrested White as he tried to escape through an air vent. They charged White with one count of attempted murder and multiple counts of criminal confinement. A judge set White's bail at $500,000.

****

On March 25, 2007, 34-year-old John Baugher failed to return his two children, four-year-old Remi and two-year-old Lars, to his ex-wife following a scheduled visitation with them. Joelle Remillard, his ex-wife, called the police in Waitsburg, Washington, and reported the abduction. The authorities quickly issued an Amber Alert for the two children and a brown Volkswagen van the police believed they were traveling in. However, soon after Joelle reported the abduction, the police found the Volkswagen van abandoned in Stevens County in northeast Washington State.

Following a lead of credit card use, the police discovered that John had used an ATM card in Missoula, Montana. They also recovered video footage of John, his two children, and an unidentified woman eating at a McDonald's restaurant in Missoula. The video showed that John had tried to change the children's appearance by cutting and dying their blond hair dark. John, the police could see, was also trying to change his own appearance by growing a beard. The police additionally recovered video of John and the children shopping at a Ross Clothing store, and received information that they had visited a Wal-Mart and a beauty supply company.

The children's mother went on the news and pleaded with her husband to return the children. "Please, bring the kids home or drop them off somewhere where there's people," Joelle said to John during a news interview.[1]

On March 27, 2007, the police in Idaho Springs, Colorado, received a tip from a reporter in Spokane, Washington, that John and his two children were aboard a bus bound for Denver, Colorado. The police boarded the bus and arrested John, and then recovered the two children unharmed.

"I just essentially entered the bus, recognized Baugher from his picture, and arrested him without incident," said Idaho Springs (Colorado) police detective Brian Radulovich. "The children were with him."[2]

The police charged John with two counts of first-degree custodial interference. A judge ordered him held on $100,000 bond.

****

On April 26, 2002, Kelli Nunez abducted her two daughters, which her husband had custody of, from a daycare center in Lafayette, California, a community about 20 miles northeast of San Francisco. She then drove the girls to New York City. While living there, Kelli heard about an underground group, a San Jose support group for parents' rights, that would be willing to hide her abducted children for her.

Kelli flew back to San Francisco and, at the airport, saw two people she didn't know holding a placard with a code word on it. Kelli handed her two daughters over to the strangers and then left. Later arrested, Kelli spent six months in jail rather than tell the authorities where the two girls were. Reportedly, the underground group continuously moved the little girls around in order to confuse the authorities.

Finally, a local television station began an investigation into this underground group, and found that its leader, a man named Junior Manning, was a convicted child molester. Within minutes of the television station broadcasting this story, members of the underground group, apparently not knowing the truth about their leader, called the television station and made arrangements to turn the two little girls over to them.

A judge later sentenced Kelli to the maximum sentence for the abduction, five years and eight months in prison. He also sentenced a member of the underground group to four years in prison. Additionally, the judge sentenced Junior Manning, the leader of the underground group, to nine years in prison, both for his part in the abduction and for his failure to register as a sex offender.

Kelli's ex-husband, Danny, told reporters that he felt his ex-wife's sentence was certainly appropriate and would give his daughters time to heal. "I wanted the girls to have time to recover and time to develop the skills they need so they can be prepared for when they see their mother again."[3]

****

On July 21, 2007, three masked individuals, two women and a man, the man armed with a handgun, broke into the home of Jennifer and Matt Erickson in Itawamba County in northeast Mississippi. Matt wasn't at home, and so the intruders tied Jennifer up with electrical cord and then abducted five-month-old Madison Erickson. The abductors, however, left another young child of the Ericksons behind.

In a few minutes, Jennifer managed to free herself and called the police. Since the abductors had left the one child behind, and the one they took had been adopted, the focus of the police investigation naturally went to the abducted child's biological mother, Jamie Kiefer. The authorities quickly learned that Jamie had recently changed her mind about the adoption and had started legal action to void it.

"Apparently (the kidnapping) was related to the adoption of the baby," said FBI Special Agent Jason Pack. "Apparently Ms. Kiefer had changed her mind about the adoption."[4]

Sheriff Phil Crane of Itawamba County added, "I think this had been in court not too long ago. So this was an ongoing situation."[5]

The authorities soon discovered that Jamie had a sister, Rikki Swann, who lived at Fort Bragg, North Carolina. Itawamba County authorities called the military police at Fort Bragg and asked them to search the area. The police there found a white van with Mississippi plates on it parked near the apartment of Amanda Bell, a friend of Rikki Swann. Bell and Swann had become friends when their husbands, both in the same Army unit, had been deployed to Afghanistan.

The police obtained warrants, and once inside the apartment they found Jamie Kiefer, Rikki Swann, and Madison Erickson. Officers arrested the two sisters, Kiefer for the abduction and Swann for assisting her afterward. The authorities are still looking for the other individuals who helped Kiefer in the abduction. The police didn't file any charges against Bell, whom they believe didn't know about the abduction.

"I knew that Rikki was (in the home)," Bell said. "I had no idea about the kidnapping."[6]

****

On January 8, 2007, 23-year-old Jose Dominquez sneaked in through the backdoor of the home of Betzabeth Perez, his estranged wife. Carrying a knife, Jose reportedly confronted and threatened Betzabeth and another woman in the house. But when he tried to abduct his 10-month-old daughter Keely, his estranged wife struggled with him and Jose injured her. Dominquez then grabbed the baby girl and fled the house.

"He forcibly took the child from her mom and used a knife to threaten the mom and another woman that was in the home," said Sergeant Jimmy Manrrique of the Brownsville (Texas) Police Department.[7]

The next day the police caught up with Jose. They found him wandering the street near where a friend of his lived. The police recovered the baby and returned her to her mother.

Authorities charged Dominquez with two counts of aggravated assault with a deadly weapon, injury to a child, child endangerment, and evading arrest. The baby, according to the mother, although safe, was dirty, desperately needed a diaper change, and hadn't been fed for some time.

****

On February 19, 2006, Rachna Prasad was working her shift as the cashier at the parking garage of the University of California, Davis campus, about 15 miles west of Sacramento. She was giving change to a man who was leaving the garage when she noticed a little girl lying unsecured on the front seat of the car. Feeling that something might be wrong, she contacted the police and gave them a description of the car and its driver.

As it turned out, the driver, 23-year-old Jason Bentsen, had just abducted his 20-month-old daughter from the University's Medical Center. While the child had been outfitted with a security bracelet, he had apparently cut it off. Jason had had visiting privileges with his daughter, but some months before, custody of the child had been taken away from him and the child's mother, and given over to the El Dorado County Child Protective Services.

Several hours later, using the information provided by Rachna, the police stopped Jason and his daughter on Highway 50, and recovered the child unharmed. The authorities believe Jason was headed back to his home in South Lake Tahoe.

****

Many readers may think that this seems like a lot of anecdotes compared to the previous chapters, and it is, but that is only because a lot of family child abductions occur every year in our country. It is a huge crime in America, making up almost 80 percent of all the child abductions that occur each year.

According to the U.S. Department of Justice, Office of Juvenile Justice and Delinquency Prevention, in 1999, the study year for the report we talked about earlier, the *National Incidence Studies of Missing, Abducted, Runaway, and Thrownaway Children—Children Abducted by Family Members: National Estimates and Characteristics,* family members committed an estimated 203,900 child abductions in the United States.[8] While this may sound like a large number, keep in mind that the number is probably much larger. In many cases of family child abduction, the members of the family work out the situation themselves without having to involve the authorities.

Despite their large numbers, however, unless a family child abduction ends in murder, or something almost as tragic, these incidents seldom make the news like stranger child abductions do. But regardless, the odds are much better, four to one, that if a child is abducted, it will be by a family member.

Even with these odds, many readers may not see any real physical danger to the children, and think, "Oh well, at least the children are with a parent, grandparent, etc. They will be all right." These readers couldn't be more wrong. Children abducted by noncustodial parents or other relatives have a high risk of neglect, sexual and physical abuse, and possibly even worse, as the following anecdote illustrates.

* * * *

During the last part of February 2007, 47-year-old Eric Johnson had taken his eight-year-old daughter, Emily, for a weeklong vacation in Cancun, Mexico. On March 5, 2007, he was supposed to drop Emily off at school in Bedford, Indiana. Her mother, Beth, would then pick Emily up after school let out.

But instead, Eric drove his daughter to the Bedford, Indiana, city airport, where he was a student pilot. He rented a single-engine Cessna, and then took off in it with Emily.

Beth and Eric had had a rocky marriage and an even rockier divorce. In July 2006, a judge issued a protective order for Beth when she told him how Eric had pulled a gun on her and threatened to kill her if she didn't stop the divorced proceedings against him. In order to get Eric to put the gun away, Beth told him she would, but then later divorced him anyway.

Explaining later to her mother what had happened during the confrontation with Eric, Beth said, "Mom, you'll tell anybody anything when you've got a gun pointed at you."[9]

Beth naturally checked to be certain that Eric had dropped Emily off at school, and when she found out that he hadn't, she reported the abduction to the Bedford police. But before she did this, she called her ex-husband on his cell phone. Reportedly, he told her, "I've got (Emily) and you're not going to get her back." The mother could hear Emily in the background crying, "Mommy, come get me!"[10] Beth didn't know at the time that they were in an airplane.

A little later, the Cessna aircraft crashed into Eric's ex-mother-in-law's house, killing Eric and Emily. The mother-in-law, who was at home when the plane crashed into her house, wasn't hurt.

* * * *

As the incident above shows, just because an abducted child is with a family member is no assurance that the child is safe. Of course, while the murders of family abducted children, as in the case of Emily above, do happen every year, not every child kidnapped by a family member is in danger of becoming a homicide victim. Yet still, these abducted children can and often do become the victims of other crimes. In a national government study of 354,100 family abductions, researchers found that in about four percent of these (approximately 14,000), the abducted children suffered serious physical injury. Another four percent experienced physical abuse. In about one percent of the cases (approximately 3,500), the children suffered sexual abuse.[11] Some studies of this crime have found even higher rates. For example, two leading researchers in the field of child abduction found that seven percent of the family abduction victims they studied suffered sexual abuse, 23 suffered physical abuse, and five percent suffered both.[12]

But the largest harm done to family abducted children is not always physical. The government study talked about in the above paragraph found that 16 percent of the family abducted children (approximately 56,000) suffered serious mental and emotional harm.[13] Another study found that family abducted children often suffer from uncontrollable crying and mood swings, loss of bladder/bowel control, eating and sleeping disturbances, aggressive behavior, and fearfulness.[14]

In an article titled "Parental Kidnapping: A New Form of Child Abuse," the author stated, "In child stealing the children are used as both objects and weapons in the struggle between parents, which leads to the brutalization of the children psychologically, specifically destroying the sense of trust in the world around them."

This author lists a number of detrimental outcomes for the victims of family abduction:

1. Depression.
2. Loss of community.
3. Loss of stability, security, and trust.
4. Excessive fearfulness, even of ordinary occurrences.
5. Loneliness.
6. Anger.
7. Helplessness.
8. Disruption in identity formation.
9. Fear of abandonment.[15]

Much of this emotional and psychological damage to family abducted children comes from the ripping of the children away from their known, comfortable environment, and making them hunted fugitives, who must often change schools, friends, and even their names. Family abductors, in order to avoid arrest and the return of the children, must many times live on the run, seldom staying in one location for any length of time, and occasionally living on the street or in homeless shelters. Also, the abducted children have often been torn away from parents whom they love and who love them. The children many times don't know if they will ever see these parents again.

The author of a report on family child abduction that was presented to a UN conference said, "Generally, the abductor does not even speak of the abandoned parent and waits patiently for time to erase probing questions like 'When can we see mom (dad) again?'"[16] Eventually, the abductor hopes, the children won't even think about the other parent any longer.

An article in the *San Francisco Chronicle* stated, "While children kidnapped by relatives may not experience the terror of being held captive by a stranger, they suffer lasting trauma of another kind. A landmark 1991 study by the National Center for Missing and Exploited Children, published in the journal

Child Welfare, revealed that for every minute, hour, and day children remain abducted, the deeper the emotional and psychological scars they will bear for life."[17]

The Department of Justice study mentioned earlier, the *National Incidence Studies of Missing, Abducted, Runaway, and Thrownaway Children,* besides giving statistics on the number of family child abductions and the harm they cause, also provided some other interesting facts about child abductions by family members. It found that 44 percent of the children abducted by family members were under the age of six, and that while 46 percent of these abducted children were gone for less than a week, 21 percent were gone for a month or more. Of the 203,900 children abducted by family members during the study year, 53 percent were abducted by the father, 25 percent by the mother, 14 percent by a grandparent, and the remainder by aunts, uncles, etc. Interestingly, many of the family abductions, the study found, took place in the child's home or yard (36 percent) or someone else's home or yard (37 percent). In 63 percent of the cases, the abducted child was legally with the abductor when the abduction took place.

Another study, "Early Identification of Risk Factors for Parental Abduction," provided some more interesting facts about family child abduction:

1. A large percentage of the children abducted by family members were preschool age.
2. Mothers were more likely to abduct after a custody order went against them, while fathers were more likely to abduct before a custody order was issued.
3. Fathers were more likely to use force during an abduction.
4. The percentages of the races of abducting family members closely mirror that of society at large.
5. One-fourth of family abductors had a network of family and social support they could depend on during and after the abduction.
6. Allegations of neglect and physical or sexual abuse as a reason for the abduction were high among family abductions, though very often these allegations were unsubstantiated.
7. Spousal abuse claims were also very high in family abduction cases.
8. The recidivism rate for family abductors was about 30 percent.
9. In family abduction cases, nearly one-half of the abductors and two-fifths of the left-behind parents had criminal records.[18] Also, another study of child abductions found that 75 percent of male abductors and 25 percent of female abductors had exhibited violent behavior in the past.[19]

After reading all of the above, readers may ask, why do family members want to abduct children from a parent who has custody? There are several reasons. While the number is small, there are a number of legitimate cases in which the abducting relative is rescuing the children from a hazardous environment, such as a new boyfriend who is attempting to molest the children or is physically abusive to them. In many cases, the mother won't do anything about it, and consequently the father or other relative abducts the children in order to save them from this. Also, some parental abductors may take their children hostage because they hope to be able to force a reconciliation with the other parent, a person who usually wants nothing to do with them.

However, despite the small number of children that are abducted for the reasons above, noncustodial parents commit the vast majority of child abductions for one reason—revenge. The noncustodial parents want to strike back for losing their children in a bitter custody battle. The losing side wants to hurt the side that won, and the best way to do this is through stealing the children, and then keeping the children away. This threat of abduction, incidentally, isn't a danger just for a short time after the divorce and child custody hearings either. Researchers at the Department of Justice, Office of Juvenile Justice and Delinquency Prevention, found that the risk of a child abduction lasts for five years after a divorce is final.

According to the testimony given at a congressional hearing on missing children, a representative of the organization Child Find had this to say about family child abductions, "Searching parents worry and wonder, constantly tormented by this act. It is a revenge far sweeter and longer lived than a beating or even murder, for it never ends."[20]

Of course, after the abduction the danger of abuse and neglect to the abducted children increases tremendously because, while the abducting parent may want revenge and for the other parent to suffer, he or she may not really want to raise the children alone. This, as it turns out, can often be a lot of trouble and hard work. However, to keep the revenge going, the parent cannot give the children back, and so he or she is stuck with them. Consequently, neglect and/or abuse will often follow.

Fortunately, for parents worried about a family abduction, several years ago the federal government sponsored a study that revealed a number of risk factors that can show when there is an increased likelihood that a parent will become a child abductor. Using these, the other parent can know when extra precautions should be taken. The study, talked about above, "Early Identification of Risk Factors for Parental Abduction," was a collaboration between the Judith S. Wallerstein Center for the Family in Transition and the American Bar Association Center on Children and the Law. This research group found six categories of parents who were the most likely to become child abductors (highlighted words below are the risk factors found by the study, while the other comments are by the author of this book). Keep in mind, however, that these only show an increased likelihood, and that being in one of these categories isn't an absolute guarantee that a parent will become a child abductor, nor does not fitting into any of these categories absolutely guarantee that a parent won't become a child abductor.

1. *When there has been a prior threat of or an actual abduction.* Past performance is the best indicator of future performance. Therefore, a person who has previously abducted a child is much more likely to do it than one

who hasn't. In addition, if a parent has previously abducted a child, or has made a credible threat to do so, the custodial parent, fearing an abduction, will naturally try to keep the child away from the other parent, which may then push him or her into taking action. This also applies to legal orders and court sanctions that keep a parent away from his or her children.

2. *When a parent suspects or believes abuse has occurred and friends and family members support these concerns.* In some cases of family abduction, the abducting parent believes that the other parent is abusing, molesting, or neglecting the children. Often, the abducting parent may have reported this abuse to the police, but the authorities have not acted on it (occasionally, but not always, because there is no proof of the abuse). However, the abducting parent, particularly if he or she has supporting family members or friends, feels that something has to be done to rescue the children, and this will often lead to an abduction.

3. *When a parent is paranoid delusional.* Parents with a serious mental disorder such as paranoid delusions can be extremely dangerous as child abductors. The custodial parents have no idea how the delusional parents see the children or what plans the delusional parents may have for them. Since the abducting parents suffer from paranoid delusions, they may see the children as an evil extension of the custodial parents and feel the need to kill them. Or, since the parents are paranoid delusional, they may abduct the children because they believe the custodial parents mean to harm them. And of course, the stress of going through a divorce and child custody hearings can often aggravate the paranoia.

4. *When a parent is severely sociopathic.* Sociopathic individuals are generally very egotistical, self-serving, and believe that they are special, privileged people. They have little regard for anyone else, and feel that since they are superior to everyone else, it is only right and proper to use others for their own benefit. Consequently, when one of these parents abducts a child, it is not because of love for the child, but rather because the parent wants to use the child for some selfish purpose. Severely sociopathic people have little or no conscience, and often have absolutely no qualms about using, or even harming, their own children in order to manipulate or hurt others.

5. *When a parent who is a citizen of another country ends a mixed-cultural marriage.* The danger of child abduction in these cases is very high when the abducting parent has a strong social network in another country. The abducting parent will naturally feel rejected and lonesome during the divorce, and may decide to return to his or her roots, where there will be the emotional support he or she needs. In addition, some cultures consider children as property, and so consequently, when these abductors return to their home country, they will often take their children with them. Also, many of these abductors may blame the "decadent" American culture for their divorce, and want to raise their children in a different culture, the one they were raised in.

6. *When parents feel alienated from the legal system and have family/social support in another community.* When parents believe that they have gotten a raw deal from the courts in a divorce and child custody hearing, they may feel the need to take matters into their own hands and abduct the children the courts didn't, but should have, awarded to them. This is especially true

if there is a location that the abductors can take the children to where there will be social and emotional support for the abductor. This category also includes parents who are the victims of domestic violence. In cases in which the courts fail to recognize this violence, and consequently award the children to the abuser, the other parent may feel the need to take action.

Along with the above report, there have been several additional studies that have shown other warning signs of parental child abduction:

1. *When a person has no strong ties or links to the community or state.* Individuals who have just gone through a divorce and have lost custody of their children often feel abandoned and rejected. If these individuals have no pressing reason to stay in the community, and want to pay back the other parent for the rejection and abandonment, child abduction becomes a very real possibility.
2. *When a person has no financial reason to remain in the community or state.* Often, parents who have lost custody of their children cannot abduct them and leave the community because of the financial need (i.e., a good job) to stay in the community. They know that if they leave the community they will suffer a dramatic financial loss. But the opposite situation, where parents feel that they could do just as well or perhaps even better financially in another community, heightens the risk of child abduction.
3. *When a person has become involved in abduction planning activities, such as selling a home, acquiring a home in another community or state, quitting a job, liquidating assets, requesting copies of their children's school records, etc.* When a custodial parent finds evidence of this kind of activity, serious action needs to be taken, which we will talk about in a later chapter. A non-custodial parent who has engaged in these kinds of activities has obviously given child abduction some serious consideration.
4. *When the relationship with an ex-spouse is volatile and the ex-spouses argue often over child visitation.* The noncustodial parent may feel that he or she is not getting a fair deal from the ex-spouse, and, since they can't agree on visitation, will want to correct the situation by abducting the child. And since the relationship with the ex-spouse is volatile, the abduction can also become an act of revenge.

Readers should keep in mind that, often, abducting parents will not fit into just one of the above categories. They may have traits from several of them.

While the abduction of a child to another community or state is stressful enough for the left-behind parent, there is another type of family abduction that is much worse. This is an international abduction. As we will see in the next chapter, the parents of internationally abducted children quickly find out that the custody orders of American courts often mean little or nothing in foreign countries, and that the courts in foreign countries may many times unfairly favor the abductors. But worst of all, the left-behind parents also discover that the U.S. government usually offers little or no help to the parents of internationally abducted children.

International Abductions

In 1988, talented and hugely successful artist Jeff Koons met Italian porn star Ilona Staller. Staller had once made international news by being elected to the Chamber of Deputies of the Italian Parliament. She ran as a representative of the "Party of Love." Koons used Staller as a model for a while, and eventually fell in love with her. The couple married in Hungary in 1991, and produced a son, Ludwig, in 1992. In 1993, the couple divorced. Then the real trouble started.

Both parents wanted custody of Ludwig, and started legal proceedings to get it. Staller, however, exacerbated the custody problem by taking Ludwig to Italy, supposedly on a business trip. However, once there, she decided that, rather than return to New York City, she would just stay and live in Italy with her son.

Koons would have none of this, however. He flew to Rome and found that his wife was in Ecuador on business. However, he also found that she had left Ludwig there in Rome. Having a duplicate passport for Ludwig, Koons took his son and flew back to New York City with him. Koons then hired a high-power law firm and they managed to persuade a New York Supreme Court judge to issue an order not allowing Ludwig to be removed from New York until the divorce proceedings were final. Staller, returning from Ecuador to find her son gone, also came to New York, and a court awarded her shared custody of Ludwig.

And so, the divorce and child custody proceedings dragged on. In 1994, Staller, apparently afraid that the U.S. courts would grant custody of Ludwig to her estranged husband, and in violation of the court order, took her son and fled back to Italy.

Finding his son missing again, Koons then returned to Italy, hired an Italian attorney, and, in 1998, the Civil Tribunal of Rome awarded him custody of Ludwig. Staller, however, appealed the decision and eventually a higher court overturned the custody order and instead ruled in her favor.

"I felt like a dog chasing his tail, dealing with the injustice we were receiving," Koons said of the legal proceedings in Italy. "It was very hard to go through. It went on for years."[1]

Staller though had her own feelings about the child custody battle, "If they took away my son, you can forget about the Hague Convention because I would have come to America with a tank to get my son back."[2]

The legal battle raged on, costing both parents huge sums of money. It appears, however, that Staller will likely prevail and keep custody of Ludwig, now 15, because of a loophole in the Hague Convention, a treaty the United States has signed with Italy and almost 80 other countries. This treaty is supposed to immediately return internationally abducted children to their home country for that country's courts to decide who should have custody. However, as we will discuss at length later in this chapter, the Hague Convention has a number of loopholes that can be used by a parent who internationally abducts a child. In this case, Staller's attorneys used the loophole of not having to return an internationally abducted child who has been in a country for over a year. This loophole in the treaty is based on the belief that returning a child after this length of time would probably be more upsetting and unsettling than allowing the child to remain where he or she has likely become acclimated. In addition to loopholes though, the treaty itself is often not always adhered to by all countries, even though signed by and in force in these countries.

"I always felt my government would do the right thing and get my child back," Koons said. "Now I realize that I might not be able to see and live with my child again."[3]

In May 2004, Koons lost another court case concerning the child custody battle. He unsuccessfully attempted to have a judge reduce the legal bill he had received from the law firm he had hired to retrieve Ludwig from Staller. The bill was for $3.9 million.

* * * *

Many readers might wonder about the relevance of the above incident since it involves celebrities, albeit minor ones, and most international child abductions involve ordinary people. But it has strong relevance. In Koons' case, he has had several courts both side with and rule for him, yet he still doesn't have custody of his child. And he has spent nearly $4 million in this fight. So, if a person who has this much money to spend, and a celebrity status to back him up, cannot successfully recover an internationally abducted child, what chance does an ordinary person with limited resources have? Often, as we will see in this chapter, not much, though there is hope.

International child abduction is not a huge crime in comparison to ordinary family abductions, with the U.S. State Department estimating that every year parents internationally abduct approximately 1,000 children.[4] This is less than one half of one percent of all family abductions. Of course, this total is only an estimate based on the number of left-behind parents who contact the U.S. State Department. No one knows how many left-behind parents of internationally abducted children hire lawyers, mercenaries, etc. on their own without involving the U.S. government. Still, the number likely pales in comparison to the total number of family child abductions every year.

But yet, while this 1,000 or more internationally abducted children is a small number in comparison to the over 200,000 ordinary family child abductions that occur each year, in many ways international child abductions are much, much worse than ordinary family abductions. This is because, in ordinary family abductions, if the abductors take the children to another community, or even to another state, and the custodial parents can find out where the children have been taken to, the laws are usually pretty straightforward. The custodial parents can usually, but not always, have their custody orders enforced and their children returned.

In international abductions, on the other hand, the abducting parents often take the children to countries that don't have any treaties in effect with the United States concerning the return of abducted children. In many of these countries, a court order from the United States means absolutely nothing. As a matter of fact, in some countries local laws will favor the abducting parent, particularly if that parent is a citizen of the country. This makes the retrieval of an abducted child from one of these countries nearly (but not totally) impossible for the custodial parent.

However, while worse than ordinary parental child abductions, international parental abductions are in many ways very similar to the ordinary ones. The victims are usually young children, the abductor often has a social support network in the country he or she is abducting the child to, the abductor generally does not place any value on the other parent's role in the child's life, and the abductions are often committed as revenge for a bitter divorce and child custody battle. One major difference, however, is that 80 percent of internationally abducted children have claim to more than one nationality.[5] This fact often makes the abduction easier since the child is usually entitled not just to a passport from the United States, but also a passport from the other country of citizenship. Custodial parents are many times unaware of the existence of this foreign passport, and consequently cannot stop their children from leaving the United States with the abductors.

The American Bar Association Center on Children and the Law conducted a study in collaboration with three national missing children organizations.

They interviewed 97 parents of children who had been internationally abducted. The results showed that:

1. The children of these parents had been taken to 46 different countries. One-third of these children had been taken to countries in Latin America, one-fourth to Muslim countries, and one-fifth to European countries.
2. Sixty-two percent of the abductors were not American citizens, but citizens of a foreign country.
3. Eighty-three percent of the marriages were of mixed nationality.
4. The abducting parent was likely to make less money than the left-behind parent.
5. Mothers and fathers were equally likely to be international abductors.
6. An equal number of girls and boys were internationally abducted.
7. The mean age of the abducted child was five.
8. Half of the abductions took place during a court-ordered visitation.
9. The left-behind parents spent an average of $33,500 for search and recovery efforts involving their internationally abducted children.[6]

In 1980, in order to straighten out the confusing web of conflicting laws in different countries regarding child abduction and custody, a group met at The Hague in the Netherlands, and, on October 15, 1980, they produced a document called "The Hague Convention on the Civil Aspects of International Child Abduction." (This document can be viewed in full at www.incadat.com.) What this document did was state that all countries that sign and ratify the Hague Convention agree that a child illegally abducted to a country that is a signatory of the treaty will be promptly returned to the child's home country, and that the courts in the child's home country will be the ones to decide all custody issues.

According to Article 1 of the Hague Convention, "The objects of the present Convention are: a) to secure the prompt return of children wrongfully removed to or retained in any Contracting State; and b) to ensure that rights of custody and of access under the law of one Contracting State are effectively respected in other Contracting States."[7]

The Hague Convention requires that a decision on the return of an abducted child must be made within six weeks of the commencement of proceedings. Interestingly, a parent doesn't have to have a custody decree in order to make use of the Hague Convention. The parent must, however, have been exercising a "right of custody" at the time of the abduction. In addition to this, one of the main points of the Hague Convention is that it should be the courts in the home country of the abducted child that make the custody decisions. Basically, what the Hague Convention says is that the courts in the country the child has been abducted to are not to look into the merits of the case. It is not their job to decide who would be the best parent. That is for the courts in the child's home country.

As of 2007, 78 countries have signed and ratified the Hague Convention. The United States ratified it in 1988. How often does this treaty come into play for U.S. citizens?

The American Bar Association Center on Children and the Law conducted a survey of countries that have signed and ratified the Hague Convention. They found that these countries most often identified the United States as one of the three countries they most frequently dealt with for all categories of international child abduction cases. As a matter of fact, the United States accounted for more than 50 percent of all the cases these nations dealt with.[8]

However, as with most legal documents, there are exceptions to the Hague Convention. Once such exception states that the custodial parents must begin the Hague Convention proceedings within a year of their children being abducted. The reasoning for this exception is that the developers of the treaty felt that if children have been situated in a country for a year or more, they have likely become acclimated to the country, and moving them would probably cause a serious disruption in their lives. For the sake of the children's stability, they felt, it would probably be better to just leave them where they are.

The exception above is the legal argument that Ilona Staller, in the incident at the beginning of this chapter, is using to keep her son Ludwig in Italy. Her lawyer, in court pleadings, doesn't deny that Staller took Ludwig in violation of a New York court order, but rather his argument is that Ludwig has been living for so many years now with his mother in Italy that it would be unfairly disruptive to his life to suddenly make him move back to New York City with his father. Many legal experts think this argument will likely prevail.

Other exceptions in the Hague Convention include the cutoff of the treaty's provisions when children reach the age of sixteen, and the provision that abducted children don't have to be returned to their home country if they will be in danger there. Unfortunately, the Hague Convention doesn't spell out what the dangers are that fit into this last exception. Instead, this decision is left up to the courts in the country the child is abducted to.

The exact wording of the Hague Convention on this last exception is, "Notwithstanding the provisions of the preceding Article, the judicial or administrative authority of the request State is not bound to order the return of the child if the person, institution or other body which opposes its return establishes that...there is a grave risk that his or her return would expose the child to physical or psychological harm or otherwise place the child in an intolerable situation."[9]

The Hague Convention, though it is all that many left-behind parents of internationally abducted children have to work with, is certainly not a perfect instrument. Maura Harty, assistant secretary of state for Consular Affairs, said in testimony before Congress in July 2003, "While the Hague Convention has facilitated the return of many children to the United States, and while it is a vast improvement over the lack of any international mechanism whatsoever, it is an imperfect instrument. The Hague Convention does not guarantee a satisfactory result for every left-behind parent. Compliance with the Convention varies among foreign jurisdictions. Even when the left-behind parent has filed an application in a timely fashion, hired legal counsel, and literally done everything 'right,' that parent, and the United States, may be bitterly disappointed with the result."[10]

As Assistant Secretary of State Harty stated, even in countries that have signed and ratified the Hague Convention, left-behind parents of internationally abducted children often find that the courts in some of these countries don't abide by the requirements of the treaty. Jeff Koons found this out in the incident at the beginning of this chapter when with dealing with Italian law concerning the abduction of his son Ludwig. Italy, however, isn't the only signatory country to the Hague Convention that disregards its requirements.

In a report demanded by a U.S. senator of all the countries that have failed to return abducted children, of all the current cases of child abduction to European countries that haven't been resolved, and of all the countries that give protection to child kidnappers, the U.S. State Department produced a very watered down report, coached in diplomatic terms. The State Department did, however, list the five worst offending Hague Convention signatory countries: Austria, Honduras, Mauritius, Mexico, and Sweden. Many people who read the report were shocked that the authors of the report didn't name Germany as one of the top offenders. U.S. State Department records show that of 243 Hague Convention cases filed in Germany, only 40 children have been returned.[11]

"These records should be available for every parent," said Joseph Howard, whose ex-wife abducted their 10-year-old daughter to Germany. "Why is the State Department covering up for Germany's criminal behavior?"[12]

Tom Sylvester, another left-behind parent, had some years before fallen in love with and married a woman from Austria. However, when the marriage went bad and Tom found that his wife had abducted their daughter to Austria, he did what he was legally supposed to do. He filed a petition under the Hague Convention. Yet, even though Tom prevailed in the Austrian court system, and had an order from Austria's highest court that gave him custody of his daughter, Austrian officials simply refused to comply with it.

"I was deceived," Sylvester said. "I trusted in the idea that Austria was a civilized country that would live up to its obligations."[13]

Sweden, another nation that has signed and ratified the Hague Convention, also seldom returns abducted children. Tom Johnson, who works as an attorney for the U.S. government, had his daughter abducted by his Swedish ex-wife. Tom also followed all the proper procedures and obtained an order from the Swedish courts to return his daughter. Officials, however, wouldn't enforce the order. Interestingly, Sweden paid for all of the legal expenses of Tom's wife, while Tom had to shoulder all of his legal expenses himself.

Tom eventually testified before the House International Relations Committee about the problem of getting the Hague Convention enforced, but little has been done because of his testimony. Sweden's Supreme Administrative Court maintains that it is following the Hague Convention. By the time it got the case, two years had passed, and by this time forcing Tom's daughter to move back to the United States would be disruptive to her stability, as the exception in the Hague Convention states.

"Swedish culture says that all children would be better off in Sweden and certainly the ones that belong to Swedish mothers," Tom Johnson said.[14]

Yet, while the Hague Convention is certainly imperfect, not having it is often much worse. In countries that aren't signatories to the Hague Convention, local law usually decides child custody cases. In many instances, this can work against custodial parents. For example, in many Muslim countries, most of which haven't signed the Hague Convention, Islamic Family Law applies to international child abduction cases. Women will often find that Islamic Family Law doesn't favor them. In most Islamic countries, for example, women and children cannot leave the country without the husband and father's permission. Also in most Islamic countries, the father is considered to have the ultimate custody of all children born of any marriage.

In addition to many Islamic countries, a number of other nations have also not signed and ratified the Hague Convention. These include, for example, Russia, China, Saudi Arabia, The Philippines, and Japan.

In Asia, many left-behind parents consider Japan to be the worst abuser of custodial parents' rights. "A Japanese court will never give custody to a foreign parent," said international family lawyer Jeremy Morley. "If the child is a Japanese national, the system will only see it as his right to be raised in Japan. They feel it would be extremely unfair to a child to deprive him of the opportunity to live in a wonderful place like Japan."[15] According to a December 2006 Scripps Howard article, the U.S. State Department has 32 open cases of child abduction to Japan. They have not had one success yet in getting a child returned.[16]

Still, despite all the problems in both countries that have and have not signed the Hague Convention, the chances are usually much better of having an internationally abducted child returned from a signatory nation to the Hague Convention than from one that is not. For readers wanting a list of countries that have signed and ratified the Hague Convention, they can find it at http://patriot.net/~crouch/hague.html.

One of the primary requirements of the Hague Convention is that signatory nations provide an agency called the Central Authority, whose job it is to deal specifically with the issue of internationally abducted children. According to the Hague Convention, Central Authorities of the signatory nations are required to work with each other to discover the whereabouts of a child wrongfully abducted, to insure the welfare of the abducted child, to first attempt to obtain a voluntary return of the child, and then to pursue legal avenues if a voluntary return isn't possible.

In the United States, the Central Authority agency that deals with children abducted from the United States to a foreign country is the Office of Children's Issues of the U.S. State Department. According to the Department of State's Web site, the Office of Children's Issues, (888) 407–4747, can help the parents of internationally abducted children by:

1. Assisting with the filing of a Hague Convention petition in a foreign country.
2. Assisting in locating an abducted child and reporting on the child's health and welfare.
3. Giving parents pertinent information on the legal issues involved in the country their children have been abducted to.
4. Assisting the parents with locating the correct officials who can help them in the foreign country.[17]

However, the State Department also warns that it cannot be involved in any attempt to re-abduct a child or give refuge to a parent and child involved in a re-abduction. Nor, the Web site states, can the U.S. government help with the many legal and other expenses left-behind parents will encounter.

For children abducted to the United States from a foreign country, the agency that has been designated to deal with these cases is the National Center for Missing and Exploited Children. This is a government-supported, nonprofit agency. We will talk about this organization at length in another chapter.

Most readers will, of course, be much more concerned about children abducted from the United States rather than to, and will therefore more likely have to deal with the U.S. Department of State. The U.S. State Department's Web site contains the following statement, "The Department of State considers international parental child abduction, as well as the welfare and protection of U.S. citizen children taken overseas, to be important, serious matters. We place the highest priority on the welfare of children who have been victimized by international abductors."[18]

This sounds impressive, and while some parents whose children have been abducted to a foreign country might believe the above statement and expect that the U.S. State Department would use its considerable clout to protect its most vulnerable and innocent citizens, often they find just the opposite. They find that, other than lip service, the U.S. State Department offers very little assistance to the families of internationally abducted children.

Ray Mabus, a former ambassador to Saudi Arabia, said, "Embassies take pretty good care of Americans who lose their passports overseas. But if you lose your kids, it's going to be harder than it ought to be to get anyone to listen."[19]

Many parents of internationally abducted children, after dealing with the U.S. Department of State, complain that the State Department is more

concerned with keeping foreign governments happy than with helping
parents regain abducted children. Many left-behind parents feel that the State
Department, rather than wanting to help them, instead sees them as an
annoyance. Tom Johnson, the father we talked about above, whose daughter
had been abducted to Sweden, testified before a Congressional Committee
and complained about the total lack of help he received from the State
Department. He even told them that a top State Department legal advisor
said to him, "I don't work for the American people, I work for the Secretary
of State."[20]

So many left-behind parents have expressed dissatisfaction with the performance of the U.S. State Department in dealing with international child
abductions, and these parents' protests to Congressional members have
become so great, that the federal government's GAO (General Accounting
Office) conducted an audit of the U.S. State Department's response to
international child abduction. Their review was much less than glowing.

The GAO report stated, "Over the past several years, many left-behind
parents have criticized the federal government's performance in responding
to international parental child abductions. They maintain that the federal government's response has been uncoordinated, insensitive, and ineffective."[21]
The body of the GAO report then pretty well confirmed these complaints.

The GAO report found four major problems with the State Department's
handling of internationally abducted children:

1. Gaps in federal services to left-behind parents, which make it difficult for
    parents to recover their abducted children. [The report commented on
    the fact that the U.S. government gives no financial assistance at all to the
    parents of internationally abducted children, while most Hague Conven-
    tion countries do. These expenses can easily reach six figures.]
2. Weaknesses within the existing State Department case-tracking process,
    which impair case and program coordination. [The report commented on
    the fact that parents are often never updated on the status of their cases.]
3. Lack of systematic and aggressive diplomatic efforts to improve
    international responses to parental child abductions.
4. Limited use [by the Department of Justice] of the International Parental
    Kidnapping Crime Act of 1993 to pursue abducting parents and bring
    them to justice.[22]

In a follow-up report, the GAO found that in the two-and-a-half year time
span it studied, the State Department had received reports of 2,347 abductions
of children to foreign countries. Only 503, or 21 percent, of these children
were returned to the left-behind parents.[23]

The follow-up GAO report also ended with a much less than glowing assess-
ment of the State and Justice Department's plans to improve their abducted
children return success. It basically said that though the State Department
and Department of Justice had promised to improve, they gave no concrete

plans for how they would do it. The report stated, "Although State and Justice have made some progress, most actions they have identified as necessary to improve the federal response have not been implemented, and many steps are not clearly defined." The report then goes on to state, "[W]e question whether these actions will be implemented because the State and Justice Departments have no comprehensive plan for moving forward with their actions."[24]

Some left-behind parents of internationally abducted children have found that the U.S. government is so powerless and unwilling to help them that they have been forced to take drastic and less-than-legal means to recover their internationally abducted children. Some left-behind parents have been forced to hire mercenaries who will go into foreign countries and recover their children for them. While this is usually illegal in most countries, and the U.S. State Department warns sternly against it, this method has nevertheless proven successful a number of times.

A number of organizations, many of then run by ex-Special Forces or Green Beret personnel, advertise their services in recovering abducted children. The Web site of one such company states, "[Our] personnel are selectively recruited from various elite military, intelligence, law enforcement and medical agencies from around the globe with expertise in their own specific fields. Such experience is not readily available elsewhere in the private and commercial sector."[25] We will talk in more detail about this option in a later chapter.

Since the Hague Convention doesn't always work, even though countries have signed and ratified it, the National Center for Missing and Exploited Children convened an international forum to look at the problems with this treaty. The members of this forum found many problems.

In its report, the forum, which included members from many countries, said that problems occur in Hague Convention countries because of undue delays in processing cases, lack of support given to left-behind parents, unawareness of attorneys and judges with the requirements of the Hague Convention, improper use of the Hague Convention exceptions, and the lack in many countries of an arm to enforce Hague Convention return orders.[26] A new or amended treaty will likely be needed to fix these problems.

When most people think of international child abduction, they think of a child kidnapped from the United States and taken to some foreign country. Few people think of it in reverse, in which a child born and living in a foreign country is abducted to the United States. However, as the following incident shows, these types of abductions do occur.

****

Inga Beveridge, who lived in Australia with three children fathered by two husbands, met retired Suffolk County police officer Kenneth Quaranto while playing an online computer game. She soon fell in love with him. In September 2000, she abducted her three children from Australia, in violation of

Australian law, and brought them to live with her and Quaranto on Long Island in New York.

The fathers of the three children, John Beveridge and Christo Norden-Powers, searched diligently for them. "My ex-wife was very good at covering her tracks," John Beveridge said.[27]

However, eventually John learned of Inga's whereabouts and filed a complaint under the Hague Convention, asking to have the abducted children returned to Australia. A federal judge who heard the case, and following the content of the Hague Convention, ordered U.S. marshals to retrieve the children and return them to their fathers.

In December 2000, federal marshals did just this. They raided the Quaranto house and retrieved the children, returning them to their fathers.

＊＊＊＊

Most readers might suppose that the United States, considering the problems it experiences having its own abducted children returned from foreign countries, would have a 100 percent record of returning foreign children abducted to the United States. However, this isn't so. The United States, though sincere in its efforts, has a less than perfect record in returning children that should be returned. According to testimony before Congress by Ernie Allen, president of the National Center for Missing and Exploited Children, the U.S. return rate, though nearing 90 percent, wasn't perfect.[28]

Finally, as talked about above, while the U.S. government may be of little help to U.S. citizens trying to get their internationally abducted children returned, the U.S. Department of Justice, Office of Juvenile Justice and Delinquency Prevention, has nevertheless prepared a very comprehensive guide for parents of internationally abducted children, titled "A Family Resource Guide on International Parental Kidnapping." This guide covers such subjects as preventing an international parental kidnapping, stopping an abduction in progress, how to search for an internationally abducted child, civil and criminal remedies that can be used to recover an internationally abducted child, the various resources available to assist the parents of an internationally abducted child, and the importance of planning the reunification with an abducted child so as to keep psychological and emotional problems to a minimum. This report can be downloaded from the Internet at www.missingkids.com.

While so far in this book we have covered the major types of child abduction, there are also child abductions committed every year for reasons other than sexual assault, the desire to have an infant, or to gain revenge on an ex-spouse. Although these other types of child abduction are smaller in number than the major types, they can still be, as we will see in the next chapter, every bit as dangerous—and occasionally even deadly.

Other Types of Child Abduction

In June 2002, someone shot and killed the uncle of seven-year-old Erica Pratt. Following the murder, a rumor began spreading through the southwest Philadelphia neighborhood where Erica lived that her family had gotten a large insurance settlement for her uncle's death. This rumor apparently reached the wrong ears.

On July 22, 2002, two men in a white car snatched Erica, kicking and screaming, from a street corner in Philadelphia near her grandmother's house. Within a short time of Erica's abduction, the family received a call from the kidnappers saying they wanted $150,000 for Erica' safe return. The men then let Erica talk to her family so they would know the callers really had her.

The two men took Erica to the basement of an abandoned house on the northwest side of Philadelphia, where they duct taped her hands, feet, and eyes. They then left her there, apparently expecting to pick up the ransom money soon.

Erica though, after being left in the basement for almost 24 hours, finally decided that she couldn't just simply wait for someone else to rescue her. She began chewing on the duct tape, and finally managed to free herself. She then kicked out a panel in the basement door, afterward pushing out a window of the house and calling for help. Children playing in the neighborhood heard her cries and alerted two police officers who happened to be in the area.

"She had duct tape around her head and duct tape marks on her eyes and face," said Officer Michael Harvey, one of the two officers who had been alerted to Erica's location. "Her left eye was bulging, and we observed duct tape on her hands."[1]

The officers drove Erica to a local hospital to have her checked out. The family, naturally, rushed there to be reunited with her. "She's OK, she's fine, she's safe," Erica's mother told the news media. "That's all we're worried about."[2]

The police later arrested James Burns and Edward Johnson, two men with long criminal records. Authorities charged both men with Erica's kidnapping.

When asked about the rumors of insurance money and the reason for the abduction, a family friend laughed and said, "They don't have $150,000. There's not $150,000 in this whole neighborhood...this whole thing was a misunderstanding and misinformation that got blown out of proportion, and a little 7-year-old girl got caught up in it."[3]

****

Just before 9:00 a.m., on February 23, 2007, 13-year-old Clay Moore and a dozen other students stood waiting at a school bus stop in Parrish Florida, a small community about 30 miles southeast of St. Petersburg. Suddenly, a red Ford Ranger truck skidded to a stop in front of them. The startled school children watched in horror as a man jumped out with a gun and forced Clay to get into the truck, then sped away.

The abductor drove Clay to a wooded area, where he duct taped him to a tree. Clay, though frightened during the ride, had realized that he might not be able to depend on anyone else to rescue him, and so, during the trip to the wooded area, he unfastened a safety pin he had used to repair his school uniform jacket. He hid the pin in his mouth.

Once the man had fastened Clay to the tree, he jumped back into the red pickup truck and sped away. Clay waited until he was certain the man wasn't coming back, and then began using the safety pin to free himself from the duct tape. After getting himself loose, Clay walked until he found some farm workers, who let him use one of their cell phones to call his parents.

"I can't put into words how absolutely horrifying it was when we received the news [about the kidnapping]," Clay's mother, Traci Kelle, said. "But I have to say when I got this phone call (that he was safe), it was the best thing that ever happened in my life."[4]

The detailed information that Clay gave to the police led them to the home of 22-year-old Vicente Ignacio Beltran-Moreno, a Mexican national who lived in nearby Bradenton, Florida. "He [Clay] was right on the money with the information that he gave us," said Manatee County Sheriff Charlie Wells.[5]

Although the police didn't find Vicente at home, they did find the red Ford Ranger truck he had used in the abduction. They also found evidence in the form of a handwritten note that showed that Vicente had kidnapped Clay with the intent of ransoming him.

Even though the police quickly put an alert out for him, Vicente somehow managed to escape back to his native Mexico. Finding this out, the police contacted the Mexican authorities and requested that they pick up Vicente. Vicente, upon discovering that the police were looking for him, voluntarily surrendered to U.S. authorities at the Texas/Mexico border on March 7, 2007. The police charged him with Clay's kidnapping.

"We are truly proud of Clay," Traci Kelle said. "He did an incredible job on his own. He kept his head about him."[6]

****

The abduction of children in our country for the purpose of ransom is certainly not unheard of. Practically everyone, for example, knows about the Lindbergh baby kidnapping, in which the Lindbergh family paid $50,000 in an unsuccessful attempt to get their baby back. Most readers probably also know about the July 1976 kidnapping of 26 school children and their bus driver in Chowchilla, California. The abductors in this case had hoped to get a $5 million ransom for the return of the children. Although the Lindbergh and Chowchilla incidents occurred a number of years ago, as the two much more recent incidents above demonstrate, cases of child abduction for the purpose of ransom still occur today.

Along with ransom, another reason for child abduction that few readers are probably aware of is membership by a parent or relative in a cult or extreme religious sect. Child abductions of this type occur because the leader of one of these cults or sects will order a member to abduct a child that the cult or sect member doesn't have custody of so that the child can be raised under the cult or sect control. If a cult or sect is to survive, it must bring in new members, and this is one of the ways cults and sects obtain them.

Why, readers might ask, would parents or relatives do this? First, they do it because these parents or relatives are often totally committed to the cult or sect ideals and goals and think the children should be too. Also, the parents or relatives many times can't say no to their leaders. Through various mind control techniques, cult and sect leaders often hold absolute, total control over their members, who have been known, besides child abduction, to do much worse things, such as torture people or even commit murder simply because a cult or sect leader told them to.

As most readers are aware, there were many stories about cults and extreme religious sects in the news media during the 1970s, 80s, and 90s, with probably the last major news story about them in the United States being the mass suicide of the Heaven's Gate cult during the passage of comet Hale-Bopp in 1997.

However, as the following two incidents show, cults and extreme religious sects are still around and active today, and in large numbers.

* * * *

In April 2005, Michael Hari, a former county sheriff, was supposed to have appeared with his two daughters at a child custody hearing. "I got a call from Michael," his ex-wife said. "He told me, 'We're running late. We'll be there in a few hours.'"[7] Michael and the girls, however, never showed up for the hearing.

After Michael and his daughters didn't show up at the custody hearing, and no one knew where they were, Michael's ex-wife and her family contacted the National Center for Missing and Exploited Children. The Center put them in touch with representatives of national talk show host Dr. Phil McGraw. Representatives of the show offered to help the family by paying for a private investigator and giving the family an expense account to have the girls returned once they were located.

"We jumped at it," a family member said. "We didn't have the money to go to all that."[8]

Michael's ex-wife eventually found out that he was with his two girls in the Central America country of Belize, where a religious group he belonged to called the Old Brethren German Baptist Church had a compound. In this church compound the conditions were reportedly very primitive, with no electricity or running water. Michael's ex-wife naturally became concerned, and not just about the physical and emotional welfare of her daughters, but also about the fact that her two girls were no longer attending school. Allegedly, the Old Brethren German Baptist Church believes that girls should not receive any education beyond the eighth grade.[9]

Once Michael and the two girls had been located in Belize, nationally renowned television host Dr. Phil used an on-air plea to persuade Michael to bring his two girls back to the United States. Upon Michael's return, the police arrested him and charged him with the girls' abduction. On November 14, 2006, a court found Michael guilty of abducting his two daughters.

In an even more recent case, on August 6, 2007, French commandoes stormed a cult compound on La Reunion Island and rescued an abducted 12-year-old boy. A cult had abducted Alexandre Thelahine from his parent's home on August 3, 2007 because the cult believes he is the "New Messiah." This same cult had also abducted him on July 9, 2007, but police rescued the boy the next day.

The French police had been especially anxious to find this abduction victim because the leader of the cult, 25-year-old Julien Verbard, had been convicted in absentia of raping two young boys. According to the police, Verbard held total control over the cult members, who devoted their lives to protecting him. While hiding Verbard from the police, the cult members used extreme security measures to be certain the authorities couldn't find them.

"All the members of the sect protected him all the time," said police detective Francois Perrault about the cult members' devotion to leader Julien Verbard, "traveling only at night and using three vehicles to be sure nobody would follow them."[10]

* * * *

As talked about above, cults and extreme religious sects have not been highly visible or in the news lately. During the 1970s and 80s, readers were used to seeing, for example, Hare Krishna devotees, with their shaved heads and saffron robes, begging in airports and other public places. And even up to the turn of the twenty-first century, readers were used to hearing about atrocities such as the Jim Jones mass suicide in Guyana in 1978, the deaths of the Branch Davidians and government agents in Waco, Texas, in 1993, and the mass murder of over 1,000 cult members in Uganda in 2000. These kinds of tragedies became so common that many readers were no longer stunned when they heard about them.

Although events involving cults and sects have seemed to have quieted down since the Uganda atrocity, that doesn't mean that cults or extreme religious sects are gone. Quite the opposite, they're still here, and still several million members strong. It is only a matter of time before another cult or extreme sect makes the news somewhere with some atrocity.

However, in the context of this book, cults and extreme sects, as the two incidents above point out, are often involved in child abduction. While there are many reasons for child abductions by these groups, the major reason is because cults and sects, if they are to survive as their members die or leave the group, must constantly recruit new members, and one way to do this is through raising children under the control of the cult or sect. This way, as adults, they will already be indoctrinated and conditioned to be members. Unfortunately for these groups though, a large number of their members with children, because of their lack of stability, don't have custody of their offspring. So, many times cult and sect leaders will have these noncustodial parents abduct their children and bring them to the cult or sect compound, where they can be hidden from the authorities and brought up under the strict control of the group.

[For readers wanting more information about cults and their dangers, see my book *Deadly Cults* (Praeger 2003)].

There is a final type of child abduction that makes the news quite a bit. This is a pseudo-abduction. A pseudo-abduction is when parents murder their own children, hide their bodies, and then report to the police that someone has abducted their children.

* * * *

At around 9:00 p.m., on October 25, 1994, Shirley McCloud, who lived just a quarter-mile from the John D. Long Lake in northern South Carolina, near the small town of Union, heard a woman wailing on her front porch. When she went to see what the commotion was about, she found a young woman crying and babbling hysterically about how a black man had taken her car and abducted her two children. Shirley immediately had her son call 911.

Deputies from the Union County Sheriff's Department responded quickly to the scene and listened as 23-year-old Susan Smith told them about how a black man had jumped into her car while she was stopped for a traffic light in Monarch Mills on the east side of Union. She said the man told her to drive or he would kill her. She then related to the deputies how the carjacker, after he ordered her to stop near a sign for John D. Long Lake, shoved her out of the car and then drove off. Her two little boys, three-year-old Michael and 14-month-old Alex, she sobbed, had still been strapped into their child seats in the rear of her car.

The Union County Sheriff's Department immediately began a large-scale search for Susan's car and the two young boys. They first searched the area around John D. Long Lake, and even had a helicopter with heat-seeking equipment look for anything in the water. The officers didn't find a thing.

"We do not have a car, we do not have the children, we do not have the suspect," said Union County Sheriff Howard Wells. "An investigation of this kind is very frustrating. Our primary goal is getting the children back."[11]

On October 26, 1994, Susan, accompanied by her estranged husband David, stood on the steps of the Union County Sheriff's Department. They made a plea on national television for the return of their children. "To whoever has our boys, we ask that you please don't hurt them, and bring them back. We love them very much."[12]

On October 27, 1994, the Union County Sheriff's Department had both David and Susan take lie detector tests. David passed without difficulty. Susan, however, didn't do as well. Her test showed deception when asked if she knew where her two boys were. Investigators afterward continued questioning Susan and found a number of inconsistencies in her story.

Detectives learned, for example, that the red light Susan claimed she had stopped at just before the carjacker jumped into her vehicle only turns red if another car is approaching on the cross street. Susan had told the officers that she saw no other cars that night. Also, several times during the questioning Susan talked about her boys in the past tense, as if she knew they were already dead. She additionally told the investigators conflicting stories about where she'd gone on the night the carjacker took her car and her boys. When the police pointed out these inconsistencies to her though, Susan simply changed her story.

On the morning of November 3, 1994, Susan appeared on three national television shows, again appealing for the safe return of her children. Later that day, the sheriff of Union County sat down alone with Susan and confronted her about all of the inconsistencies in her story. Susan finally broke down crying and told the truth about how she had been extremely depressed that night. She admitted to the sheriff that she had backed her Mazda Protégé up to the boat ramp at John D. Long Lake and then let it roll into the water with her two boys still strapped inside. She claimed that she had wanted to commit suicide and that she had originally meant to die with her boys, but changed her mind at the last moment and jumped out.

Authorities later found out that a week before Susan murdered her two little boys, a man Susan had hoped to marry had sent her a letter saying that, though he cared for her, he didn't want to raise someone else's children. Susan later said that she had "never felt so lonely and so sad in my entire life."[13]

After Susan's confession, divers immediately went back to John D. Long Lake and found Susan's car submerged upside down in the water, the hand of one of her little boys pressed against one of the car windows. The helicopter that had earlier searched the lake with its heat-seeking equipment had apparently missed the car because it had searched in a different part of the water on the assumption that a person who wanted to hide a car in the lake would have sent it into the water at a higher speed than just at a roll.

Interestingly, when investigators had the Mazda pulled out of the lake, they discovered that the car lights had been on. Some observers believe that Susan wanted to watch the car to make certain that it went all the way under. Autopsies would later show that both boys had died from drowning.

Family members held a funeral for Michael and Alex at the local Methodist Church on November 6, 1994. They were laid to rest next to other family members.

Once the public found out that Susan had confessed to killing her two little boys, a number of the black residents of Union expressed anger over the fact that Susan had accused a black man of taking her children. But they expressed even more anger over the fact that a lot of people in the community had accepted the accusation without argument. Susan's brother, Scott Vaughan, apologized to the black community.

"It was a terrible misfortune that all this happened," Scott said. "My family feels betrayed, like everyone else."[14]

On January 16, 1995, Thomas Pope, the county solicitor, filed a motion of his intention to seek the death penalty for Susan. Upon finding this out, Susan's defense attorney attempted to work out a plea bargain, under which Susan would plead guilty to Michael and Alex's murders and receive a sentence of 30 years to life. The county solicitor, however, refused to bargain with Susan and insisted on going for the death penalty.

On July 10, 1995, Susan Smith's trial began in the Union County courthouse with the jury selection. The judge had earlier sent Susan for a mental evaluation, and a court-appointed psychiatrist found her competent to stand trial. Opening statements in her trial began on July 19, 1995.

At 7:53 p.m. on July 22, 1995, following closing arguments, the jury began deliberating the case. Two and a half hours later, the jury returned with a verdict of guilty to two counts of murder.

Next, on July 24, 1995, the sentencing phase of the trial began. The prosecution and defense began offering evidence as to why Susan should die for her crimes and why she shouldn't. After four days of testimony, the same jury that had convicted her went back into deliberations about Susan's fate. After two and a half hours, the jury, apparently believing Susan to be an extremely disturbed woman, rather than a vicious one, decided not to recommend the death penalty, and instead recommended a life sentence for her crimes. The judge sentenced Susan to 30 years to life.

****

While the Susan Smith story garnered a huge amount of media attention, she is certainly not the only parent to have murdered a child and then claimed to the police that the child had been abducted. In January 2007, 25-year-old Lucila Rojas reported to the police that a man dressed in black had abducted her baby outside of the Jacobi Medical Center in the Bronx, New York. However, her story had so many inconsistencies in it that it immediately made the police suspicious.

Eventually, Rojas admitted to the police that the baby had been unwanted and the result of a violent encounter. And so, she had used a baby blanket to smother the infant and then placed the baby's body into a plastic bag and dumped it in a trashcan in Queens.

"The most significant thing from my point of view is the claim that the child was conceived as the result of the defendant having been raped in Mexico and the defendant having said that she placed a blanket over the child's face saying that now the baby will sleep forever," said Queens District Attorney Richard Brown. "Apparently, her claim is that the child reminded her of the fact that she was raped in Mexico."[15]

The police charged Rojas with murder, evidence tampering, and endangering the welfare of a child. Although the authorities searched several landfills, they didn't find the infant's body.

Of course, fake abductions to cover up the murder of a child aren't committed only by women. On September 8, 1999, 27-year-old Richard W. Spicknall, the manager of a sports bar, told the police that he had gotten into an altercation with a hitchhiker on a bridge over the Choptank River near Easton, Maryland. The hitchhiker, Spicknall claimed, threw him off the bridge and into the water, and then took his Jeep Wrangler with his two children, three-year-old Destiny and two-year-old Richard Spicknall III, still strapped inside.

Construction workers later found the Jeep parked with both children still inside near a home under construction less than a half mile away from where

Richard said the altercation had taken place. Both children had been shot. Two-year-old Richard was dead at the scene, but the workers found Destiny to still be alive. The authorities rushed her to a hospital, but she died the next day.

At the time of the reported abduction, Richard and his wife Lisa were in the process of getting a divorce. Lisa had gotten a protective order against Richard because of several bouts of physical abuse she claimed to have suffered at his hands. However, despite this, they had shared custody of the children. The police, upon listening to Richard tell what happened, found far too many inconsistencies in his story to believe him.

For one thing, the first 911 call to the police came in three hours after Richard said the abduction had taken place. Also, witnesses saw Richard get out of the water within sight of the location where workers later found his two children. In addition, the bridge is 50 feet high, and the strong current of the river would have taken Richard opposite of the direction he said he went. The police arrested Richard and charged him with the murder of his two children.

"We obviously don't believe his original story," said Major Greg Shipley of the Maryland State Police.[16]

Although at first maintaining his innocence, Richard eventually broke down in court and admitted to killing his two children. A judge later sentenced him to life in prison. He told the police in an interview that he had killed his children because he didn't want to see them grow up in a new family.

Richard's wife Lisa now works as a counselor for victims of domestic violence. "It's very empowering work," Lisa said. "I look at this as turning negative energy into positive energy."[17]

****

No one knows how many children reported to be abducted every year in our country have actually been murdered by their parents. No one knows how many parents are cold enough that they can carry off the deception. But certainly a percentage of the children reported to the police as being abducted every year will never be found because they are dead and carefully hidden, murdered by their parents.

So far in this book we have looked at the many different types of child abduction that occur in our country, and at the young people who are victimized. However, as we will see in the next chapter, there are other victims of child abduction beyond the children who are taken. These are the secondary victims of child abduction. These secondary victims, which can include family members of the abduction victim and occasionally just witnesses to the abduction, often suffer physical injuries as well as lifelong emotional and psychological damage as a result of this crime.

Secondary Victims of Child Abduction

On July 15, 2002, at around 7:00 p.m., five-year-old Samantha Runnion played with a friend, Sarah Ahn, in front of her grandmother's home in Stanton, California, a community just south of Los Angeles. Suddenly, a stranger walked up to the two little girls and asked if they'd seen his Chihuahua puppy that'd run away. When Samantha approached the man and told him she hadn't, the man grabbed her and dragged her into a nearby car.

Samantha fought and tried to pull away, yelling to Sarah, "Help me! Tell my grandmother!"[1]

Sarah raced home and told her mother what had happened. The mother immediately called 911, and a massive search by the police began. Sarah gave the police the description of a Hispanic man with a moustache and slicked-back black hair. She said he drove Samantha away in a light green car. Because of the violent crime she had witnessed, Sarah received counseling from a trauma intervention team.

Immediately upon finding out about Samantha's abduction, Samantha's mother, Erin Runnion, overcome and in a total panic, called her ex-husband in Massachusetts. "She just broke down," her ex-husband told reporters. "She told me Samantha had been abducted, and she was hoping it was me."[2]

On July 16, 2002, an obviously frightened man called 911 and told the Riverside County Sheriff's Department that he had found the nude body of a little girl along highway 74 in rural Riverside County. This is an area that is a popular spot for hang gliders, and is located about 50 miles from where the abductor had grabbed Samantha. The caller pleaded with the police, "Please hurry. I'm scared, and I want to get out of here."[3] The little girl turned out to be Samantha.

Apparently, the person who had left Samantha's body along the road had also posed it in a manner that shook and traumatized the man who found it. "We believe he wanted us to find the body, and it was a calling card for future activity," said Orange County Sheriff Mike Carona, telling reporters that, because of the positioning of the body, he believed that they had a serial abductor/killer on the loose.[4]

CNN anchor Paula Zahn, talking about the finding of Samantha's body, said, "Investigators, who released a sketch of Samantha Runnion's killer, say he left a calling card, posing the five-year-old's body in such a way that said, 'Here I am, come and find me.'"[5] FBI criminal profilers who looked at the case (specialists who examine all of the evidence in a criminal case and, from it, develop a probable profile of the offender) said they believed the murderer had molested children before, and would likely molest and kill again.

An autopsy would later show that Samantha had been sexually assaulted, physically abused, and then suffocated to death by intense pressure on her chest. The sheriff of Orange County, Michael Carona, went on the news and told the killer, "Don't eat, don't sleep, because we are coming after you."[6]

According to family members, Samantha's mother, Erin, who had gone on the news to plead for her daughter's safe return, was totally devastated by the news of Samantha's death and immediately went into seclusion. Sadly, Erin had moved to the condominium in Stanton because she thought it would be safer for her children.

Detectives, true to the sheriff's word, soon located and identified Samantha's abductor and murderer: 27-year-old Alejandro Avila, a production line supervisor at a plant that manufactured medical devices. The police served search warrants at Avila's mother's home and at the home of his sister. In addition, they towed away several vehicles belonging to Avila, including a light green one.

Sheriff Carona, commenting on the identification of Avila as Samantha's abductor and murderer, and referring to his earlier promise to catch the man who did it, said, "If you thought for one moment that I was joking—that we were joking—tonight you know that we were deadly serious."[7]

Further police investigation showed that Avila had previously been in the area where Samantha had been abducted. The daughter of a woman Avila had dated lived with her father in that area. In 2001, the police had arrested Avila and charged him with molesting the girlfriend's nine-year-old daughter and another girl. Avila's girlfriend told the police that she had broken up with him because he always wanted to be alone with her daughter. To everyone's surprise, including Avila's attorney, a jury acquitted Avila of all charges in the case.

In the Samantha Runnion case, the police charged Avila with murder, kid-napping, and two counts of lewd acts with a child under 14. The police told the news media that Avila had left some very incriminating evidence at the spot where he dumped Samantha's body. He also left evidence, detectives said, in front of Samantha's grandmother's home and in his car. They said that they felt they had enough evidence to go ahead and charge Avila without having to wait for DNA tests to come back from the lab. Avila, of course, denied being Samantha's killer and claimed that he had been 30 miles away when her abduction occurred. However, cell phone and credit card records retrieved by the police placed him in the area of the abduction at the time it occurred.

"I'm 100 percent certain that Mr. Avila is the man who kidnapped and murdered Samantha Runnion," said Sheriff Carona. When talking about the intensity of the effort put into the investigation, Sheriff Carona added with a tone of deep emotion, "Samantha had become 'our little girl.'"[8]

On July 24, 2002, Samantha's parents held her funeral at the huge 3,000-seat Crystal Cathedral in Garden Grove, California. An astonishing 5,500 people attended the funeral. Most of these people didn't know Samantha other than what they had read or heard about from various news media sources. When the cathedral filled up, several thousand people stood outside and listened to the funeral over loudspeakers.

"It's not fair that we're looking at a tiny casket," Reverend Robert A. Schuller, II told the audience. "It's not fair. It's wrong. What is good is what brought all of you here today."[9]

The day following Samantha's funeral, her mother Erin spoke on the Larry King Show. "There's very little room for anger," she told Larry King. "It's all hurt. It's all sadness."[10] She also told about her reaction the night Saman-tha was abducted, about her panic and frenzied search for Samantha, about pounding on car trunks and calling for her child. She even told about jump-ing onto the hood of a passing car and demanding that the driver let her look in his vehicle for Samantha.

Erin also appeared extremely upset about the fact that in the year before Samantha's abduction a jury had turned Avila loose to prey on her daughter. "I blame every juror who let him go," she said. "Every juror who sat on that trial and believed this man over those little girls, I will never understand."[11]

Avila's attorney in his earlier molestation trial told reporters that even he had been shocked at the verdict because at the time he had thought there was more than enough evidence to convict Avila. "Quite frankly, I was surprised," he told reporters about Avila's acquittal. He said that Avila's arrest for the abduc-tion and murder of Samantha Runnion was making him rethink his career. "It has thrown my entire world off course," he said. "It has stopped me on a personal level to contemplate whether I did anything wrong."[12]

Orange County District Attorney Tony Rackauckas, on July 22, 2002, announced that, "Mr. Avila is charged with the murder during a kidnapping, with two special circumstance allegations of murder in the commission of a lewd and lascivious act upon a child under the age of 14."[13] The special circumstance allegations Mr. Rackauckas spoke about made Avila eligible for the death penalty. On August 5, 2002, Mr. Rackauckas announced that he had decided he would seek the death penalty against Avila.

On March 21, 2005, the trial of Alejandro Avila for the abduction and murder of Samantha Runnion finally got underway. Early in the prosecution's case, the two girls who had accused Avila of molesting them testified. The prosecutor also presented evidence that showed that DNA in the material the police found under Samantha's fingernails came from Avila. In addition, crime lab personnel testified that DNA from teardrops found in Avila's car came from Samantha. Finally, the prosecution presented evidence that showed that Avila had kept a collection of child pornography on his home computer, and that his credit card bills and cell phone records put him in the area of the abduction at the time it occurred.

The jury in the case, after nine hours of deliberations, returned with a conviction on all counts. "He is guilty! Guilty! Guilty! Guilty!" Erin Runnion shouted in the hallway outside of court after the verdict was read. "And that feels really good!"[14]

The same jury that had convicted Avila then went back into deliberations about his punishment. After two days, they came back with the recommendation that Avila receive the death penalty for his crimes. "If there was ever a crime in the...history of Orange County, this one begged for the death penalty," said jury foreman Terry Dancey. "It was a heinous, heinous crime."[15]

Judge William R. Froeberg, acting on the jury's recommendation, sentenced Avila to death. He ordered Avila to be taken to Death Row at San Quentin prison. "For the temporary gratification of his lust, the defendant destroyed an entire family's future," the judge said. "He has forfeited his right to live."[16]

****

In the abduction case above, Samantha Runnion was the central victim. However, in the whole matter of her abduction there were many more victims. Because of what happened to Samantha, her mother, father, and other family members all suffered extensive psychological trauma that they will carry with them for the rest of their lives.

While most people certainly see parents as being secondary victims of a child abduction, victims many people forget about in child abduction cases are the siblings of the abducted child. This is true even in cases in which a child is not harmed, just abducted. The abducted child's siblings are often abandoned emotionally while the parents focus all of their attention on getting the abducted child back. Also, older siblings must often care for younger ones because the parents are many times too preoccupied with getting the abducted child back to be real parents to the rest. As a result, the siblings become victims of the abduction since they have not only lost their abducted sibling, they have also lost the love and affection of their parents.

In addition, while most people, when they think of a child abduction, see much of the sorrow and despair that comes from the incident as falling on the parents, grandparents too can be seriously affected by the loss of their grandchildren. They can suffer many of the same detrimental psychological and emotional effects as the parents. As one study said, "In cases where the children have not been returned, the interviewed parent has spoken of the additional burden of having to watch aged parents coming to terms with the permanent loss of their grandchildren, knowing that they will probably die without ever seeing them again, which the interviewed parent has identified as 'the biggest pain of all' to bear."[17]

We also mustn't forget any witnesses to an abduction, such as Samantha's little friend Sarah, who witnessed both the abduction and its outcome. She too will likely have difficulty psychologically and emotionally because of this incident.

And while few might see him as a victim, though he certainly was one, the man who found Samantha's body will also likely experience detrimental effects because of it. Stumbling onto a body like this, particularly when it is a small child, is not something that normally happens to people. Few individuals could experience something like this without suffering some psychological trauma.

I found when I worked in law enforcement that most people consider police officers to be tough individuals who can see the absolute worst things imaginable and then brush them off. Actually, this is not the case at all. Crime, particularly when it involves children, affects police officers the same way it affects other people. For example, when I was commander of the Indianapolis Police Department's Homicide Branch, I went to the scene of over 500 murders. Most of these have dulled in my memory because they involved adults who had voluntarily gotten themselves entangled in hazardous situations that ended in their deaths (purchasing narcotics, selling narcotics, robbing people, etc.). But I remember, and remember with absolute clarity, the murders that involved children. These victims, I knew, were totally innocent, and the memory of them will be with me until I die. The same holds for police officers who work with abduction victims like Samantha Runnion.

Finally, the entire population of the United States becomes victims when they hear or read about cases of child abduction. Incidents such as the Samantha Runnion case, the John Wayne Gacy case, the Adam Walsh case, all received intense amounts of media attention because they involved children. Members of the public see the smiling faces of these children on the news, in pictures of them taken at school, at some family function, and so forth. But they know that these children have suffered horribly. It makes all parents just a little more afraid for their own children.

But even in abduction cases that haven't ended in murder, still members of the public see the faces of these missing children on billboards, on posters, and on milk cartons. No one knows what has happened to them. Have they been beaten, tortured, raped? All of these unknowns spark a fear in parents, who then worry a little bit more about, and keep a little tighter rein on, their own children. People everywhere become a bit more paranoid, but at the same time wonder how the parents of abducted children can deal with it, and wonder how they would deal with it.

Erin Runnion, Samantha's mother, speaking at Avila's sentencing, said, "This was not about me and my family versus this man. This was about our community—the people—versus this man. Because when someone commits a crime like this, when someone hurts an innocent child, it is really a crime against all of us."[18]

An article in *Time* magazine told about how the community dealt with the results of the Samantha Runnion abduction, "But it was local residents who were having trouble sleeping. Suddenly those garage doors closed, those backyards emptied and a place that had been a community became a collection of condos behind a gate."[19]

When I talk, as I did above, about everyone in America being a victim when it comes to child abduction, consider: what would make over 5,000 people who didn't even know Samantha Runnion show up at her funeral? Would this many people have shown up if she had died from some childhood disease or through a car accident? No, they wouldn't have. Would this many people have shown up if her mother, her babysitter, or her mother's boyfriend had murdered her? No, they wouldn't have. This many people showed up at Samantha's funeral because child abduction is one of the worst fears most parents have for their children. This many people showed up at Samantha's funeral because they imagined the pain that Samantha's parents must have felt. This many people showed up at Samantha's funeral because they wondered how they would handle it if something like this happened to them.

Lisa Genera, who brought her three-year-old daughter to the funeral, said, "It could have been in our neighborhood, it could have been one of our children. She [her three-year-old daughter] doesn't understand killing, so I told her (Samantha) was up in heaven. She understood that."[20]

Another woman, who brought her six-year-old son to a memorial for Samantha, said, "I'm scared to let him go out." The six-year-old said, "I'm only allowed to talk to friends of my mom."[21]

A representative of the organization The Joyful Child Foundation said, "All parents live with fear in their heart that something's going to happen and then when something does happen, I think that's one of the reasons it touches all of us."[22]

As stated above, cases of child abduction fuel the paranoia and fear in every parent's heart that something like this could happen to them, and how powerless they would be. The jury foreman in the Avila trial, Terry Dancey, said, "That poor little girl sat out there, waiting for someone to save her, and nobody could save her—not you, not me, not her mother."[23]

A radio talk show host gave the perfect description of a parent who has lost a child to abduction. She described Erin Runnion hours after the abduction (but before the man found Samantha's body). "See it and you'll never forget it," the talk show host said. "It's a portrait of pure despair and grief. The woman's eyes were tear-filled and pleading. Her mouth was framed tension; you could almost hear her silent cries for help." The talk show host then went on to say, "The news photos of Erin Runnion capture the deepest grief, frustration and fears of any mother whose child has been stolen."[24]

When family members first hear the news about the abduction of one of their members, they are, of course, immediately overcome with terror and disbelief. Then comes the soul crushing stress and anxiety of being totally powerless while others, such as the police, search for the abducted child.

Adding to this stress and anxiety, the parents of abducted children often don't know who has abducted their children, or how their children are being treated. Are their children being beaten, raped, tortured, or perhaps even murdered? Because there have been so many cases like that of Samantha Runnion published in the media, parents often fear the absolute worst when a child is abducted, and this intense fear, stress, and anxiety will continue until the child is recovered. And if the situation isn't resolved, and the child is never found, then the fear, stress, and anxiety never stops. On the other hand, if the case ends like the Runnion case, a new, even higher-level stress sets in.

Most people would likely agree with the study that summarized its findings as, "The psychological literature states that the loss of a child is one of the most distressing events an adult can experience. The loss represents a change in the parents' everyday interactions, a redefinition of social roles, or, as some parents describe, a loss of a part of oneself."[25]

Fortunately, most abducted children aren't murdered, but still a child abduction affects parents deeply. Adding to the misery of the uncertainty of not knowing what has happened to an abducted child, parents will often isolate themselves from those who might be able to help them. One study said, "Several of the parents explained how they shunned society during the time that the children were away because they found that everything in society revolves around children and, not even knowing where their own children were, they did not want to be part of a child-centered lifestyle, nor did they feel entitled to be so."[26] Many parents will say that having a child abducted is like having a medical test done for what could be a deadly condition. The world stops until the situation is resolved one way or the other. A national survey by Honeywell and the National Center for Missing and Exploited Children found that child abduction is the second largest fear parents have for their children, surpassed only by substance abuse.[27]

Of course, since child abduction is an event that doesn't occur in most people's lives, when it does, the individuals it happens to usually have no basis to work from when dealing with it. They usually have no life experiences to draw from that will work in this situation. Additionally, many times friends and other family members also don't know how to respond or what to do. According to one study, "Because child abduction is so rare, parents are surrounded by individuals who may not know how to appropriately respond to the event. If their efforts do not result in noticeable change, outsiders may become frustrated by their inability to provide helpful support, and withdraw their support."[28]

In addition, often the amount of support family and friends give to the parents of abducted children depends on how much to blame they feel the parents are for the situation. If family and friends believe the parents should have seen the abduction coming, and been more prepared, they are less likely to be supportive.

And naturally, if the parents of abducted children have been involved in high-anxiety situations before the abduction, such as a hotly contested divorce or a bitter child custody hearing, they may already be highly stressed. The child abduction can then push them to the edge of an emotional breakdown, no matter how supportive family and friends are.

There have been a number of studies about the negative effects of child abduction. Left-behind parents have reported experiencing many negative physical and psychological effects, including:

1. Depression.
2. Anxiety.
3. Anger and rage.
4. Feelings of irritability and wild mood swings.
5. Loss of appetite.
6. Loss of hair.
7. Impaired sleep patterns.
8. Having suicidal thoughts.
9. Feeling unable to carry out everyday functions.
10. Isolation.
11. Worry about finances because of unexpected expenses (travel, attorney costs, court fees, etc.).
12. Feeling totally helpless and in limbo.
13. Becoming dependent on pills and alcohol.
14. Experiencing sudden, unexpected physical illness.
15. Feelings of guilt for not being able to protect the child. In addition, since child abduction, particularly infant abduction, is often accomplished through deception (e.g., the abductor pretending to be a nurse) and the parents actually hand their child over to the abductor, many parents suffer intense guilt afterward because they feel partly responsible for the abduction. This guilt just adds a little more stress to a system that has already been stressed almost to the limit.
16. Unfortunately, most of the above symptoms will only increase in intensity at special times, such as the abducted child's birthday, Christmas, family reunions, etc.

Of course, in addition to all of these negative symptoms while a child is missing, parents and family members, once a child has been recovered and returned, don't just go back to normal. They often become hypervigilant, panicking every time they don't know where the child is. And if the abducted child isn't recovered, then this hypervigilance still occurs, but with their other children. Before the abduction, the parents may never have feared for their children, but now the threat has become very real, and will likely never leave them. One study, for example, found that after a child abduction, 71 percent of mothers quit work to stay home with their children, and 90 percent instituted firmer family structures, rules, heightened security, and more accountability.[29]

Expanding on the above, a study of the parents of recovered abducted children found, "However, the stress and trauma of the experience did not necessarily end when the child was recovered. Many parents in the study related that their psychological stress was higher after reunification with their child than it had been prior to the abduction, possibly because of concerns about a re-abduction and/or stress associated with the reunification."[30]

Besides a fear of re-abduction, other things can also add stress after a recovery and re-unification. Often, for example, abducted children have been told over and over by their abductors that the other parents were dead, didn't care about them, didn't want them back, etc. Also, abducted children may feel that the left-behind parents didn't do enough to try and get them back. In a study of 18 children being seen for psychiatric evaluation after an abduction, 16 of them reported grief or rage toward the left-behind parent.[31] This, of course, only adds to the parent's stress level.

Parents of recovered abducted children also report experiencing, even years after the abduction, problems such as an elevated startle response, abduction nightmares, and trouble concentrating. They also report a high level of anxiety whenever they are reminded of the abduction by things such as a news story about a child abduction or anything else that brings back the memories, even though their child is now safe.

In addition to all of this, mental health experts find, many individuals who suffer through a child abduction can also develop symptoms of PTSD (Post-Traumatic Stress Disorder). This is a condition that comes about when an individual experiences a terrifying event outside the scope of ordinary human experience. Soldiers in combat, police officers in deadly force situations, etc. often develop symptoms of PTSD. Abducted children and their families can also develop it.

According to the Web site for the National Institute of Mental Health, "Post-traumatic Stress Disorder (PTSD) develops after a terrifying ordeal that involved physical harm or the threat of physical harm. The person who develops PTSD may have been the one who was harmed, the harm may have happened to a loved one, or the person may have witnessed a harmful event that happened to loved ones or strangers."

The Web Site goes on to describe the symptoms of PTSD, "People with PTSD may startle easily, become emotionally numb...lose interest in things they used to enjoy, have trouble feeling affectionate, be irritable, become more aggressive, or even become violent." The Web site then tells how individuals with PTSD can have flashbacks triggered by events reminding them of the incident. These flashbacks can involve any or all of the senses, and they may be so intense that the person can believe they are actually happening.[32]

Unfortunately, as we talked about above, even after an abducted child has been recovered and returned, the stress and anxiety level the parents experienced during the abduction will many times continue, and even heighten, as the family tries to return to normal. But often, many parents find, along with the stress of reunification, they must also deal with the stress brought on by the legal system. Every time a parent must attend a court hearing because of criminal charges against the abductor, or testify in a civil suit brought against the abductor or individuals who helped make the abduction possible, this only re-awakens all of the old feelings and memories of the abduction.

Interestingly, there is a specific type of child abduction can have negative psychological effects on individuals only marginally involved in it, and that is infant abduction. Studies have shown that nurses, doctors, and others who work in a hospital or other such setting where an infant abduction occurred can suffer significant psychological trauma.

The U.S. government sponsored study "An Analysis of Infant Abductions," for example, stated, "Parents were traumatized by the loss of their infant, and the experience often created serious and long-lasting psychological symptoms." Then the report added, "The nurses on duty when the infant was abducted from a healthcare facility suffered from trauma as well. They frequently felt blame, believing that somehow they could have prevented the abduction, perhaps by being more aware of the imposter, or that they should have caught the abductor taking the infant off the unit." The report also noted that often after an infant abduction the nurses on duty when the abduction occurred will resign or transfer to another unit.[33]

We talked above about how child abductions can affect the police officers working the case. Much like doctors and nurses in an infant abduction who experience psychological trauma because they didn't do enough to protect the infant, police officers can feel the same way if an abducted child is killed or never recovered. In the incident involving Samantha Runnion, Sheriff Carona made the statement, "Samantha is now our little girl." He also said, "Little girls aren't supposed to die. Little girls aren't supposed to die the way Samantha died."[34] Police officers, because of their role in society, can have a strong, almost overpowering need to safely rescue a helpless child. When they fail at this, psychological and emotional difficulties can often set in, making them victims of the child abduction.

So far in this chapter we have talked about all of the serious emotional and psychological traumas individuals other than the child victim can suffer because of a child abduction. As the following anecdote shows, there is also a very real physical threat to these individuals.

****

Shonelle Melvelle-Grant and Jessica Liriano had been coworkers and friends, and Shonelle had often babysat for Jessica's daughter Kiki. Shonelle, however, apparently developed an extremely strong attachment to Kiki, and in 2004 Shonelle abducted the little girl for three days. Fortunately, the police found and returned Kiki safely. After being arrested and charged for the abduction, Shonelle entered into a plea agreement with the prosecutor, and, through it, escaped any serious jail time. Because of this incident, Jessica moved in order to keep her daughter away from Shonelle.

However, Shonelle had other ideas. In September 2006, she approached a man she thought was a professional hit man, and gave him a down payment to kill Jessica so that she could then get Kiki. She told the hit man that it would be all right if, in the process of killing Jessica, he also killed Jessica's 10-year-old son Andrew. Shonelle and the hit man met and discussed the plot to kill Jessica eight times. Shonelle even drove the hit man to Jessica's house, and gave him all the personal information she had on Jessica.

Unfortunately for Shonelle, she wasn't really talking to a professional hit man, but rather to an undercover police officer who secretly recorded their discussions. The police arrested Shonelle, and though at first she denied being serious about having Jessica killed, in January 2007, she pled guilty to a charge of second-degree solicitation. The judge sentenced her to 28 months to seven years in prison.

****

As the above incident shows, being in the way of a child abduction can be dangerous. Although not all child abductors will kill others who stand in their way, violence during child abductions is still very common. And sometimes violence can occur, not because individuals are trying to stop a child abduction, but simply because they are there when the abduction occurs and have become witnesses.

"An Analysis of Infant Abductions," a study commissioned by the federal government, found that in cases of infants being abducted from a home, one-third of these incidents involved violence. In the *National Incidence Studies of Missing, Abducted, Runaway, and Thrownaway Children,* talked about in previous chapters, researchers found that abductors used force in 14 percent of all parental abductions.

In this chapter, we have talked about the detrimental effects that a child abduction can have on people other than the child being abducted. Often, the longer the abduction lasts, the more severe these effects. However, strangely enough, sometimes the abducted children themselves can decide to prolong the abduction by voluntarily staying with their abductors. Why would they do this?

As we will see in the next chapter, through certain psychological changes, some abducted children can find themselves becoming strongly attached to their abductors, even though the abductors may be harsh to them, and even though excellent chances of escape present themselves. As we will see, some children choose to stay.

Why Some Children Stay

In the afternoon of January 8, 2007, 13-year-old Ben Ownby stepped off of a school bus at the stop near his home. Ben, a straight-A student at Union Middle School, lived in Beaufort, Missouri, a sleepy little town about 50 miles southwest of St. Louis. It seemed to be the end of just another day at school. However, it would soon turn out to be anything but an ordinary day for him. Suddenly, a man jumped out of an older model white Nissan pickup truck and brandished a gun. He then forced Ben into the truck and sped away. Fifteen-year-old Mitchell Hults witnessed the abduction and gave the police a very accurate description of the truck.

Several days later, two police officers, with the intention of serving a warrant, went to the South Holmes Apartment complex in Kirkwood, Missouri, a western suburb of St. Louis. While in the apartment area they noticed a white Nissan pickup truck that matched the description of the truck used in the Ben Ownby abduction. The officers soon learned that the truck belonged to 41-year-old pizza shop manager Michael Devlin. The officers knew Devlin from having visited the pizza shop many times.

The two officers finally located Devlin and began talking to him. However, they noticed a very obvious change in his demeanor when the first mention of the recent abduction came up. "It went from a casual conversation, 180 degrees from that," said Kirkwood police officer Chris Nelson.[1] "As the questions began to get more specific, that's when the attitude changed. It threw a lot of red flags up for us," said Officer Gary Wagster."[2] Wagster and Nelson, feeling uneasy about their conversation with Devlin, notified the FBI of their suspicions.

At about the same time, the owner of the pizza shop where Devlin worked also became suspicious. He knew that the truck Devlin drove matched the description of the truck the police were looking for. In addition, Devlin had very uncharacteristically taken the day of the abduction and the day afterward off work. When the manager checked Devlin's truck, he saw that it was covered with road dust. Ben Ownby, he knew, had been abducted on a dirt road. The pizza shop owner called the police with his suspicions.

Within hours, the police obtained a search warrant and raided Devlin's apartment in Kirkwood. Inside, they found Ben Ownby alive and well. They arrested Michael Devlin, and charged him with Ben's kidnapping. However, the police found something else in the apartment they hadn't expected to find.

Inside the apartment the police also discovered a 15-year-old boy who everyone in the apartment area knew as Devlin's son Shawn. He turned out instead though to be Shawn Hornbeck, a boy who had been reported as abducted over four years before.

In October 2002, Shawn Hornbeck had been abducted at gunpoint while out riding a bicycle near his rural Richwoods, Missouri, home. For months, the authorities, along with over 1,600 volunteers, had searched the area in vain for Shawn. The police, when looking for Shawn, had once even had a lake drained of four million gallons of water. Shawn's family, in desperation, had set up a Web site for tips about his disappearance, and had once even reportedly picketed the sheriff's office because they were unhappy about the lack of results in the case.

After the arrest of Devlin and the recovery of the two abducted boys, Franklin County Sheriff Gary Toelke held a press conference, at which he told reporters, "We have some good news and we have some probably unbelievable news."[3]

Naturally, Shawn's parents, who after all of this time had likely begun to believe that Shawn was probably dead, were ecstatic when the police told them that he had been found alive. He had been missing for 51 months. But of course, questions soon arose from all quarters about how Shawn could have been held captive for so long.

"The questions that arise from this are going to be pondered for a great long time," said Kirkwood Police Department spokesperson Tom Ballman.[4]

In October of 2007, Devlin decided to plead guilty to all of the charges against him in four jurisdictions. According to his attorney, the evidence against him was overwhelming. On October 8, 2007, Franklin County Circuit Court Judge Stanley Williams sentenced Devlin to life in prison for kidnapping and 20 years for armed criminal action. Devlin received over 20 more life sentences from the other jurisdictions.

"This is a predator," said Franklin County Prosecutor Bob Parks. "This guy is evil. This is evil incarnate."[5]

****

Of course, upon hearing about Ben's safe return and Shawn's miraculous recovery, which the press dubbed as "The Missouri Miracle," the public was extremely happy for the families, but also had many questions. How had Devlin been able to keep Shawn a prisoner for all of these years? Even more questions arose when investigators found that Shawn had had contact with the police at least four times since his disappearance, but hadn't said anything to them about who he really was.

On August 15, 2003, less than a year after his abduction, Shawn had reported to the police that someone had stolen his bicycle from in front of Devlin's apartment, and on September 29, 2006, the police had stopped Shawn for wearing dark clothing and having no reflectors on his bicycle after dark. Both times Shawn had told the officers that his name was Shawn Devlin. Two other times the police had stopped Shawn for being out late at night. Why, the public wondered, hadn't he told the police who he really was when he had contact with them?

Still more questions arose when the investigation also showed that Devlin had often left Shawn alone at the apartment for long periods of time. In addition, Shawn had friends in the apartment area where he lived, and had reportedly even gone out on a date with a girl from the nearby Visitation Academy. Yet, no one knew the truth about him.

Even stranger though, Shawn had had a contact of sorts with his parents during his captivity. After Shawn's abduction, his parents had started the Shawn Hornbeck Foundation. This organization helps the families of missing and abducted children. On their Web site, Shawn posted the message, "How long are you planing [sic] to look for your son?"[6] He signed the message Shawn Devlin.

A large number of experts in child psychology and in the field of coping with extreme traumatic events weighed in on this case, and almost all of them said that this wasn't such an unusual situation. They felt that Shawn's behavior was perfectly normal. For example, Dr. Robert Butterworth, a psychologist specializing in trauma, said this about the Shawn Hornbeck case, "He might have been in the situation where everything he knew, every kind of activity he once did was taken away. No school, no friends, no parents and maybe all the stimulus was gone...[His captor] had the power of all of this over him."[7]

Dr. Butterworth also added, "When trying to understand what did or did not happen, it's important to realize that the rest of us don't know what sort of psychological techniques may have been used to control Shawn...Abductors sometimes tell their captives that if they try to escape, others dear to them—family or even pets—will be hurt. They use psychological chains, which can be just as bad as physical."[8] Supporting this viewpoint, Devlin reportedly had Shawn so cowed, even after four years, that when he ordered Shawn to guard Ben while he was away from the apartment, Shawn obeyed.

Child kidnappers "know how to create a paralyzing sense of fear so even when the captor is not present, the child feels he is omnipresent," said Dr. Terri Weaver, a professor of psychology at St. Louis University. "Their mental package is very coercive, very convincing, very mean. They don't just say, 'I'll kill your family.' They tell how they'll do it in graphic detail and manner—how they'll kill the child's family and even pets."[9]

Dr. Weaver, in explaining why Shawn never told anyone who he really was, said, "When a young child is taken from his family and isolated and perhaps threatened, and those threats are backed up by violence—all that plays a tremendous role in silencing the child."[10]

As a confirmation of what Dr. Weaver says, a reader wrote to *The Sheboygan Press* about the Shawn Hornbeck case, "I was abducted when I was 15 years old and my abduction lasted months not years, but the beatings, torture and threats of murder to those I loved kept me under his control even though I had been left alone on numerous occasions. I felt to blame for years for what happened to me."[11]

Dr. Weaver went on to add, "I think it's a real mistake to judge this child. Whatever he did to this point to stay alive is to his credit." She went on to say that children in such situations kick into survival mode, "doing what needs to be done to keep yourself going day-to-day."[12] She then made the point that repeated contact with outsiders can actually reinforce an abducted child's sense of helplessness. While adults would know that they have to explain their situation to others in order to get help, children expect grown-ups to know what's going on and to offer help without being asked. When they don't, the children's feelings of helplessness are reinforced.

A forensic pediatrician at the University of North Carolina—Chapel Hill, Dr. Sharon Cooper, said that because abductors often threaten to kill the children's family if they try to escape, the children will "sacrifice their own desire to escape as a means to protect the family."[13]

Dr. Cooper then added, "Most 11-year-olds taken from their support systems are in a state of shock. Their worry is who is going to provide their basic needs."[14]

Dr. Stephen Golding, a forensic psychologist, said, "People are led to believe, through someone taking advantage of their vulnerabilities, that leaving is not an option, that things will get worse for them or will get worse for others."[15]

Jeffrey Lieberman of Columbia Medical Center said on the Larry King Show, "The initial dynamic, which really defines the response, is one of fear. 'I have to figure out a way to get through this and survive.'"[16]

Also appearing on the Larry King Show, Dr. Paul Ragan of Vanderbilt University said, "I think that it's really important that we not judge this young man, this young boy. He may be 15, but I think there's probably been a lot of psychological arrest in his development and I'm very concerned that he was actually probably very, very heavily coerced and threatened and shamed into this very subordinate relationship with Devlin and that there were probably very, very strong, unseen psychological bounds that kept him—kept him imprisoned."

Dr. Ragan added, "But also, captors will mix up negative or punishment with some kind of reward, and that just actually strengthens the relationship, strengthens the attachment, strengthens the control, because they're saying to this person, 'I have complete control. I can make you happy. I can make you sad. I can give something as a reward, I can take it away. I can punish you.'"[17]

After reading all of the expert opinions above though, what do we really know about the case that would show that Devlin really did use these coercive techniques? Actually, quite a bit.

A probable cause statement accompanying Devlin's arrest for Shawn's abduction stated that Devlin had terrorized him with a gun to get him to cooperate. The affidavit also states that Devlin "abducted [Shawn] utilizing force for the purpose of terrorizing the victim. After securing [Shawn], Michael Devlin flourished a handgun in order to gain compliance of the minor child."[18]

We also know that early in Shawn's captivity Devlin would wake him up every 45 minutes.[19] Sleep deprivation is a technique professional interrogators like to use to make an interrogation subject more compliant and cooperative. In addition, we know that Devlin regularly sexually assaulted Shawn. We know this because, on February 5, 2007, the prosecutor charged Devin with 69 counts of forcible sodomy. Seventeen of these counts referred to his rape of Ben, who he allegedly sexually assaulted four times a day during his captivity. The remainder of the charges refers to his numerous reported sexual assaults of Shawn. This, of course, would also naturally terrorize a young boy.

Neighbors of Devlin in the apartment area where he lived said that they often heard "weird sounds, like whimpering, screaming, and pleading, coming from Devlin's apartment. It was like Shawn was trying to get [Devlin] to stop doing something."[20]

On April 17, 2007, the authorities filed seven more charges against Devlin. These included attempted murder, transporting a minor across state lines for sexual purposes, and armed criminal action. As to the attempted murder charge, according to the charging affidavit, Devlin had attempted to kill Shawn soon after abducting him, which, of course, would only add to Shawn's terror and to his belief that Devlin would carry out any threats he made.

In court, following his arrest, Devlin told how after sexually assaulting Shawn for several days following his abduction, he had driven him back to the rural area where he'd originally kidnapped him from, with the intent to kill him. He told the court that he pulled Shawn from the truck and started strangling him, but then stopped.

"I attempted to kill [Shawn] and he talked me out of it," Devlin said.[21]

In addition to all of the above, the authorities also charged Devlin with possession of child pornography after they discovered a considerable amount of child pornography on Devlin's home computer. However, more important, they also found that Devlin had taken both photography and video of his sexual assaults of Shawn.

U.S. Attorney Catherine Hanaway, referring to Devlin's photographing and videotaping of sex acts with Shawn, said, "This is by far the worst thing that we have seen."[22]

Of course, these photos and videos would become just another way of keeping Shawn from leaving, with the threat that if he ever did leave then his family and friends would see them. But even without the photos and videos, we must remember that Shawn had been forced into homosexual activity many times, and he knew that if he escaped from Devlin then all of this would eventually come out. This is something few 15-year-old boys would want others to know about. In the Steven Stayner case, which we will talk about a little later in this chapter, after Stayner had escaped from an abductor who had forced him into homosexual activity repeatedly, his schoolmates teased and taunted him unmercifully about it for years.

We also know, referring to Dr. Ragan's comments above about abductors mixing reward and punishment, that Devlin, along with sexually assaulting Shawn, reportedly also gave him an Xbox 360, an iPod, a computer, and a bicycle. In addition, he was allowing Shawn to drive his truck. Mixing rewards like this with punishment cements an abductor's hold over a child.

Readers, however, may wonder why Devlin, after over four years of getting away with abducting and sexually assaulting Shawn, would take the tremendous chance of abducting Ben Ownby, knowing the consequences if it didn't work. The reason is that child molesters, experts have found, usually have a preferred age range for their victims, and they often don't sexually desire children outside of this age range. Shawn had grown up considerably during the four years of his captivity, and this change had likely made Devlin think about wanting someone new and younger.

As to Shawn's thoughts and hopes during his abduction, after his rescue by the police, Shawn and his parents appeared on the Oprah Winfrey Show. On the show, he told Oprah that, "I prayed that one day my parents would find me and I'd be united."[23] Shawn also said that he had posted the message on the Shawn Hornbeck Foundation Web site because, "I was hoping it would give some kind of hint."[24] When asked by Oprah, "How often did you think about your family?" Shawn answered, "Every day."[25] Off-camera, he told Oprah that during his captivity he had been "terrified to contact his parents."[26]

Since his return home, Shawn has expressed an interest in becoming involved in the Shawn Hornbeck Foundation. "Nobody knows what it is like unless you have been there," Shawn said.[27] He told his parents that he didn't want other children to have to go through what he did.

In July 2007, the Shawn Hornbeck Foundation announced that it had entered into a partnership with several stock car drivers to put age-progressed pictures of abducted children on their race cars. "They could be living two doors down from somebody in a different county," said stock car driver Christina Lemons.[28]

Along with all of the expert opinion above, there is also one other explanation for Shawn's behavior that a number of experts alluded to, and that is a psychological condition called the Stockholm Syndrome. This is a condition often seen in individuals who have been held hostage for long periods of time.

* * * *

The Stockholm Syndrome got its name from a bank robbery that took place on August 23, 1973, at the Sveriges Kreditbank in downtown Stockholm, Sweden. On that day, Jan-Erik Olsson walked into the bank and fired a gun into the ceiling, announcing a holdup. Two police officers quickly responded to the bank's alarm, but Olsson wounded one and disarmed the other. After making the disarmed police officer sing of few stanzas of *Lonesome Cowboy,* he sent both officers out of the bank. That left Olsson in the bank with four employees as hostages.

Thus began a hostage standoff that would last for 131 hours. Olsson's first demand to the police was that his former prison cellmate, Clark Olofsson, be released from the penitentiary and brought to the bank. He then added that he also wanted three million Swedish kronor (then worth about $730,000), two more guns, bulletproof vests, and a fast car. The police had Olofsson brought to the bank, but they refused Olsson's other demands.

The police, after conferring with experts, had agreed to the demand of sending Olofsson into the bank because they felt he was much more rational than the seemingly spastic and hyper Olsson. They also felt that Olofsson would have a strong self-interest in keeping the situation calm and down to earth.

The two robbers took the four hostages into the bank's 11 by 47 foot vault, where Olsson put nooses around their necks. He threatened to yank them and kill the hostages at the first sign of a police assault.

After the situation had worn on for several days, Olsson finally let one of the hostages speak on the telephone with the Swedish prime minister. Election time was nearing, and so the prime minister had a personal interest in wanting to peacefully end the hostage incident, which was the top news story every day in Sweden. He reportedly feared that a violent end would hurt him and his party at the polls. To the surprise of the prime minister, the hostage scolded him for not fulfilling the hostage-taker's demands. She also chided the prime minister for allowing the police to endanger the hostages' lives, and then told the prime minister that, "The robbers are protecting us from the police."[29]

During the incident, Olsson also allowed several people, including the Stockholm police chief and criminologist Nils Bejerot, who is credited with coining the term "Stockholm Syndrome," to come into the bank to check on the welfare of the hostages. Everyone who saw them was surprised at how upbeat and cheerful the hostages were. Also, as a part of their rescue strategy, the police had drilled a hole into the vault from the floor above, and had lowered in a microphone. Stunned police officers heard the hostages and hostage-takers chatting as if they were lifelong friends.

On August 28, 1973, the police, deciding it was time to end the incident, dropped tear gas through the drilled hole. Olsson and Olofsson surrendered without hurting the hostages, even though they had threatened constantly to do so if the police tried to rescue them.

However, when the hostage standoff finally ended, stunned police officers charging into the bank found the hostages volunteering themselves as human shields so that the police would not kill the hostage-takers. The former hostages, following their release, also pitched in and set up a defense fund for Olsson and Olofsson. Even six months after the incident, reporters found that the hostages still felt very positive about the hostage-takers, and said that they felt the only real threat they were under during the incident was from the police.

* * * *

Social scientists studying the Stockholm Syndrome have found it to be an unconscious survival mechanism that, as in the incident above, remains long after the hostage incident has been resolved and the danger gone. These researchers, however, have also found that in order for the Stockholm Syndrome to develop certain conditions must exist. The hostages and hostage-takers must be in danger together, and there must be positive contact between them. The hostages must be able to see the hostage-takers as human beings with very real needs and feelings. However, while positive contact can make the syndrome appear, negative contact can keep it from appearing. Still, in some situations, such as when the hostages are expecting beatings, rapes, torture, or even murder, the mere absence of these can be seen as positive contact.

Researchers have found that even the smallest kindness by a hostage-taker can be seized upon by the hostages as a sign that perhaps they won't be beaten, raped, tortured, or murdered, and, because of their survival instinct, the hostages will unconsciously attempt to bond with their captors in order to expand on this kindness. The hostages will try to act in ways that will win their captors' approval, and this can cause emotional bonding.

Scientists also believe that individuals who develop the Stockholm Syndrome do so because they are totally isolated from any outside sources of help, they see their situation as very likely to end in death, and they believe that the possibility of escape is nonexistent. The hostages must therefore look to their captors for survival, and consequently they will unconsciously attempt to bond emotionally with them. Interviews with former hostages have shown that they very often felt that their only chance of survival was through allying with their captors. Doing this, though, makes the hostages see their captors as human beings with feelings, needs, and weaknesses. But in addition to this, they also begin to see events from their captors' point of view. Consequently, individuals suffering from the Stockholm Syndrome begin to see authority figures the same way their captors do, thus explaining their antagonism against them. As a testament to the strength of the Stockholm Syndrome, experience has shown that hostages under the influence of the Stockholm Syndrome, because of their intense bonding with their captors, will often not attempt to escape even if an excellent chance to do so presents itself, as it did in the Shawn Hornbeck case.

Interestingly, the Stockholm Syndrome can also work in reverse, with the hostage-takers developing very strong emotional bonds with the hostages. This, of course, can work to the advantage of the hostages, since hostage-takers will be reluctant to harm individuals they have developed strong emotional bonds with. For example, during the South Moluccan hostage incident a number of years ago in The Netherlands, a hostage selected for execution by the hostage-takers wasn't executed after all because his captors, through the Stockholm Syndrome, had developed strong emotional bonds with him.

For the above reason, police hostage negotiators will often attempt to get the Stockholm Syndrome to develop since it will make the hostage-takers much more reluctant to hurt the hostages. They do this by asking the hostage-takers about the welfare of the hostages, about any medical conditions they may have, and about their general needs, hoping to make the hostage-takers see the hostages as human beings with real feelings and needs.

There have been a number of notable cases of the Stockholm Syndrome since the incident in Sweden. Later that same year, for example, another case of the Stockholm Syndrome occurred during a bank robbery in Brooklyn. This incident later became the basis for the movie *Dog Day Afternoon*. And of course, probably the most highly publicized example of the Stockholm Syndrome is that of Patty Hearst. In this case, because of the Stockholm Syndrome, a rich young heiress actually joined a ragtag outfit that called itself the Symbionese Liberation Army, and even took part in one of their bank robberies.

"You have been so abused and so robbed of your free will and so frightened that you come to a point that you believe any lie that your abductor has told you," said Patty Hearst. "You don't feel safe. You think that either you will be killed if you reach out for help, or you believe your family will be killed. You've, in a way, given up, you've absorbed the new identity they've given you."[30]

The Stockholm Syndrome is so strong and so pervasive that all police SWAT teams must be on the watch for it. SWAT teams, for example, know from some very unfortunate incidents that they cannot take at face value anything that hostages, even released hostages, tell them. Hostages under the influence of the Stockholm Syndrome will often tell the police untruthful things that they hope will help the hostage-takers. SWAT teams also know that they have to carefully check all hostages at the conclusion of a hostage incident to be certain that one of the hostage-takers isn't masquerading as a hostage, often with the help of the real hostages. In addition, it is standard practice for hostage negotiators to closely watch each other during a SWAT incident to be certain that none of them have fallen under the sway of the Stockholm Syndrome.

Could this psychological condition explain the actions of Shawn Hornbeck? Of course it could, and it would make sense of many of the things he did that didn't seem to make sense.

While the Shawn Hornbeck case made national headlines for weeks, his is certainly not the only case of an abducted child who possibly fell under the spell of the Stockholm Syndrome. His is not the only case of an abducted child who began to identify with his or her captor and stayed there even though excellent chances of escape presented themselves. For example, Hollywood made the Steven Stayner abduction case into a movie called *I Know My First Name Is Steven*.

* * * *

On December 4, 1972, convicted pedophile Kenneth Parnell and an accomplice abducted seven-year-old Steven Stayner as he walked home from school in Merced, California, a small community near Yosemite Park. After the abduction, Parnell drove Steven to a cabin near Yosemite, where he had laid out a collection of toys for the boy to play with. He told Steven that he had called his mother and she said it was all right for him to stay the night. To the seven-year-old, everything seemed to be okay.

Parnell moved Steven continuously during the next seven years in order to prevent anyone from becoming suspicious and asking questions. Parnell convinced Steven that his parents couldn't afford him any longer and that they had given Parnell the okay to adopt him. During Steven's captivity, Parnell gave him many gifts that boys his age would like, but he also sexually molested Steven on a regular basis. In addition, Parnell supplied Steven with drugs and alcohol while he was still a preteen.

Parnell also gave Steven a new name, Dennis Parnell, and a cover story to tell teachers and anyone else who might ask about him. Surprisingly, Steven attended schools that had received posters from Steven's desperate parents, who untiringly searched for him. Yet, none of Steven's teachers made the connection between the picture on the poster and the little boy in their class.

After Steven had been with Parnell for seven years, during which time Steven had had many excellent opportunities to escape, Parnell did something that finally made Steven decide he had to leave. As Steven grew older, and as we talked about earlier with Michael Devlin, Parnell apparently decided that he needed a younger boy in order to satisfy his pedophile desires, and so he and an accomplice abducted five-year-old Timmy White as he walked from school to his babysitter's house.

That night, Parnell dyed Timmy's blond hair dark brown so that he wouldn't look like the little boy on the inevitable missing child posters. Parnell also told Timmy the same story he had told Steven seven years earlier about his parents not wanting him any longer, and how he would be Timmy's new father. Steven, though, knew what would be in store for little Timmy, and he decided that he just couldn't let that happen to another little boy.

"I couldn't see Timmy suffer," Steven said. "It was my do-or-die chance..."[31]

On March 1, 1980, while Parnell worked the night shift as an employee of a hotel in Ukiah, California, Steven took Timmy and fled. Trying unsuccessfully to find Timmy's home, the two boys eventually walked into a police station and told their story to stunned police officers.

The police, after verifying the story, arrested Parnell. Later, two separate juries found Parnell guilty of the abductions of both Steven and Timmy. A judge, following the convictions, sentenced Parnell to prison.

However, prison didn't change Parnell's pedophile desires. On February 9, 2004, after Parnell had been paroled for the two abductions, a jury found him guilty of attempting to buy a young child. Parnell had offered his caretaker (he was by this time having serious health problems) $500 if she would bring him a little African-American boy. The caretaker, however, immediately contacted the police, and then, working with them, returned to Parnell and told him that she had the little boy out in her car. He gave her $100 and told her to bring the little boy in. Instead, the police came in and arrested him. Officers found that Parnell had a collection of sex toys in his house, and the other $400 in his pocket. A judge sentenced Parnell to 25 years to life for the attempted abduction.

****

In another similar case, on March 2, 1998, Wolfgang Priklopil abducted 10-year-old Natascha Kampusch from the street in Vienna, Austria, as she walked to school. Her family and the police, though searching desperately for her, couldn't find out what had happened to her. Witnesses said that they saw Natascha being pulled into a white minibus, and though the police interviewed the owners of over 700 white minibuses, including Priklopil, they couldn't find anything to connect any of the owners to the abduction. Priklopil had no criminal record.

Before the abduction, Priklopil had designed a hidden chamber under his house, where for the first six months he kept Natascha confined, telling her that the doors were rigged with explosives. But soon, Natascha's captor began giving her more and more freedom, even one time taking her on a skiing trip. Priklopil reportedly told her, however, that he would kill anyone she asked help from. Yet, at the same time he also gave her presents regularly. In addition, he supplied Natascha with books, magazines, a television, and other comforts.

Finally, on August 23, 2006, after eight years with Priklopil, Natascha decided she wanted to leave, and escaped while Priklopil was distracted talking on his cell phone. She eventually persuaded someone to call the police for her.

When Priklopil discovered that Natascha had left and that the police were looking for him, he committed suicide by jumping in front of a train. As to whether Priklopil had sexually molested Natascha during her captivity, she said in a letter to the press, "Intimate questions: everybody wants to ask intimate questions, but these have nothing to do with anybody else. It may be that one day I speak to my therapist about it and maybe not. At the end of the day the private life is mine alone."[32]

However, in the same letter to the press, Natascha had this to say about Priklopil's death, "He has been a big part of my life, and as a result I do feel I am in a sort of mourning for him."[33]

An Associated Press article about Natascha's letter to the media said, "Her statement—which surprised many people with its eloquence—suggested she may be suffering from the 'Stockholm Syndrome,' in which victims cope with intolerable situations by identifying with their captors."[34]

As for Natascha's condition since her escape, an article in the *San Francisco Chronicle* said, "Although experts who have examined Kampusch say she is suffering from a severe case of Stockholm Syndrome, in which kidnapping victims or hostages sympathize with their abductors, she has also shown herself to be alert and decisive, as reflected in her request not to be sent to live with either of her now-divorced parents."[35]

* * * *

In addition to the cases above, many people who have looked into the Elizabeth Smart abduction also believe that she may have fallen under the control of the Stockholm Syndrome. According to reports of the case, she had a number of excellent chances to escape, but didn't. Also, she reportedly at first denied being Elizabeth Smart, and then her major concern when identified by the police was what was going to happen to her two captors after the police arrested them.

According to an article in the *Chicago Tribune,* "Marta Weber, a clinical psychologist in San Francisco who specializes in trauma cases, concurred that Smart could have suffered from the Stockholm Syndrome. 'If you have to be in a room with your captors, you have to get along with them in such a way so that you don't provoke them to harm you,' Weber said. 'What the ego does is, it will rearrange your perceptions so that you can believe you like these people so you don't have to lie about it and be found out. You actually believe you have a positive relationship with them.'"[36]

Abducted children and hostages, however, aren't the only ones to fall under the spell of the Stockholm Syndrome and then stay in relationships that they know are destructive. For example, a large number of mental health professionals believe that the Stockholm Syndrome is involved in many cases of violent domestic relationships. Very often, individuals will stay in these violent relationships, even though they know they should leave, and even though excellent opportunities to leave present themselves. The Stockholm Syndrome, many mental health professionals believe, instead binds them to the other person, even though the other person may be abusive and violent towards them. And this attachment can be strong indeed.

According to the article "Love and Stockholm Syndrome: The Mystery of Loving an Abuser," by clinical psychologist Joseph M. Carver, "The Stockholm Syndrome reaction in hostage and/or abuse situations is so well recognized at this time that police hostage negotiators no longer view it as unusual." He then goes on to say, "Local law enforcement personnel have long recognized this syndrome with battered women who fail to press charges, bail their battering husband/boyfriend out of jail, and even physically attack police officers when they arrive to rescue them from a violent assault."[37]

Confirming Dr. Carver's words above, all veteran police officers have experienced the situation of attempting to arrest someone who has assaulted a person he or she is in an intimate relationship with, only to have the abuse victim physically attack the police and try to stop them. The Stockholm Syndrome can be a powerful glue that can hold people, including abducted children, in relationships that are not healthy.

While it can often be difficult for people to understand why children would choose to stay with an abusive abductor, frightened parents desperate for an abducted child's safe return also often have a difficult time understanding the lukewarm response they many times receive when they first contact the police about a child abduction. As we will see in the next chapter, dealing with the police during a child abduction can many times only add more stress and frustration to an already traumatic event.

Police Response to Child Abduction

Nine-year-old Jessica Lunsford of Homosassa, Florida, a small town on the Gulf coast, 75 miles north of Tampa, loved the purple stuffed dolphin her father had won for her at a county fair. When the police found Jessica's corpse several weeks after her reported abduction, they discovered her still clutching the stuffed animal.

On the morning of February 24, 2005, Jessica's father, Mark, went to Jessica's room to be certain she was getting up for school. To his surprise, he found the room empty, both Jessica and her favorite stuffed animal missing. Alarmed and panicking, Mark immediately called 911.

The police officers responding to the call began a search for Jessica. Yet, even though family and friends joined in the search, as evening fell, they had found no trace of the missing nine-year-old.

The following day, hundreds of volunteers joined in the search for Jessica. However, after a week of effort, the searchers had found no sign of the little girl.

The Citrus County Sheriff's Department, as a part of its investigation into Jessica's disappearance, routinely began a check of all of the reported sex offenders who lived or worked in the area. During this inquiry they discovered that a 46-year-old sex offender named John Evander Couey wasn't living at his reported address and hadn't registered any new address, a violation of Florida law.

Couey, the Sheriff's Department found, had a long arrest record, which, besides sex offenses, also included drug charges, burglary, weapons charges, and fraud. The sheriff's department investigators, after a little digging, learned that Couey was now staying with Dorothy Marie Dixon, his half-sister, and several other people, all of whom lived in a trailer within eyesight of the Lunsford home.

When detectives from the sheriff's department went to the address, the individuals living in the trailer at first denied that Couey lived there. The detectives, however, didn't believe them, and characterized them as "a bunch of cracked-out individuals. Just a bunch of druggies."[1] However, for some reason, the detectives didn't obtain a search warrant to do a thorough search of the trailer at that time.

"For some reason, they came to our house but they didn't come in and search," Couey would later tell detectives in his confession, "but I wish they would have cause they would have found her, but they didn't."[2]

Some days later, however, the detectives did return to the trailer with a search warrant, and found blood on a mattress where they believed Couey had slept. The detectives didn't know it but, though Couey had lived in the trailer for some time, he didn't any longer. Several days after Jessica's disappearance, he had caught a bus for Savannah, Georgia, where he stayed at a homeless shelter. While there, the local police had questioned him about drug possession. However, the officers in Savannah didn't know that the police in Florida were looking for Couey, so they let him go.

Even though the police in Savannah hadn't taken Couey to the station, he worried that they might return and do so. Consequently, he decided he needed to move again, and so he headed for Augusta, Georgia, checking into a Salvation Army shelter there. By this time, the news media had begun broadcasting information about the Jessica Lunsford disappearance, and listing Couey as a suspect in her abduction. A worker at the shelter recognized the photo of Couey on television and called the police. Responding officers arrested Couey and charged him with failure to register in Georgia as a sex offender. They notified the Citrus County Sheriff's Department of Couey's arrest, and the department immediately sent two detectives to question him.

The sheriff's department detectives, during their interrogation of Couey, felt certain that he was guilty, but holding out, and so they kept up their intense questioning. Couey, however, insisted over and over that he didn't know anything about Jessica's disappearance. During the questioning, when one of the detectives asked Couey if he would be willing to take a lie detector test, Couey told them he wanted an attorney.

Under standard police procedure, if during an interrogation a suspect states that he or she wants an attorney, the questioning must stop until an attorney is obtained and the suspect is allowed to confer with him or her. Otherwise, any incriminating statements made by a suspect will very likely not be allowed as evidence during a trial. The Citrus County detectives, however, ignored Couey's request for an attorney and continued their interrogation.

The following day, during a lie detector test, Couey finally broke down. He told the detectives how he had abducted, sexually assaulted, and then murdered Jessica Lunsford. He told them that he had buried her in his half-sister's backyard.

"You know what I am?...I'm a convicted child molester," Couey told the detectives. "I didn't know what to do. You know, I got scared. I panicked."[3]

According to Couey's confession, he entered the Lunsford home through an unlocked door at around 3:00 a.m., and then slipped into Jessica's bedroom. He awoke her and then ordered the startled and frightened little girl to be quiet and to follow him back to his half-sister's house. There, he raped her several times and then placed her in a closet in his bedroom, ordering her not to move. The terrified little girl obediently stayed in the closet all day while Couey went to work.

Couey told the officers that he kept her hidden in his bedroom for three days, raping her repeatedly. He said he wouldn't even let her out to use the bathroom, because he didn't want the other people in the trailer to know she was there.

After several days, when Couey found out that the police had listed him as a suspect in Jessica's disappearance, he panicked. He knew he had to get rid of her. So, he bound Jessica's hands with speaker wire, and then placed her in two trash bags, afterward burying her alive in his sister's backyard. The coroner would later say that Jessica had died of suffocation, taking three to five minutes to die after being buried. It appeared that she had unsuccessfully tried to tear the trash bags to get out. When the police dug her up, they found her still clutching her purple dolphin. In the coroner's examination, traces of cocaine were found on Jessica, believed to have come from her being present while Couey smoked crack cocaine. The coroner also confirmed that Jessica had been raped, and that she had not been fed for a long time before her death.

The police charged Couey with burglary, kidnapping, sexual battery, and murder. A judge ordered him held without bond.

During pretrial motions in June of 2006, defense attorneys successfully persuaded Judge Richard Howard to throw out Couey's confession because the Citrus County detectives had not gotten an attorney for him as he had requested. Also, before this, due to the intense pretrial media coverage of the case, obtaining a local pool of unbiased jurors proved impossible, and so the trial was moved across the state from Citrus County to Miami-Dade County.

Couey's trial finally began in early 2007. Even without Couey's confession, the police still had plenty of evidence against him. They had found Jessica's blood mixed with Couey's semen on the mattress Couey had used in the trailer. They also found some of Jessica's blood on the floor of the closet in

Couey's bedroom. Crime lab technicians additionally discovered Jessica's fingerprints several places in Couey's bedroom. Along with all of this, the speaker wire used to bind Jessica's hands was identical to the wire Couey had used in building a homemade television antenna for the trailer.

On March 7, 2007, after four hours of deliberation, a jury found Couey guilty of murder, kidnapping, sexual battery, and burglary. A week later, after more deliberations, the same jury recommended that Couey be put to death for his crimes. On August 24, 2007, Judge Howard, following the jury's recommendation, sentenced Couey to death.

"I wanted to cry out but we were told we weren't supposed to," Jessica's mother told reporters about the verdict. "It made me feel a little better on the inside. He finally got what he deserved."[4]

Jessica's father, distraught over what had happened to his daughter and wanting to spare other parents the same pain and suffering he went through, tirelessly lobbied Florida lawmakers for tougher penalties for crimes committed by sex offenders. On May 2, 2005, Florida governor Jeb Bush signed the Jessica Lunsford Act. This law requires a minimum sentence of 25 years in prison for sex offenders who prey on children under 12. It also requires lifetime electronic tracking of these offenders if they are ever released from prison. In addition, the law makes it a felony in Florida to harbor an unregistered sex offender.

****

In the above case, why didn't the police obtain a search warrant the first time they went to the trailer to look for Couey or Jessica? This is a particularly troublesome question since they apparently had enough probable cause to obtain a search warrant several days later. While this is easy for me to ask, it's hard to say why they didn't do this without knowing all of the particulars of the case, and what information the police had available to them at the time.

But could they also have gone into the trailer and looked around even without a search warrant? Yes, they could have. And this likely would have saved Jessica's life. The courts permit the police to make warrantless entry into structures if they feel someone's life is in danger. Was that the case here? Yes, it was. Did the police know that? We can't be sure, but I'm certain that every officer who was involved in this incident has gone through his or her own personal hell wondering what he or she did wrong and what he or she could have been done differently that might have saved Jessica's life.

As a detective's guide for the investigation of child abductions said, "Abductions which result in a child's death present great investigative and emotional obstacles for law enforcement officers."[5] This can be especially true if the officers fail to do something that might have saved the child.

And yet, strangely enough, even though police officers who don't rescue a child alive can suffer both emotionally and psychologically, many parents of missing children, who may have been abducted, complain that the police often answer their calls for help with a much less than enthusiastic response. Many parents have complained over the years that unless they have solid, undeniable proof that their child has been abducted and is in danger, the police don't want to take a report, or tell the parents that they must wait 24–48 hours after the child is missing before they will take a report.

While the above response by the police may sound cold and unfeeling, there is actually a basis in logic for it. According to the NISMART Bulletin "Nation Estimates of Missing Children," between 1.3 and 1.5 million children turn up missing in the United States every year.[6] However, well over 90 percent of these children return home on their own within 24–48 hours of their disappearance. Consequently, the police know that they would "waste" millions of man-hours every year if they took reports right away and immediately went out looking for every missing child.

Of course, while the police response to parents wanting to report a missing child may have a logical basis, this is certainly not very comforting to the fearful parents of a child who has never been any kind of problem, and suddenly turns up missing. Is the child really just missing at the moment or is it possible that he or she has been abducted? And this fear by the parents is only compounded by the fact that children who are killed after being abducted are usually murdered within the first three hours of the abduction. Consequently, waiting 24–48 hours only puts the child's life in more danger and peril.

Also, very often police departments are less than enthusiastic about getting involved and taking missing child reports on possible child abductions by noncustodial parents because they believe that custody issues are not criminal, but civil matters. This is not so, however. As a bulletin by the Office of Juvenile Justice and Delinquency Prevention says, "Although many individuals, including some law enforcement personnel, perceive parental abduction as 'civil in nature' and a private family matter best handled outside the realm of the criminal justice system, it is a crime in all 50 States and the District of Columbia and, in most cases, constitutes a felony."[7] (A felony is a serious crime punishable by a sentence of a year or more in prison, as compared to misdemeanors, which are less serious acts punishable by a fine or a sentence of less than a year in the county jail.)

"We must treat these offenses as serious criminal matters," said Ernie Allen, president and CEO of the National Center for Missing and Exploited Children, talking about parental child abduction. "They are violations of the criminal law in every state, and under most circumstances are now felonies in every state. They must be investigated seriously, and require a high level of knowledge and expertise by the investigator."[8]

Actually, despite the belief by police departments otherwise, the expeditious taking of a missing child report and immediate action by the police can often make the difference as to whether or not a child abductor can escape apprehension. It is much easier to apprehend a child abductor and recover the child safely while the abductor is still within the police department's jurisdiction, since the dissemination of information about the wanted person and abducted child can be handled much quicker. Yet still, many police departments continue to delay or refuse to take these reports.

To combat this problem of police reluctance to take a missing child report, readers need to be aware that the federal National Child Search Assistance Act of 1990 (42 U.S.C, section 5780) requires that any police department requested to do so must immediately (all waiting periods are prohibited) enter the particulars about a missing child into the NCIC (National Crime Information Center) computer system. This is a nationwide computer system maintained by the FBI that is available to every police department in the United States. Consequently, entering a missing child's information into this computer system can insure that if the police in another community encounter this child they will know that he or she has been reported missing, and the parents will be notified.

Still, despite the federal law above, a survey of local police departments, sponsored by the U.S. Department of Justice, found that, "Agency personnel reported varying practices as to the entry of information on parentally abducted children and perpetrators into the NCIC database. It was the practice in some jurisdictions not to enter information on a parental abduction case unless the child's whereabouts were 'unknown,' an arrest warrant had been issued, or the abductor had fled out of State."[9] Of course, all of these practices are in direct violation of the federal law mentioned above. Yet still, these practices continue to exist in many local police departments.

Readers, therefore, who find themselves facing police departments that, regardless of this federal law, still refuse to take a missing child report and enter the information into the NCIC system, can go to the nearest FBI field office and have this information entered into the NCIC system. The Missing Children's Act of 1982 (28 U.S.C., section 534a) requires the FBI to do this. As might be imagined, a federal agency such as the FBI would be much less likely than a local police department to disregard federal law.

However, even if parents are successful in persuading officers to take a missing child report, many police departments still do not give high priority to child abduction cases, particularly family child abduction cases. For example, a study sponsored by the U.S. Department of Justice found that police departments in the United States make arrests in only about 15 percent of all parental abduction cases reported to them.[10] And parental child abduction cases are, by far, the largest number of child abduction cases reported to the police. From a police officer's point of view, I find this to be a totally unacceptable arrest percentage, particularly considering that the police know exactly who the suspect is, and very often know just where to find him or her.

This same study, sadly enough, also discovered that almost 70 percent of the police departments studied did not have written policies and procedures for handling parental child abduction cases, and only 10 percent said that they had received any training in the handling of these types of cases. The study concluded that, "Emerging from this study is a picture of a criminal justice system paying relatively scant attention to the crime of parental abduction."[11]

Another study of police departments found, however, that certain attributes of all types of possible child abduction cases, listed below in their order of importance, will cause police departments to categorize them as having high investigative priority, and consequently force the police departments to immediately begin a search and investigation.

1. The child is less than eight years old.
2. There is an eyewitness to the abduction.
3. There is a danger to the child of sexual exploitation.
4. Physical evidence of an abduction exists.
5. The child has a requirement for prescription medicine.
6. The child has a mental handicap or disability.[12]

Fortunately, not all police departments have this cavalier attitude about waiting 24–48 hours before taking reports of missing, and possibly abducted, children. In the early 1980s, for example, the Indianapolis Police Department gained international acclaim, including a feature article in the April 1984 issue of *Reader's Digest,* when in 1982 they recovered every single one of the 1,592 children reported as missing that year. They did this by taking missing children reports immediately, and then going out right then and looking for the children.

Today there are a number of police departments that still hold to this belief that delay is a dangerous tactic when looking for missing, and possibly abducted, children. A number of cities have even formed special units just for the purpose of looking for these children.

Many of these specialized units are attached to the state police or the district attorney's office, which then makes them available to smaller jurisdictions that don't have enough child abductions each year to make having their own unit feasible. As an article about child abduction investigation said, "Agencies with limited resources can become quickly overwhelmed when a high profile [child abduction] case occurs."[13]

Another article about child abduction investigation agreed with this when it said, "The investigation of a missing child who possibly was abducted, however, constitutes the most serious and perplexing challenge facing law enforcement agencies. It can rapidly overwhelm and exhaust all available resources (e.g. financial, personnel, logistical) and impose a heavy personal and professional burden on investigators, support personnel, and management."[14] The simple truth is, without having these specialized units made available to them, most small police departments simply could not successfully resolve many child abduction cases.

Having these specialized units to investigate child abductions, units that are manned by highly trained investigators, is critical to the proper handling of child abduction cases because police officers who don't specialize in child abduction cases can very often make wrong assumptions about them. For example, the report from the Attorney General's Office for the State of Washington, talked about in previous chapters, said, "Homicide investigators, through no fault of their own, sometimes fail to realize that the investigations of the murders of abducted children are very different from the other murders they usually investigate. Consequently, they sometimes makes decisions about the direction of the investigation that are not 'high percentage' choices."[15] Supporting this statement, I found when I headed the Indianapolis Police Department's Homicide Branch that the large majority of our murders involved either narcotics dealing or violent domestic relationships. The experience gained in solving these types of murders, I found, proved of little value to detectives when investigating child abduction murders.

And while the above quote involves child abductions that result in murder, the same problem exists for ordinary child abduction cases that don't end so drastically. Police officers untrained in child abduction cases will assume that they can apply their experience in burglary or auto theft investigations to these cases, but very often these experiences are simply not relevant to child abduction cases.

In addition, having these specialized child abduction units is also critical because in a survey of the parents of abducted children, 62 percent said they were "somewhat" or "very dissatisfied" with the police handling of their case.[16] Another study of the parents of abducted children found that two-thirds of them said they received little or no assistance from the first law enforcement official they spoke with.[17] Readers will recall that, in the incident in the previous chapter involving Shawn Hornbeck, his parents once picketed the local sheriff's department because they were so dissatisfied with the handling of their son's case. The parents of abducted children need to be able to contact a team of police officers who are knowledgeable about child abductions, experienced in investigating them, and supportive of the parent's plight.

One such unit is the Kern County (California) Child Abduction Unit. This group of officers operates out of the Kern County District Attorney's Office. Their stated purpose is, "The Child Abduction Unit of the Kern County District Attorney's Office exists to help parents recover children who have been abducted, to prosecute those who violate criminal laws related to child abduction, and to represent the Superior Court...when the Court orders the District Attorney to locate and recover missing children."[18]

Another excellent child abduction unit is the Santa Clara County (California) Parental Child Abduction Unit. This unit recovers from 60 to

80 parentally abducted children every year, and also operates out of the district attorney's office.

"Our mission in some ways is simple," said Deputy District Attorney Julianne Sylva. "We are trying to protect the children."[19]

Georgia Hilgeman-Hammond, the executive director of The Vanished Children's Alliance, had high praise for the Santa Clara unit. "Many see these cases as two warring parents. But these are complicated cases, and to handle them we have dedicated and caring people who are knowledgeable, readily available, and who do this as their primary job."[20]

However, as the following anecdote shows, having properly trained and motivated police officers can not only make a huge difference when it comes to the finding and recovery of abducted children, but also to the ability to stop an abduction as it is occurring.

****

On February 24, 2004, Customs and Border Protection Officer Luis Astete, who is assigned to the Portland International Airport in Portland, Oregon, received a call from an agent at U.S. Immigration and Customs. The agent told Officer Astete he had information that a man who had illegally abducted his two children was headed with them out of Portland International in route back to Peru in South America. He gave Astete the name of the man and the abducted children, and asked him to check it out.

When Officer Astete checked he found that the man had entered the United States the previous November, and had been carrying $23,000 in cash. Knowing how child abductors work, Astete realized that the man likely needed this money to buy forged travel documents for his children. However, Astete found out something else that was much more disturbing. The man had already left Portland International with his two children and was at that time waiting in Dallas for a connecting flight to Lima, Peru, a flight that left in 35 minutes. The children, as Astete suspected, were traveling under false names and forged travel documents.

Officer Astete called the gate in Dallas, but found that he received much less cooperation than he had hoped for from the gate agent. The gate agent didn't want to delay the aircraft or take three people off the plane without concrete proof that he should.

"Look, man, I can't just yank them off the plane," the gate agent told Astete. "What if it's the wrong guy?"[21]

Officer Astete, knowing that if the abductor got the children out of the country, the mother would be hard pressed to get them back, simply wouldn't give up. Astete managed to get the Dallas Police Department to send an officer to the gate. There, the Dallas police officer took the child abductor into custody and recovered the two children. Two hours later, the police had the children on an airplane in route back home to their mother in Oregon.

****

Besides being aggressive and knowledgeable as Officer Astete was in stopping the above abduction in progress, another area where knowledgeable and concerned police officers can also make a huge difference is in the handling of the recovery of an abducted child. A child who has been abducted by a family member, for example, will often have confused, mixed feelings about the abducting parent. Progressive police departments know that it is best for the child's welfare that he or she not witness the police placing the abducting parent under arrest, putting the abducting parent in handcuffs, etc. Otherwise, the child can feel guilty, can feel that he or she is somehow to blame for what is happening to the parent.

Of course, sometimes having the child be a witness to the arrest of the abducting parent cannot be avoided. In this case, as the U.S. Department of Justice book *Family Abduction—Prevention and Response* says, "If the return of the child is involuntary and involves resistance or arrest of the abducting parent, the law enforcement officer or child protective service worker will need to provide an initial explanation to the child of what is happening and will happen until the other parent arrives."[22] Obviously, someone needs to take the child to a quiet place and, after explaining what has happened, be certain the child knows that he or she is not to blame.

Progressive police departments also know that, in order to lessen the emotional damage to a recovered child, they should remove the abducting parent from the scene of the child's reunification with the left-behind parent. Otherwise, the child can be faced with a conflict of who to turn to, particularly if the Stockholm Syndrome is involved. Consequently, the police should be certain that the reunification takes place in a quiet, private place. The press, well-wishers, and distant family members should be somewhere else.

So, what are the solutions to the problems we have discussed in this chapter? First, local police departments need to forget about waiting periods, and begin taking missing children reports right away. To do otherwise is unconscionable given the facts about how soon abducted children are murdered and how much easier it is to locate abducted children if the police start right away. Second, these same local police departments need to develop training for their officers in the dynamics of child abduction, and in how police officers should ideally handle child abduction cases. The third part of the solution is that local police departments need to develop detailed written guidelines and procedures about how they will handle child abductions, so that when any of their officers receive one of these cases they can have some type of guidance to supplement their training.

An article in the *FBI Law Enforcement Bulletin* concluded, "Although missing child cases frequently are not abductions, law enforcement agencies must prepare themselves for the inevitable life-threatening case by establishing child abduction investigative protocols and memoranda of understanding with adjacent law enforcement agencies. Such planning is effective only when initiated prior to an abduction allegation and the ensuing investigation."[23]

As we spoke about in previous chapters, abducted children don't just come from poor, one-parent, or dysfunctional families. An abducted child can come from any family, at any level of society. And often, a child abduction will be the only contact, besides perhaps traffic tickets, that some citizens will ever have with the police. These citizens therefore should be able to expect that a police department will give their case the importance it deserves. Children are our society's most valuable resource, and police departments need to keep this in mind, and assign the proper level of importance to child abduction cases.

While in this chapter we have looked at how the police response can help or hinder a child abduction case, in the next chapter we will look at how the rest of our government can also make a difference. As we will see, various government entities can have a huge effect on whether or not the resolution of a child abduction case is positive.

What the Government Can Do

A surveillance camera at Evie's Car wash in Sarasota, Florida, caught the abduction as it occurred, and the event horrified America as viewers across the country watched it on the evening news. America saw an innocent child being pulled away to her death.

On February 1, 2004, Super Bowl Sunday, 11-year-old Carlie Brucia didn't return home after a sleepover at a friend's house, and her parents, naturally concerned for her safety, called the police. Responding officers began a search for her, eventually using a bloodhound, which tracked Carlie's scent to Evie's Car Wash, where it stopped. The police contacted the owner of the car wash, who came to his business and checked the security video.

"It was cold chills right up my back," said the car wash owner, Mike Evanoff, about finding the images of Carlie and her abductor on the videotape. "My manager couldn't even look at it. It's an awful feeling."[1]

Apparently, Carlie had decided to cut through the car wash on the way home from her friend's house, where she'd had the sleepover. On the videotape viewers can see that a man approaches her, and it is apparent that Carlie doesn't know him and tries to avoid him. However, the man says something to her, and then grabs her arm and pulls her off camera.

"It was apparent that (Carlie) did not recognize this subject and... attempted to pass by him when he stopped her and forcibly walked her out of camera view," said a later police probable cause affidavit.[2]

The video also showed that the man wore a mechanic's uniform, and that he had tattoos on both arms. The video, however, wasn't clear enough for the police to make an identification of the man. Consequently, for several days after finding the video no one knew what had happened to Carlie.

The police investigation continued, however, with an attempt, using technology made available by NASA, to enhance the videotape and perhaps make out the name on the patch on the suspect's shirt. "It appears to be a short name, maybe three or four letters," said FBI agent Carl Whitehead. "We're in an effort to try to enhance that to clarify that."[3]

The police, in addition, established a nationwide hotline for tips on the case, and offered a reward of $50,000. The case finally broke though when, after the police released the video to the public, two people who saw it, including a woman who lived with a man named Joseph P. Smith, called the police to say the man in the video was Smith.

Consequently, the police investigation quickly focused on a 37-year-old auto mechanic named Joseph P. Smith. Detectives soon discovered that the police had already arrested Smith the day after Carlie's disappearance on an unrelated probation violation charge, and that he still sat in jail. Smith had a long police record, including arrests for kidnapping and attacks on women. The police questioned Smith, who denied being near the car wash on the day the man in the video abducted Carlie Brucia. However, the security video clearly showed a car Smith had borrowed from a friend parked there.

Despite Smith's denials to the police, during a visit to the jail by Smith's brother and mother, he reportedly confessed to them that he had kidnapped, raped, and killed Carlie Brucia. The family members, following the visit, told the police where they could find Carlie's body. The police went to the Central Church of Christ on Proctor Road near Interstate 75, a few miles from Evie's Car Wash. There they found Carlie's body.

On February 20, 2004, a grand jury indicted Smith on the charge of first-degree murder. An autopsy showed that her abductor had strangled Carlie to death. The prosecutor also charged Smith with kidnapping and capital sexual battery.

The trial for the abduction, rape, and murder of Carlie Brucia began in November 2005. The prosecutor had, along with the car wash security video, several other pieces of damning evidence. DNA from a semen stain on the shirt worn by Carlie came back to Smith. The jurors also heard a recording of Smith's confession to his brother and mother, in which he said that he had killed Carlie during some "rough sex" with her.

"In this case, there truly is overwhelming evidence," said Prosecutor Craig Schaeffer. "There's mountains of evidence in this case."[4]

Smith's defense attorney stunned the court, however, by deciding not to give a closing statement before the case went to the jury. The jury deliberated for six hours and agreed with Prosecutor Schaeffer, finding Smith guilty of first-degree murder, sexual battery, and kidnapping. The same jury then went back into deliberations, and voted 10 to 2 in favor of the death penalty for Smith.

In his defense during the sentencing phase of his trial, Smith said that he had been high on both cocaine and heroin when he killed Carlie, and didn't know what he was doing. He pleaded with the judge to spare his life for the sake of his family.

Judge Andrew Owens, Jr., however, didn't give much sway to Smith's explanation or to his pleas for mercy. He instead followed the jury's recommendation and sentenced Smith to die for his crimes. "Joseph Smith, based upon your actions, you have forfeited your right to live freely among us... and you have forfeited your right to live," said Judge Owens.[5]

****

While this is a horrible case with a horrible outcome, still positives can come from such a case. Because of the Carlie Brucia abduction and murder, the federal government decided that it needed to form regional teams of criminal investigators that could respond to and assist the local authorities in the investigation of abducted children. The federal government named these units CART (Child Abduction Response Teams).

"As many of you know, the CART program began as a result of the tragic abduction of 11-year-old Carlie Brucia in Sarasota, Florida, in February 2004," Deputy Assistant Attorney General Cybele K. Daley told a conference in San Diego in January of 2006. "Members of the Orlando Regional Operations Center working on the Brucia case determined that they needed trained experts in the field of child abduction investigation and response. These experts needed to be able to respond to an abduction immediately, assist the lead local law enforcement agency, and bring additional regional resources to the recovery effort."[6]

A number of local police departments attending this conference received training in child abduction investigation and recovery. Police officers from communities as far away as Warren County, Ohio; Maryville, Missouri; Montesano, Washington; and Shakopee, Minnesota attended the conference and training sessions.

"When a child is abducted, time is of the essence," said Daley. "Trained regional teams will soon be poised to bring additional resources to help recover children safely and return them to their families."[7]

In addition to the above, the FBI has also established its own program of specially trained officers that can be called upon to assist in child abduction cases. These teams are called CARD (Child Abduction Rapid Deployment). Under the "Lindbergh Law," the FBI has the authority to investigate the mysterious disappearance or kidnapping of a child.

"The CARD Teams are designed to deploy teams of 4 to 6 experienced personnel to provide on-the-ground investigative, technical, and resource assistance to state and local law enforcement," said an FBI press release. "The CARD Teams consist of Crimes Against Children Investigators, who have in-depth experience in child abduction cases."[8]

FBI Special Agent Janice Mertz, who heads the FBI's Crimes Against Children Unit, said, "We want our best people moving as fast as they can and using every skill they've got to find missing kids and bring them home safely. That's the bottom line of this initiative."[9]

While this is a wonderful addition to the law enforcement effort in child abduction cases, what else can the government do in addition to developing and training these federal CART and CARD units? What can be done to expand these programs to the local level?

What needs to be done is that every major police department in the United States needs to have a unit specifically trained in child abduction. A unit with this training wouldn't make all of the false starts and travel down all of the blind alleys that police departments without such units many times do when they have a sudden, high profile child abduction. These problems come about, as we talked about previously, because police departments often tend to assign these cases to detectives who have no training or experience in child abduction, and who consequently often follow low percentages paths. These specially trained units, on the other hand, would know that child abduction cases have specific attributes about them that other cases don't, and would also know the best, high-percentage routes to take to safely recover the abducted child.

It has been found that police departments and local prosecutor's offices that have these specialized child abduction units take reports of child abduction much more seriously, and pursue the cases more thoroughly. For example, a report by the Office of Juvenile Justice and Delinquency Prevention found that, "Extradition was more likely to occur in jurisdictions in which prosecutors' offices had a unit employing staff who specialized in parental abduction cases."[10] On the other hand, many prosecutor's offices that don't have these units often simply drop the charges against abductors arrested out of their jurisdiction rather than go through the lengthy, complicated procedure of extradition.

Of course, in many jurisdictions there wouldn't be enough cases of child abduction to keep these units working full time, and so they would instead have to be on call. There is precedent for these types of police units. In many cities, the members of the police department's SWAT team have other jobs within the police department and only come together as a SWAT team when a SWAT situation develops. Still, they receive regular training on SWAT tactics to keep them sharp and up to date. Local police department CART units could operate in the same manner.

Fortunately, the federal government is helping local police departments set up these units. In January 2006, the U.S. Department of Justice held its first ever training session for local CART units. The federal government designed this training specifically to assist local law enforcement agencies in setting up units to respond to child abduction cases.

Since then, specialized training in child abduction investigation and recovery has been given in many locations, including Cleveland, Ohio; Tarrant County, Texas; and Fargo, North Dakota. "A lot of jurisdictions are really taking a look at it," said West Fargo (North Dakota) police detective Greg Warren. "A missing or abducted child is going to happen around here somewhere eventually, and you want to be prepared."[11]

All major police departments need to take advantage of this federal training, and prepare themselves for the inevitable high-profile child abduction. Major police departments need to use this training to become proactive about child abduction.

As a member of a government agency for 38 years, I know that the government, at any level, at least in the past, was seldom proactive. We usually only reacted after a tragedy struck. It was quite often only then that we realized we must do something that would stop these kinds of tragedies from occurring again. For example, the Amber Alert system, which today operates in every state to alert citizens of an abducted child who is in danger, came about, as the following incident shows, through a tragedy that perhaps could have been avoided.

****

Nine-year-old Amber Hagerman loved to ride bicycles. On January 12, 1996, Amber, along with her mother and her five-year-old brother Ricky, visited her grandmother's house in Arlington, Texas, a small suburb located between Dallas and Fort Worth. Amber's grandmother kept bicycles at her house for her grandchildren to use when they visited. Amber asked if she and her brother could ride them.

"OK, but just go once around the block," Amber's mother told her.[12]

Amber and her brother pedaled away to the parking lot of a nearby Winn Dixie grocery store that had been shut down for some time. The store's parking lot had a ramp that kids liked to ride their bikes over. A little while later, Ricky returned to his grandmother's house by himself. The grandmother asked Ricky where Amber was, and he said that she had wanted to ride on the ramp some more. The grandmother told Ricky, "You tell Sissy to get back home."[13]

Ricky pedaled back to the Winn Dixie parking lot, but then a few minutes later returned home alone again. He told the family that he didn't know where Amber was. The grandfather jumped into his truck and drove to the Winn Dixie. There, Amber's grandfather saw a marked police car, and he hurried up to the officer, who told Amber's grandfather that the police department had received a call from a man who had heard a little girl screaming and then saw a man dragging her to a truck. The grandfather found Amber's bicycle lying on the Winn Dixie parking lot.

The next day, Amber's mother appeared on television and pleaded for her daughter's safe return. "Please don't hurt my baby," she cried. "She's just an innocent child."[14]

Although the police conducted an intense search, they never turned up the truck or the suspect. Since Amber didn't live in the area or frequent the parking lot, detectives theorized that it had been a crime of opportunity. The abductor had seen his chance when Ricky left and Amber was alone in the parking lot.

The police, unfortunately, did recover Amber's body several days later in a creek bed several miles from where she had been abducted. A man walking his dog found her nude body, her throat slit. The police, during their investigation, put out a likely psychological profile of the suspect, hoping that someone would recognize the person.

"Our hope is...someone out there will hear this and will think, 'Gee, this sounds like someone I know,'" said an Arlington (Texas) Police Department spokesperson.[15]

And yet, though the police received thousands of tips, none of them led to the killer. The search continues to this day for Amber's murderer. In July 2007, police from Arlington, Texas, began investigating possible leads between child abductor and murderer Terapon Adhahn and Amber Hagerman. Terapon's abduction of Zina Linnik in Tacoma, Washington, talked about in Chapter 2, bore some very striking similarities to the Amber Hagerman case. Also, Terapon had reportedly lived in Texas for several years.

In February 2007, Arlington, Texas police sergeant Mark Simpson retired from the police department after 32 years. Simpson had been the lead detective on the Amber Hagerman case, and continued to work the case for over 10 years. The group of detectives he led investigated more than 5,000 leads and spent more than $1 million on the investigation.

"We're not done," Simpson said. "The case is not finished, and it won't be finished until we make an arrest."[16]

On the tenth anniversary of Amber's abduction, her mother spoke to the media. "It's all the same to me: one year, 10 years, 20 years," she said. "The pain is still there, and I miss her just as much."[17]

****

The police and other officials, through the Amber Hagerman case, realized that they needed the public's help in apprehending child abductors before they had a chance to harm the abducted children. In Amber's case, the police had quickly gotten a description of the abductor and his truck. They knew that if they could have gotten this information about the abduction out to the public right away, they would have had thousands or even millions of eyes looking for the suspect and abducted child. This, they knew, could not only have possibly saved Amber, it could likely save the lives of many abducted children.

Along with these officials, many people in the northern Texas area where the Amber Hagerman incident occurred also began asking the question of why, when a child has been abducted and every minute counts in the safe return of the child, doesn't the media and the police department get together and put out the information about the abduction to the public? After all, they break into television and radio programs to warn about severe weather. Why not also alert the public about a child abduction?

In response to these questions and concerns, in October 1996, the police and the Dallas/Fort Worth Association of Radio Managers unveiled the Amber Plan, a system that would put out media alerts on confirmed child abductions for television and radio broadcast. Following this announcement, in July 1997, the Dallas Amber Plan began. The alert system quickly showed its value when a babysitter with a serious drug problem abducted an eight-day-old baby. An Amber Alert went out and a driver spotted the abductor's car. The police rescued the baby unharmed.

Soon, other cities began following suit, and started instituting their own Amber Alert programs. In February 2005, Hawaii instituted its Maile Amber Alert program (Maile Gilbert was a six-year-old girl abducted and murdered in Hawaii). This means that now all 50 states have an Amber Alert program. In addition, Canada has now also adopted the Amber Alert program.

"In 11 years, we have seen a single, local program grow into a powerful national network," said Regina B. Schofield, National Amber Alert Coordinator. "Amber's tragedy sparked the creation of the Amber Alert program, now one of the most effective tools employed to protect children."[18]

Along with having television and radio announcements of child abductions, which use the Emergency Alert System (formerly the Emergency Broadcast System), the same system used for severe weather, many communities now also use electronic road signs to broadcast Amber Alert information. This means that many millions of more eyes can now look for abducted children.

To date, nationwide over 300 abducted children have been rescued because of Amber Alerts. The Amber Alert program, naturally, wants to continue this success by advancing with technology. And so, the alerts can now be broadcast on cellular telephones at no cost to subscribers. When cellular telephone customers sign up for the program they designate up to five zip codes from which they want to receive Amber Alerts.

In addition, in January 2007, MySpace.com, the Internet social gathering place, teamed up with the National Center for Missing and Exploited Children and agreed to post Amber Alerts on their Web site. "MySpace Amber Alerts will allow the online community to be part of a nationwide effort to bring even more children home," said Ernie Allen, president and CEO of the National Center for Missing and Exploited Children. "We are grateful that MySpace has agreed to help us distribute these important alerts."[19]

A problem, however, exists within the Amber Alert program that proponents fear could dangerously dilute its effectiveness. The problem is that there are no national standards for when Amber Alerts can be issued. Instead, each community sets its own requirements. Consequently, these alerts have been used for missing Alzheimer's patients, children involved in custody disputes, and for missing children not known to be abducted. Many people fear that overuse of the system like this will dilute its effectiveness by having so many Amber Alerts that the public will become numb and complacent. Officials worry that the public will get "Amber Alert fatigue."[20]

Many parents though disagree. When a parent has a child missing, that parent doesn't care about guidelines or oversensitizing the public. That parent wants the child found—end of discussion. In 2004, according to one newspaper report, 20 percent of the Amber Alerts issued that year were for lost children, runaways, or simple misunderstandings about the child's location, and not abductions.[21]

Of course, even in locations with strict requirements for the issuance of Amber Alerts, there are still occasions that require judgment calls on the part of the police. This, naturally, angers parents when the judgment call is not to issue an Amber Alert. And naturally, the police don't want to be wrong and have a child turn up dead. But still, tough decisions must be made. Proponents line up on both sides of this question.

"Too many kids get left out and are lost because of arbitrary decisions by law enforcement. It's unconscionable," said Judy Martin, a victim rights advocate in Cleveland.[22]

"It has not ever been meant for missing children, lost children or child custody cases," counters Fort Worth (Texas) Sheriff Dee Anderson, who helped establish the first Amber Alert program. "Almost at times the plan is a victim of its own success, because now everyone wants it used when a child is missing."[23]

A news article about Amber Alerts stated, "Some police officials agree that with the power of Amber, less is more. Fewer alerts and strict enforcement of guidelines mean that the public respond better because they understand alerts are issued only after serious consideration."[24]

Amber Hagerman's mother, Donna Norris, agrees. "I do think it's being overused. It was just supposed to be used for kids they knew were in danger, in cases where they knew there had been an abduction. Now they use it for runaways all the time, but there are thousands of runaways. You can't use an Amber Alert for a runaway."[25]

The solution, of course, to this problem is that a national standard for issuing Amber Alerts needs to be formulated and accepted by all communities nationwide. The federal government, for example, presently recommends that Amber Alerts should be issued only for children under 18, who have been abducted, and who are in imminent danger. In order to make this a national standard, the federal government need only attach such a requirement to road funding, etc.

The federal government, incidentally, already involves itself heavily in Amber Alerts. For example, in October 2002, Attorney General John Ashcroft appointed the first national Amber Alert Coordinator. This person's job is to provide support and assistance to the growing number of local Amber Alert programs. Also, in April 2004, the U.S. Department of Justice issued its "Guidance in Criteria for Issuing Amber Alerts" in the hope that this document could set guidelines for communities to use when deciding whether or not to issue an Amber Alert.

However, the biggest assistance the federal government has given to the Amber Alert program came in April 2003, when President Bush signed into law a bill that gave states the money they desperately needed in order to begin Amber Alert programs. "It is important to expand the Amber Alert systems so police and sheriff's departments gain thousands or even millions of allies in the search for missing children," President Bush said at the signing of the bill. "Every person who would think of abducting a child can know that a wide net will be cast."[26]

While the Amber Alert program is an area where the government is attempting to meet the needs of the left-behind parents of abducted children, unfortunately there are many other areas where the government isn't. For example, many left-behind parents have complained about the lack of certain government services that are available in many other countries. Often, for instance, when children are abducted to a foreign country, that country will pay all of the legal expenses of the abducting parents, while the left-behind parents from the United States are usually required to pay all of their own legal expenses. Also, many left-behind parents feel there should be social services available to assist them in coping with the huge emotional and psychological strain that a child abduction puts on them.

According to a study that interviewed the left-behind parents of internationally abducted children, "Another repeated message from the adult interviews concerns the lack of after-care facilities available to those who have been through the abduction process, and the desperate need for such provision for all parties involved, including those who may have lost custody, those who are suffering ill-health and loss of livelihood or home, those who have recovered their children and the children themselves."[27]

But of course, even more than providing these services, the federal government needs to become more actively involved in resolving international child abductions. While the U.S. State Department will assure the left-behind parents of internationally abducted children that they are doing everything they can to recover an abducted child, seldom will they put any serious pressure on foreign governments to return abducted children. Instead, they will talk to the left-behind parents and others about the delicate nature of diplomacy and how carefully they have to tread.

An article in *Insight Magazine* said that a federal task force report on international child abduction reported that, "'The federal government has limited power to respond to international abductions once the abductor and child reach a foreign country.' But parents see this as a bold-faced lie, considering such potential remedies as freezing financial assets of kidnappers who continue to do business in the United States, denying visas and passport renewals to kidnappers and their families or even cutting off U.S. assistance to countries such as Egypt that continue to hold American children illegally."[28]

Considering the above, many people may wonder: if terrorist groups or other individuals kidnap American citizens abroad we are outraged and the government immediately uses its diplomatic clout to get something done. Why aren't kidnapped children just as important?

"Any country that condones abductions should be given a penalty in their foreign aid," said Barbara Mezo, whose children were abducted to the Middle East in the mid-1980s. "This would get these countries to cooperate more." However, according to a *Newsday* report, in 2000, five nations that had almost 300 abducted children they refused to return received $476 million in foreign aid from the United States.[29]

As we talked about in Chapter 6, the General Accounting Office looked into this lack of action by the federal government concerning internationally abducted children. They found some glaring inconsistencies in the government's efforts, and issued a report with a number of suggestions for improvement.

The GAO report said, "The State and Justice Departments, the National Center for Missing and Exploited Children, and left-behind parents have identified problems and issues with the federal government's response to international parental child abduction. These problems include the need for more systematic diplomatic efforts to work with foreign governments to resolve problems of noncompliance with The Hague Convention and the lack of services such as financial assistance and counseling to left-behind parents."[30]

And though the State and Justice Departments quickly responded to this criticism with plans they said would improve their services to the left-parents of internationally abducted children, the GAO wasn't impressed. "Although State and Justice have made some progress," the GAO report said, "without clear resource commitments it will be difficult to implement the remaining recommendations in a timely manner...neither department has been able to provide us with information about such resources."

The GAO report then went on to add, "In addition to lacking resource commitments, many of the remaining recommendations we reviewed fail to identify the specific actions the State and Justice Departments will take to achieve their objectives."[31]

In dealing with the international abduction of their children, parents already face enough obstacles without the government putting up more, but still the government does. Many left-behind parents of internationally abducted children, for example, complain that judges are often totally unaware of the laws dealing with international abduction, and will many times make rulings that run counter to the law. A study by the Office of Juvenile Justice and Delinquency Prevention found that 60 percent of judges have never handled an international child abduction case, or have handled just one case. The study recommended that judges receive training in international law pertaining to child abduction.[32] In addition, in 1998, an international forum on parental child abduction, attended by representatives from many countries, also recommended the creation of a training team and core curriculum for judges and the legal profession, showing that this is not just a problem in the United States.

However, a child doesn't have to be internationally abducted for a parent to experience problems that the government could solve. Parents of children abducted and kept within the United States also experience a multitude of problems. A research paper, also by the Office of Juvenile Justice and Delinquency Prevention, titled "The Criminal Justice System's Response to Parental Abductions," listed a number of recommendations for local, state, and federal level government that could greatly assist left-behind parents of abducted children. (Highlighted words are recommendations from the report. Other content is the author's.)

1. *Recognize that parental abduction is a serious form of child maltreatment and is a crime that must be effectively investigated and prosecuted.* All too often in parental child abduction cases, government officials want to look at the incident as a civil or even private family matter that doesn't warrant government intervention. But it is not. Child abduction is a crime in every state, and should be recognized as such.

2. *Develop and implement written policies and procedures addressing the handling of parental abduction cases.* Far too many studies have found that police departments, prosecutor's offices, and child protective service offices often have no written policies or procedures for the handling of child abductions.

3. *Develop initial and ongoing training programs for all criminal justice system personnel on the handling of parental abduction cases, including the psychological aspects of the crime and the interrelationship of criminal and civil forums in resolving custodial interference disputes.* This training should include police officers, prosecutors, judges, and child protective service workers.

4. *Establish specialized units made up of law enforcement personnel and prosecutors skilled in investigating and prosecuting the crimes of parental abduction and visitation interference.* Through comprehensive training, these types of units would be well versed in the laws concerning child abduction, and consequently the cases would be handled quicker and more professionally.

5. *Consider establishing local law enforcement missing children's clearinghouses.* These organizations often function as focal points for information about child abductions and can be useful information sources for detectives working child abduction cases.

6. *Develop and implement written interstate and intrastate protocols for handling cases that involve the investigation and/or prosecution of parental abduction in more than one State or within more than one municipality in a State.* The hardest part of a child abduction case shouldn't be trying to straighten out jurisdictional disputes. These should be agreed to beforehand.

7. *Clarify the role of the FBI in investigating cases of parental abduction and actively seek the FBI's assistance in appropriate cases.* The FBI can be a valuable asset because they can many times bring resources to a case that the local police don't have access to.

Local communities can also do their part to assist in the resolution and prevention of child abductions. A research project by the Office of Juvenile Justice and Delinquency Prevention concerning the early identification of risk factors for parental abduction had a number of suggestions for what communities could do to reduce the risk of child abduction.[33] (Highlighted words are recommendations from the report. Other content is the author's.)

1. *Develop public education programs that discuss relevant laws for parents.* Interestingly, the police often find that abducting parents don't realize they are breaking the law and could go to jail for abducting their own children. Consequently, many parents would not abduct their children if they knew the laws.

2. *Develop community-based programs that increase the parents' access to legal representation.* Many left-behind parents find themselves in a quandary because they simply can't afford to hire legal representation that could resolve the case much more quickly.

3. *Pass State laws that mandate district attorneys to enforce custody orders.* Far too often, district attorneys see custody disputes as civil matters not involving them, even though parental child abduction is against the law in every state.

4. *Modify laws so that family abductions are crimes against the child.* In family child abduction the victim in the case is the left-behind parent, yet the child also many times suffers serious harm.

5. *Involve social services at each phase of decision-making that affects the child and minimize the disruption to the child's relationship with the primary parent.* The welfare, both physical and psychological, of abducted children needs to be considered throughout the investigation so as to minimize the ill effects of the abduction.

While in this chapter we have looked at what various levels of the government can do to prevent and rectify child abductions, there is also much that parents can do. As we will see in the next chapter, parents must play a leading role in preventing child abductions from occurring. However, in the event an abduction occurs anyway, there are many actions, as we shall see, that parents can take that will safely reunite them with their children.

What Parents Can Do

On May 7, 2006, three men with guns burst into a home in Burnaby, British Columbia, a suburb of Vancouver. They demanded money from the homeowner, Doug Nguyen. Although Doug pleaded with the men that he had no money, the three intruders, not believing him, ransacked the house looking for some. Not finding any money, the three men finally snatched Doug's two children, eight-year-old Diamond and her six-year-old brother Jack, likely with the idea of holding them for ransom. The intruders shoved the children into the trunk of their car and then drove off.

While many children may not have known what to do, Diamond did. Her father had taught her about interior trunk releases. When the car stopped, Diamond waited until she was certain the men weren't around, and then pulled the interior trunk release, a device installed in newer model cars that is fluorescent and, when pulled, opens the car trunk from the inside.

"Apparently, from the inside of the trunk, it's almost like a fluorescent-reflective (emergency) handle that they can pull," said Corporal Pierre Lemaitre of the Royal Canadian Mounted Police. "And they actually waited until they heard things got quiet. They heard the car stop and then just waited, and then pulled the latch."[1]

The two children climbed out of the trunk, and neighbors who lived near where the abductors had parked the car called the authorities. Royal Canadian Mounted Police quickly made an arrest in the abduction.

"I have to admit I am proud of my kids," said Doug. "She (Diamond) knows how to take care of herself and her little brother."[2]

****

This incident demonstrates one of the simple things that parents can do to thwart child abductions. Teaching children simple things, such as how to get out of a car trunk from the inside, can make the difference as to whether or not an abducted child will return home safely. Incidentally, since a child could also be put into the trunk of an older model car without a trunk release, parents additionally need to teach their children how to pull out the wiring for the taillights from the inside of the trunk. This could lead to the police stopping the car for no taillights, and discovering the children. Naturally, parents of abducted children need to tell the police that they have taught their children to do this, so the police will be on the lookout for a car with no taillights. The above are just two of the many things that parents need to teach their children in order to assure their safe return from an abduction, and perhaps prevent an abduction all together. There are many others:

1. Children should be taught that if an abductor ever puts them into the passenger area of a car, to attempt to escape at the first opportunity. Abductors will often feel that they have cowed the children, and this overconfidence can allow the children an opportunity to escape.

2. One of the most important things though that parents can do is to teach their children to *always* tell them before going anywhere with anyone. If parents don't know where their children are or whom they're socializing with, when their children are abducted, the parents may not realize it for a long time. And as we have talked about in previous chapters, taking action during the first few hours of an abduction can be crucial to rescuing children unharmed.

3. Parents must teach their children, as soon as possible, to memorize and recite their full names, the names of their parents, their address, and their telephone number. Then, if the police should stop an abductor with a small child, that child can provide the police with valuable information that will assure his or her safe return.

4. Again as soon as possible, parents should teach their children how to use the telephone to get help. In most parts of the country dialing 911 automatically informs the police operator, thanks to computer-aided dispatching, of the address the call is coming from. Amazingly, abductors will often leave young abduction victims within reach of a telephone. Children also need to be taught that if dialing 911 doesn't do anything, to dial "0."

5. Children should be taught that no one is allowed to touch them in a way that makes them feel uncomfortable, and that if it happens they need to scream loudly and try to get away. If it is an abductor making an attempt, he or she will often flee the scene, knowing that no really significant crime

has yet been committed, and that fleeing is clearly the best option. If it's not an abductor or molester, the worst that can happen is a little embarrassment, which is much easier to deal with than an abduction, rape, or perhaps even a murder.

Children should also know that if someone grabs them and tries to forcibly take them somewhere, they are not just to scream, but also to fight and resist. Children should be taught to make as much of a scene as possible. Instruct your children, for example, that if someone grabs them in a public place, such as a store, shopping mall, etc., to scream loudly and make a scene, knocking over store displays, etc. A child abductor doesn't want this kind of attention and will usually flee. Teach your children that if they are ever grabbed in a parking lot to pound on cars or to pull on the door handles to set off car alarms, or to crawl under a car. All of these things will alert others nearby that something bad is happening, and even if these witnesses won't get involved they will at least be able to give the police information about the abduction.

Parents should have their children practice how they would yell and scream if someone tried to abduct them. It's good training for the kids, and they'll love it. Also, children should be taught to yell that the person trying to abduct them is not their parent. This will alert those nearby that a possible child abduction is taking place.

6. Parents should instruct their children to always tell them if someone has tried to get them to go somewhere with them, or if a person has offered them gifts. This person could be just a nice man or woman who likes children, but maybe not. Children also need to be made aware of all of the common ruses abductors will use to get children to go with them, such as asking for help in finding a puppy or kitten, asking for directions, or impersonating an authority figure. Teach children that adults don't ask children for help. It's a sign of danger. Adults ask other adults for help.

   Parents and children need to decide on a code word. Then, if a person approaches the children and says that an emergency has occurred and one of the parents has sent him or her for them (a common child abductor ruse) that person should know the code word. Instruct children to never go with a person who doesn't know the code word.

7. Children should particularly be warned to never approach a vehicle that has stopped and motions for them to come over. It could be innocent, but it could also be an abductor.

8. Your children should know several safe areas to flee to in their neighborhood or near their schools in the event an attempted abduction occurs. These can be stores, neighbor's homes, gas stations, etc.

9. Just as they should tell you if someone has tried to get them to go somewhere with them, children need to be taught to tell you if someone is threatening them or being intrusive online. Many child molesters meet their victims online. Children should know to *never* have an unchaperoned face-to-face meeting with someone they have met online. The police get hundreds of cases every year of adult molesters and abductors pretending to be young children or teenagers online in order to entice children into meeting them somewhere.

10. Younger children should know to never give out personal information to people they don't know. This includes while online.

11. While children should be taught to be cautious, they shouldn't be taught to fear all strangers, just oddly acting ones. If children fear all strangers, they will be afraid to ask for help if they need it. And, parents should realize, to a child in need of help, a police officer would be a stranger. But along with this, children need to know that police officers are their friends and are there to help them. Far too many parents like to make the police the boogeyman who will get the children if they aren't good.

12. Children should know to never take shortcuts through unfamiliar areas, particularly by themselves. Also, most abductors like single targets, therefore, parents should teach children that there is safety in numbers and to try to always walk with friends.

13. Children need to know that if they think someone is following them, they should get to a place of safety as quickly as possible (such as a gas station, convenience store, library, etc.), and then call you or the police.

14. Older children who stay by themselves should know to never open the door to strangers. If the person at the door claims to be the police, but is not wearing a uniform, instruct your children to call 911 and report it. If it is a legitimate police officer, the dispatcher will usually know it, and, if it's not, the dispatcher can send the real police. Also, children should know to never open the door to people who say they are from the light company, gas company, cable company, etc. These individuals will almost always call and make appointments first.

15. In one of my earlier books, *The Complete Guide to Personal and Home Safety,* I advise all women to always have a cell phone with them when away from home, and not to be afraid to call the police if they feel threatened.[3] This is also good advice for older children. Parents should teach them that they need to use the cell phone if they think they need help, and that it is better to error on the side of safety and make a call that's not needed than not to make a call for help when they should have. The police receive thousands of 911 calls every year that turn out to be mistakes or misunderstandings, and we really don't think anything about it.

16. Your children need to know that you love them and want them around. Abductors, in order to discourage attempts at escape, especially in parental child abduction cases, will often try to convince the abducted children that the other parent doesn't love them or want them around any longer.

17. Your children should know, and you should tell them, that if they are ever missing you would never stop looking for them until you find them. This can assure children who are abducted that people care and are looking for them, no matter what the abductor tells them.

18. There are a number of "Escape Schools" given around the country that teach children techniques that can help them escape from potential abductors, such as how to wiggle out of clothing and backpacks if grabbed, how to wrap themselves around a bicycle and make it difficult to put them in a car, how to make a scene if grabbed, etc. These schools also teach children things that can lead to their rescue if abducted, such as stopping up a toilet and making it overflow if held in an apartment, how to use a porch light to

signal for help, and other techniques. This is great training for children and can instill self-confidence.

"It is not teaching children to fight," said Rose Cheever, a police officer who teaches a course called radKids. "It most definitely is teaching children how not to fight, how to break away from an abductor and how to yell, how to be vocal." She also added, "Let someone who might be attacking you know that it's not going to be easy for them to do."[4]

19. Children need to be taught that if they should ever hear anyone breaking into their house or if someone who shouldn't be in their bedroom (unfortunately including friends and relatives) awakens them at night, they should scream and make as much noise as possible, no matter what the person says or threatens to do. In almost all cases, the intruders will flee, knowing that capture is imminent if they don't. Such responses from children could have spared several of the abduction victims we have talked about in previous chapters.

20. Once you have taught your children all of these things, a good way to test them is to play the "what if" game. Make up some scenarios and then ask your children what they would do in these situations. Avoid the temptation to answer for them. Make them think. Most children won't get the answers right the first time, and so this is a good opportunity to review what you've taught them, and to show them how using this information could get them out of bad situations.

Children have interactions with dozens of adults everyday. While almost all of these interactions—such as with teachers, adult friends of the parents, neighbors, Sunday school teachers, scout leaders, merchants, etc.—are benign, sometimes they are not. Child molesters will often put a tremendous amount of effort into maneuvering themselves into positions of trust so they can be free, as the following incident demonstrates, to abduct and molest children.

****

Twenty-six-year-old George Richard Horner needed a place to stay and, in January 2007, a friend introduced him to the mother of a six-year-old girl, who lived in Maricopa, Arizona, a little town just south of Phoenix. Horner seemed to be a genuinely nice person who was just down on his luck, and so the mother allowed him to stay temporarily with her and her daughter.

After staying with them for three days, Horner said that he wanted to do something for them, and so he offered to take the six-year-old to school. The mother agreed, but then later became suspicious and called the school, only to find that her daughter had not shown up there that day. The mother immediately called the police, who issued an Amber Alert.

Later that day, the authorities found the six-year-old girl walking alone on a street in Casa Grande, Arizona, a town about 20 miles southeast of Maricopa. The police arrested Horner the next day and charged him with kidnapping and sexual misconduct with a minor. This incident, however, was not Horner's first brush with the law. Because of previous crimes, he was a registered sex offender. The mother later said that she would not have let him within a "hundred million miles" of her house if she had known he was a registered sex offender.[5]

****

The sad part about the above incident is that, since Horner was a registered sex offender, this crime didn't have to occur. The six-year-old's mother could have uncovered this fact about Horner's past with just a few clicks on a computer keyboard. The federal government has put together a Web site that now allows the public to access the sex offender registries for every state. This is a powerful tool that all parents should take advantage of.

However, parents should not only check on people like Horner before allowing them into their house, they should also check the national sex offender list for individuals who lead extracurricular activities their children may become involved in, potential babysitters, neighbors that they feel act oddly around children, etc. This Web site is readily available to anyone with Internet access and contains public information parents need to know. This is not invading anyone's privacy. This is protecting the safety of children. Readers can access the national sex offender list at www.nsopr.gov.

But this isn't the only thing parents can do to guard against child abductions. There are many more things:

1. First and foremost, if you see a friend's or neighbor's child walking alone or waiting for the school bus alone, be a good person and watch out for the child. After all, you'd want others to do the same for your children.
2. Never leave small children unattended, even for a short time. Don't let children play outside by themselves, especially in front of the house. Child molesters will often suddenly see an opportunity and abduct a child impulsively. It only takes a second for someone to snatch your child. Never assume, but make certain, that a spouse or some other responsible adult is watching your children when you can't.
3. If your children are very young and play at other children's homes, tell the parents of these children that you don't allow your children to play outside unsupervised.
4. You need to compile a list of the telephone numbers of friends your children play with. That way, if your children should suddenly appear to be missing, you can quickly check out these possibilities.
5. Consider establishing a "safe house" program in your neighborhood. These are homes children know they can run to and get help if they find themselves in danger.
6. Never have your children's names visible on clothing, backpacks, etc. Child abductors will use this information to appear to know the children, and, through this ruse, gain their trust.

7. Remember what your children wear everyday. This can be important because it can give the police and the public something to look for.

8. Listen carefully to your children if they want to tell you about a person acting strangely, particularly an adult. This person may be planning an abduction and/or a sexual assault.

9. Be certain that schools, daycare facilities, babysitters, and others who look after your children know who they may release your children to, and that, under no circumstances, may they release your children to anyone else. Child abductors, particularly family child abductors, will often claim that there is an emergency and that they have come to pick up the children. Give copies of custody orders to schools, daycare facilities, etc.

10. Take still photographs and videos of your children several times a year. A current photograph can help people recognize your child if abducted. In addition, keep a written record of your children's birthmarks, scars, and other unique markers that will help identify them if needed. Also, avail yourself of your local police department's program of fingerprinting children. Some police departments now also offer iris scanning and the taking of DNA samples. These can help tremendously in identifying children recovered far from their hometown.

    "You think, 'It can't happen to me,' until something happens close to home, then the reality sets in," said Margaret Green, who brought her grandson to be fingerprinted and have DNA samples taken by the St. Louis Police Department.[6]

11. There are a number of innovative technological devices that parents concerned about child abduction can purchase and use. For example, a company named Alarmwear manufactures a miniature alarm that can be concealed within clothing. Children wearing one of these alarms can activate it if abducted, and it makes a loud, piercing sound. And since the device is hidden within the clothing it will take a considerable amount of time for an abductor to find and deactivate it.

    A company named Amberstick (www.amberstick.com) manufactures a flash drive and software that can upload an abducted child's profile (picture, distinguishing marks, medical information, etc.) immediately to the police. Another innovative piece of equipment, a GPS tracking device that looks like a patch or badge, can be attached to your children's clothing. At any sign of danger the children can press a small switch on the patch or badge and the device sends a warning to the parent's cell phone and also tells the children's location. For more information on these types of safety devices, parents can go to www.brickhousesecurity.com. Along these same lines, there are also companies that manufacture children's shoes with GPS devices built into them so that the parents will always know their children's whereabouts. For more information on this, see www.gtxcorp.com.

    Finally, a device called Child Guard is an alarm that can be fastened to very young children. The parent carries a receiver that sounds an alarm if the child moves or is moved a certain distance away from the parent. For more information about this product, go to www.nacap.org/tracking_devices.asp.

12. Keep tabs on whom your children are conversing with on the computer. Sexual predators will often go into children's chat rooms and pretend to be children, eventually setting up a meeting where an abduction and sexual assault occur. Attempts to do this happen thousands of times every year. There is software available that will allow you to block your children's access to certain Web sites and that will also allow you to monitor your children's computer activities. This is not being nosy or intrusive. This is being a good parent.

13. Be particularly observant of anyone seeming to be watching your home. Call the police if it appears to be suspicious. Readers will recall that in the incident involving Shasta and Dylan Groene in Chapter 1, the child abductor cased the family home extensively before breaking in and abducting the two children. Often also, rapes and abductions can be simply opportunity crimes committed by criminals who originally only intended to burglarize your home. Make your home as burglar proof as possible. What this means is making your house so difficult to get into that a potential burglar/abductor will have to make a lot of noise getting in, which will alert you to the abductor's presence. In several of the cases we have talked about in this book, child abductors have obtained their victims by burglarizing homes. For advice on burglar-proofing your home, see my book *The Complete Guide to Personal and Home Safety* (Perseus, 2002).

14. Be observant of anyone appearing to be hanging around school bus stops. Write down the license plate numbers and descriptions of the individuals. They might just be other concerned parents, but they might also be potential child abductors.

15. Honor an estranged parent's visitation rights. Many times, a parent who is denied his or her legal visitation rights will abduct children in order to be able to spend time with them, and often to play back the other parent. Also, as much as possible, stay on good, or at least civil, terms with an estranged significant other with whom you've had children. Child abductions many times occur because one parent is angry and wants to strike back at the other.

16. If a parent has a history of child abduction, has attempted a child abduction, or threatened to, the custodial parent should ask the court to make the other parent post a bond before being allowed child visitation. This way, if a child is abducted, the bond is forfeited to the left-behind parent. This money can come in handy, particularly in international abductions. It can be used to offset the high cost of legal fees, travel, etc. The amount of the bond should be sufficient to deter any child abduction or to pay for the left-behind parent's likely travel and legal expenses in recovering the child. The Professional Bail Agents of the United States has created a child abduction prevention bond for such high-risk situations. This group can be contacted at www.pbus.com.

17. How can parents know when they should ask the court to make the noncustodial parents post a bond, and how can they convince the court of the necessity of this? One resource for this is the group PIPCA (Prevent International Parental Child Abduction). "PIPCA was formed to help protect children from international child abduction, and to increase awareness of the tragedy of international abduction and the preventative measures that can be ordered by a court when a child is at risk of abduction," Teresa

Lauderdale, one of the founders of PIPCA, told me. "PIPCA can assist in providing training, expert testimony, and general advice on this issue. PIPCA's Web site, www.pipca.org, can provide resources for attorneys, parents, and others dealing with the issue of international child abduction. This can be helpful for informing courts about the red flag indicators of risk, and consequently the safeguards these courts can order to prevent international child abduction."[7]

18. Document, if possible, and make a record of all abduction threats. Immediately report any abduction attempts to the police. This can come in handy later in court.

19. Keep good, up-to-date information on an ex-spouse or significant other with whom you have had children. Know the person's address, vehicle type and color, vehicle and driver's license number, Social Security number, passport number, etc. Also, know where the ex-spouse or significant other has family or friends living. That is often where the person will take abducted children. A federal study showed that one-fourth of parental child abductors didn't act alone, but had help from family members.[8] The more information you have to give to the police, the better the chances they will have of making a quick recovery of your children.

20. A law passed in July 2001 now requires that anyone under the age of 14 who applies for a passport must show that both parents consent to it, or that one of the applicant's parents has sole authority to approve the passport. Also, it is now possible to have the U.S. Passport Office notify you if someone, such as an ex-spouse, applies for a passport for your child. The U.S. Department of State's "Children's Passport Issuance Alert" program will alert you anytime a passport application for your child is made. The office in charge of this program, the Office of Children's Issues, can be reached at 1-888-407-4747. Information about the Children's Passport Issuance Alert program can also be found at http://travel.state.gov/family/abduction/resources/resources_554.html.

However, parents should be aware that when marrying foreign nationals any children born of these marriages are often not just American citizens but also citizens of the countries the spouses are from. This means that, rather than U.S. passports, estranged spouses can often obtain foreign passports for their children, which the other spouses will usually be unaware of.

21. Be certain you have a custody order from a court. If not, your estranged spouse often has a legal right to take the children out of state or out of the country. Also, if your estranged spouse takes the children to a foreign country, without you having a custody order, the foreign officials can rule that he or she has a right to custody of the children.

22. Some legal experts advise that if you have custodial rights and your foreign-born spouse or significant other wants to take your children to his or her country of birth, in addition to having the foreign-born parent post a bond, the custodial parent should also obtain a "mirror" custody order in that country. This "mirror" custody order is a court order in that country that recognizes your custody and parental rights. Also, find out if the country has signed the Hague Convention. If not, custodial parents should not allow travel there if there is any possibility of an abduction.

23. Before allowing spouses or significant others to take children abroad, research the laws and customs of the countries they will visit. What are their laws concerning child custody and abduction? What is the country's history of returning abducted children? Is the country a signer of the Hague Convention? Do they favor their own citizens unfairly in child custody matters? Will they recognize and accept American court orders? Are there gender inequalities in the laws of the country?

    If you are accompanying a spouse and children traveling abroad, research the countries to be visited. Some Islamic countries, for example, will not allow a wife and children to travel without the husband and father's permission. Consequently, if the husband should decide to stay in the country, the wife can't just take the children and leave.

24. In a previous chapter, we talked about the warning signs of a possible child abduction. These are not the only signs and the presence of them is not a 100 percent certainty that an abduction will occur. However, they are signs that need to be taken seriously and acted upon with extra precautions should they appear.

As we also talked about in a previous chapter, infant abduction is one of the most insidious forms of child abduction. An individual of questionable character kidnaps a child in his or her most vulnerable state. Fortunately, as shown in the anecdote below, there are steps that can be taken to minimize the risk of this happening.

* * * *

Mitchell and Juanita Slade had been charged with child abuse and neglect involving the treatment of their children, and their children had consequently been removed from the home by the Department of Social Services. So, when Juanita was in the Presbyterian Hospital in Charlotte, North Carolina, with another baby, the authorities had already arranged to take this baby away from the couple.

However, Mitchell had other ideas. He snatched his infant son and placed him in a duffle bag and attempted to leave the hospital. The hospital, though, had technology Mitchell didn't know about. The staff had placed a RFID (Radio Frequency Identification) bracelet on the child's ankle. These devices set off an alarm if they are taken out of certain areas of the hospital or are removed from the infant. Once Mitchell left the seventh-floor nursery the alarm sounded.

"I was actually out of the unit and heard the alarm," said Nursing Manager Brenda Martin. "I went directly to the nursery and the staff said we are trying to locate this baby."[9]

Hospital security officers took Mitchell into custody at the front of the hospital and recovered the baby unharmed. Mitchell later told the authorities that he had abducted the boy because he didn't want to lose custody of another child to the Social Services Department. The police eventually charged both Mitchell and Juanita in the abduction.

****

The point to the anecdote above is that technology exists that can successfully thwart infant abductions. Consequently, parents need to check with hospitals before deciding where to have a baby. Parents need to ask about the hospital's security program to prevent infant abductions. And don't be put off by claims such as, "Oh, don't worry, we've never had an abduction." You don't want to be the first. In addition to this, parents of newborns need to take other precautions:

1. Never allow anyone you don't know to hold a newborn or infant. Also, don't allow anyone you don't know to take a newborn or infant anywhere, no matter what they tell you. If in a hospital, be certain that the only ones you allow to handle your newborn or infant are medical personnel known to you. If someone who claims to work for the hospital wants to take your newborn or infant anywhere, and you don't recognize the person, call for assistance from someone on the medical staff that you do know.
2. There are many new devices coming on the market every day that can stop an abductor from removing an infant from a hospital. The hospital you choose for the delivery of your baby should employ these.
3. The Harris County Hospital District (Houston) recently installed a system of identification tags for newborns that sounds an alarm if removed from the baby or if the baby is taken out of certain areas of the hospital.

"If an alarm goes off, security forces can find the exact location of the baby through computer displays of hospital floor plans," William Jackson, the director of public safety, said about the technology being used in the Harris County Hospital District. "They're also able to identify which baby is missing by the tag number."[10] Although the Harris County Hospital District has never had an infant abduction, they have still invested in high tech equipment to be certain one never occurs.

Sometimes, however, no matter how careful parents are or how many precautions they take, a child abduction occurs. When this happens, as in the incident below, parents must then take action to see that their children are returned safely.

****

In July 1991, Joan Faber, a kindergarten teacher in New York City, married Ahmed Naby, an Egyptian college student. At first, everything in their relationship seemed fine and, in 1994, they were both overjoyed when Joan gave birth to a son, Adam. Following this, Joan helped Ahmed become an American citizen in 1995.

Problems, however, then began developing. Ahmed had trouble holding down a job and adapting to American ways, causing friction in the marriage. Eventually, the couple separated, and Adam continued to live with Joan. During their separation, Ahmed told Joan several times that he wanted Adam to grow up in Egypt, a suggestion that Joan vigorously vetoed.

However, in November 2000, when Joan went to pick up Adam from a visitation with his father, she found Ahmed's apartment vacant. She soon received an e-mail from Ahmed saying, "Adam is with me in Egypt."[11]

Then the nightmare continued. Even though a court had awarded Joan custody of Adam, Egypt has never signed the Hague Convention and doesn't recognize American court orders. Consequently, the Egyptian government wouldn't do anything to help her. Joan also found that the U.S. State Department wouldn't do much to help her either.

At wits end, Joan eventually contacted Gus Zamora of Zamora and Associates. Gus Zamora is an ex-Army Ranger. His company employees ex-military commandoes and other highly trained individuals who will go into countries like Egypt and rescue an abducted child for the left-behind parent. Zamora and Associates has successfully rescued over 50 internationally abducted children. Joan and Gus agreed on the fee, and she paid the company $65,000 for their services.

"We are dealing with a system that has limitations on just how far they can go, legally, to help a parent in the child's return," Gus Zamora told me. "That same system is full of bureaucrats who value their career and job more than they do the return of an abducted child."[12]

On September 13, 2001, Gus and Joan waited in a busy Cairo marketplace. When Adam got off of a school bus, Joan called to him, "Hi, Adam. Come to Mommy."[13]

Although Ahmed had told Adam he was no longer an American citizen and that he would never leave Egypt, the young boy raced to his mother. They all jumped into a car and sped away.

Several days later, after stays in safe houses and a nerve-shattering stop by the authorities to check identification cards, Gus, Joan, and Adam flew to Germany. Finally, on September 21, 2001, Joan and Adam arrived at JFK Airport in New York. Joan's parents, who helped finance the rescue, were so pleased they gave Gus Zamora a $5,000 bonus.

"I owe everything to Gus," said Joan. "My son would still be over there if it weren't for him. The State Department wouldn't do anything. The FBI wouldn't do anything."[14]

****

Using the incident above, am I advising left-behind parents of internationally abducted children to immediately go out and employ mercenaries such as Gus Zamora to rescue their children? No, I'm not. Do I think parents ought to give this option some serious consideration after exhausting all legal means of retrieving their abducted children from a foreign country? Yes, I do.

The U.S. State Department actively discourages this type of rescue of abducted children, yet left-behind parents of internationally abducted children also often find that this same U.S. State Department will usually offer them very little or no help at all in the quest to recover their children. Rather, the U.S. State Department seems to want the parents to just go back home and forget they ever had these children. To act as though these children were never a part of their lives. How many parents can really do that?

Before considering hiring a mercenary, however, there are many other things left-behind parents need to do. There are many steps that left-behind parents must first go through before any type of recovery of an abducted child, held either inside the United States or in a foreign country, can be possible.

1. The very first thing the parents of an abducted or possibly abducted child need to do is to contact the police and report the abduction. Also, they must make certain the police officer taking the report puts the child's information into the FBI's NCIC (National Crime Information Center) computer system. We have already discussed what to do in the event the police don't want to take a report. However, I need to add a little something more here. The parents of abducted children should be insistent to the point of being belligerent if the police do not want to take a report and begin a search. As we have also talked about, the first few hours of a child abduction are critical, and not just to getting the child back, but perhaps to saving the child's life.

2. Be certain to ask for the names and badge numbers of all police officers and other officials you speak with. Record the dates and times and the content of the discussion. If the police refuse to do anything, and your child should turn up injured, sexually molested, or perhaps murdered, you will need this information.

3. If you think an estranged spouse or significant other has abducted your child and you do not have a custody order, you need to have an attorney get you one as quickly as possible. Without a custody order, the abducting parent or significant other is often not breaking the law. And while joint custody orders may be in the best interest of children in the event the parents are on good terms and can agree on issues concerning the raising of the children, these orders are not a good idea for acrimonious couples, couples with a history of violence, or couples where one parent has a history of child abduction or threats of child abduction. Joint custody orders will only make it easier for the child abductor.

4. Parents need to be aware of all of the laws concerning child abduction. The criminal laws relating to stranger child abduction vary from state to state, and will require some research. Parental child abduction is also against the law in every state, and will require some research too. Parents need this information so that they will understand what law enforcement and the courts can and cannot do.

There are additionally a number of federal laws that cover child abduction that parents need to be aware of. A good source for information about these laws can be found in a paper by the American Bar Association, titled "Parental Kidnapping: Prevention and Remedies." This paper can be accessed at www.abanet.org/child/pkprevrem.pdf. A condensed version of these laws can also be found in the U.S. Department of Justice document "The Criminal Justice System's Response to Parental Abduction." It can be accessed at www.ncjrs.gov/pdffiles1/ojjdp/186160.pdf.

5. Contact the National Center for Missing and Exploited Children. This is a huge resource center for the parents of missing or abducted children. The Center can advise left-behind parents of the steps that need to be taken in order to recover abducted children, and of the many other groups that can help left-behind parents. The Center can also check to be certain an abducted child's information has been entered into the FBI's NCIC computer system. The Center can be reached at 1-800-843-5678 or www.missingkids.com.

6. If parents fear that abducted children may be headed out of the country, they need to contact the U.S. Department of State, Office of Children's Issues, at 1-888-407-4747. While this office's record for recovering internationally abducted children is not sterling, they have had some successes.

7. Left-behind parents may want to consider filing criminal charges against the abducting parents. To do this, the left-behind parents will need to meet with members of the local prosecutor's office to decide what charges are appropriate. Often, abducting parents don't realize that what they are doing can land them in jail. Consequently, when they find out, they many times return the abducted children. Also, if criminal charges are filed, and the abducting parents try to leave the state or the country, the FBI can charge them with Unlawful Flight to Avoid Prosecution, which means that the abducting parents can then be arrested anywhere in U.S. jurisdiction. The police, for example, might stop the abductors for speeding, and a computer check will bring up the warrant.

   Also, having a warrant filed can stop the abductor before he or she can make good on plans to leave the country. If left-behind parents are able to get the FBI to file an Unlawful Flight to Avoid Prosecution warrant for the abducting parent, they then need to also ask the U.S. State Department to revoke the abductor's passport. Be advised, however, that foreign-born abductors may possibly have a passport from their country of birth, which the United States can do nothing about. Also keep in mind that if the abductor has taken the children to a foreign country, some countries will not hunt down or extradite their own citizens. In addition, left-behind parents need to be aware that criminal charges can also occasionally interfere with the filing of a Hague Convention petition. Therefore, filing criminal charges needs to be a judgment call based on the circumstances of the abduction.

8. If left-behind parents believe that friends or family of the abductor may have helped in the abduction, thought should be given to filing a tort suit against these individuals. While friends and family may have been inclined to help the abducting parent, they usually don't want to lose bank accounts,

vacation homes, and other valuables. And so, if threatened with being sued, they may provide information on the whereabouts of the abducting parent and child.

9. If a child abduction took place inside of your house, particularly a stranger abduction, do not touch or disturb anything. The police will want to search the location for evidence and, with the newest scientific equipment available, often the tiniest of clues, involving microscopic evidence, can break a case. Do not straighten up, do not move objects, do not touch anything.

10. Give the police all of the information you have about the abduction. Sometimes information that seems to you to be unrelated, inconsequential, or unimportant can break the case. Also, the police will need a recent photograph of the abducted child and a description of any distinguishing marks the child may have. Besides photographs though, any videotapes of your child will be very useful as they give a more realistic representation of the child. In addition, the police will need to know what clothing your child was wearing when you last saw him or her.

    In addition to all of this, the police will need a list of anyone who might have information concerning the whereabouts of your child. Often, friends and relatives of a child abductor will be unsettled by a visit from the police, and will give the police information concerning your child's whereabouts that they wouldn't give to you. Along with this, make a list of everyone who has come into your house recently, and of anything you have noticed that was unusual or out of the ordinary. The police will find this useful. Keep in mind that often child abductors have been in recent contact with the child and his or her family. Also, don't assume that any person could not be the abductor. Pedophiles in particular can often appear to be the most honest, compassionate, and respected people in the community.

11. If the police don't, you might want to consider contacting the news media. A story in the newspaper or on the evening news can often bring in important tips. Also, don't forget radio. People driving to and from work will hear about your case, and then will pay more attention when they see it on television or read about it in the newspaper. If your child remains missing for a lengthy period of time, contact the news media on important dates involving your child (birthdays, anniversaries of the abduction, National Missing Children's Day—May 25th, etc.). Incidentally, if possible, a spot on *America's Most Wanted* is worth 100,000 posters. This television program reaches a huge audience and has an outstanding record of successes. Ask the detective handling your case about contacting them.

12. Keep in contact with the police detective handling your case. Don't be a pest and call several times a day, but, on the other hand, if you don't hear from the detective regularly and in a reasonable amount of time, call him or her. If the detective doesn't respond, call the detective's supervisor. When I was the Captain of Homicide, I would occasionally receive calls from the relatives of homicide victims who hadn't heard from the detective handling their loved one's case, even though they had left messages for the detective to call them. I would personally see that the detectives called these

individuals. Even if a detective didn't have any new information about the case, people still wanted to hear from him or her now and then so that they would know that they and their loved one haven't been forgotten.

13. Don't be offended or outraged if the police ask you to take a lie detector test. Particularly in the homicides of very young children, the parents are the most likely perpetrators, and, as we discussed in a previous chapter, these parents will often claim that someone has abducted a child who they have actually murdered. Put simply: until you are cleared, the police will suspect you in your child's disappearance. This is because the police are so often right in suspecting the parents. Just consider taking the lie detector test as a way to make the police want to work harder on your case, since they will then know that it is a real child abduction.

14. If you feel something needs to be done on the case that the police haven't done, insist on it. There may be a legitimate reason for not doing it, but let the police convince you of this.

15. If you haven't already contacted the National Center for Missing and Exploited Children, as advised above, ask the detective on your case to do so. The Center can fax a copy of your case to police departments around the country.

16. You might want to consider establishing a reward for your child's safe return. However, get legal advice before establishing a reward, as you are liable to pay if people perform certain acts. Your reward offer becomes a binding contract. Therefore, you want to be certain that the reward is only given for specific information or deeds that lead to specific results. Also, check to see if you can get assistance from businesses and others in establishing this reward.

Okay, your child has been abducted and you've done all of the things advised above. What next?

While it would be nice to think that law enforcement will pull out all of the stops and put a dozen officers onto the case of looking for your child, that very likely won't be the case. Unless your child was abducted by a known pedophile or you can show that for some reason your child's life is at risk, the most you're likely to get is your child's and the abductor's information put into the local police department's and the FBI's NCIC computer and a single detective assigned to the case.

This is not to say that you won't have a dedicated and thorough detective assigned to your case, however the sad fact is there are simply too many abducted and missing children every year for the police to go out and search endlessly for every one, particularly parentally abducted children. While the detective assigned to your case will take action if he or she receives good information about the case, particularly the location of your child, you must often be the one to supply this information.

Consequently, if you want your child returned safely, you must often do much of the searching yourself. So, how do you go about locating an abducted child?

1. First of all, keep in mind when searching for your child that time can be crucial. We have talked about the dangers during the first few hours of an abduction, but also if your child has been taken to a foreign country that has signed the Hague Convention, an exception to returning the child is the child's residence in the country for over a year.

2. Have posters printed with the best picture of how your child actually looks. If possible, include a picture of the abductor on these. Once these are printed, you will need help from various social agencies in order to have as many posters as possible distributed where they will do the most good. For example, you might be able to persuade a local Boy Scout troop to pass out the posters, or perhaps you can find a church group that will help you. Also, be certain to pass them out at all local and regional events. You must be very aggressive in seeing that your child's poster gets distributed where the most people will see it.

3. President Clinton, on January 19, 1996, issued an Executive Memorandum that requires federal agencies to post missing children posters in their buildings. This program is coordinated through the National Center for Missing and Exploited Children, and may bring in some vital information from someone who sees one of these posters. If your child has been missing for some time, the Center can help in developing an age-progressed picture for the poster.

4. The National Center for Missing and Exploited Children will also put your child's poster on their Web site. This Web site has tens of thousands of visitors every day.

5. Consider asking the detective assigned to your case to request that Project Alert (America's Law Enforcement Retiree Team) assist in locating your child. This is a group of retired police officers who volunteer their time to assist in finding missing and abducted children. This group can be contacted through the National Center for Missing and Exploited Children. These retired police officers can be especially helpful if the child abduction has occurred in an area where law enforcement has limited experience in such cases. This group includes seasoned investigators with many years of experience, and who, through this experience, can assist local law enforcement in their efforts.

6. There are many nonprofit organizations throughout the country that can assist left-behind parents who are searching for their abducted children. The National Center for Missing and Exploited Children can supply parents with a list of their names.

7. Since, as talked about above, you will have to do much of the searching yourself, a good place to start is with transportation centers if you believe the abductor may have used some sort of public transportation. Keep in mind, however, that many of the places you will look for information are protected by privacy laws and cannot release information to ordinary citizens. Others don't release information because of company policy, and some simply don't release information for no specific reason. However, sometimes making up a good story can get them to release the information to you. But sometimes not. It is for this reason that you will likely need an attorney. An attorney can obtain a subpoena for information, or often just

a call from an attorney requesting information that can and should be released will more likely meet with success than will a call from an unknown citizen. Call airports, train stations, and bus depots in the area to see if the abductor has recently booked tickets. You might also want to pass out copies of the posters you had printed to see if anyone in these transportation facilities remembers the abductor or your child.

8. Another good place to look for information is the last place the abductor worked. When did he or she quit? Did the abductor leave a forwarding address for paychecks or other benefits? Has a new employer called to check on the abductor's work record? Has the abductor requested that a reference be sent to a certain business?

9. If you go to the abductor's home soon after the abduction, grab the trash if you can find it. You might want to check the laws, though, since this can be illegal in some locations. However, if you can get it, you'll be surprised at what you will find. The police are often amazed at what people throw away, and how much information they can obtain from someone's trash.

10. If you believe you may know the general area where the abductor has gone with your child, check with voter's registration to see if the abductor has registered to vote.

11. Check with the bank or other financial institution the abductor used. Have accounts been closed? Have funds been transferred to another financial institution? If you have access to the accounts, examine checks and money transfers for the last several months. Do they point to a possible destination? If you have access to the abductor's credit card records, look for a pattern of purchases that points to a destination. Gasoline purchases, for example, can often show the route the abductor is taking.

12. Child abductors who have car loans, college loans, and other debts that they paid regularly will likely continue paying them. Check with these agencies to see where the payments are now coming from.

13. Family and friends of the abductor may not be involved in the abduction or even approve of it. Stay on good terms with these people because fleeing individuals, the police know, often seek out family members and friends for help. Don't rail against the abductor or threaten what will happen when the police catch him or her. This will most likely make family members and friends not want to get involved. Instead, stress your concern for the welfare of the abducted child.

14. If the abductor has always used a specific insurance company for coverage, this is another good source for information. New auto insurance will be needed in the area of destination, and you may also be able to find out where payments for life insurance, health insurance, and so forth, are coming from.

15. Does the abductor have a specific hobby? If so, you should check with organizations that cater to this hobby. Also, if applicable, check with the state fish and game agencies to see if the abductor has applied for a fishing or hunting license.

16. If the abductor is receiving any kind of federal assistance, such as VA benefits, etc., check for a change of address for the benefits.

17. The U.S. Department of Health and Human Services maintains a locator system called the Federal Parent Locator Service. The federal government developed this system in order to find parents seriously behind in child support payments. However, it can also be used to find child abductors, but only by an authorized individual, meaning a police officer, a judge, or a prosecutor. Therefore, ask the detective assigned to your case to access this system, which will search billions of public records looking for the abductor.

18. Abductors who are members of the military on active duty can be easily located through the Military Worldwide Locator Service. Information on this service can be accessed at www.defenselink.mil/faq/pis/PC04 MLTR.html.

19. Most abductors must enroll abducted children in school and will request that school records be transferred. The Family Educational Rights and Privacy Act, a federal law, guarantees that parents can find out where their children's school records have been transferred to. Get a copy of this law, or have your attorney get you a copy, in case the school doesn't want to cooperate.

20. The abductor will also likely need a copy of your child's birth certificate in order to enroll the child in school. Check with the government agency responsible in your community and see if a request for a copy has been made, and, if so, where it was sent.

21. Check with your dentist and doctor to see if a request for the dental or medical records of the abducted child has been made. Most children must show proof of immunization to be enrolled in school, and abductors will often request these records. Check to see where they are being sent. In addition, if the abductor uses a large nationwide, or even regional, drug store for prescriptions, check to see where these prescriptions are being filled at now.

22. Abductors who belong to unions will want to transfer their union membership to their new location. If the abductor needs a license to perform some sort of trade or profession, state licensing boards might have information on a new address.

23. Much of the searching for the abductor and your child can be done from a home computer. Put the abductor's name into the various search engines and see what comes up. Also, many government agencies now upload their records to the Internet, and by going to their Web sites you can search for information about the abductor. In addition, you can use Internet telephone directories and "people finders." When I was the head of the Indianapolis Police Department's Homicide Branch, a "people finder" company contacted me. This company maintained a Web site that would allow a person, for a small fee each time the person used it, to search through billions of public records. This company called me because they wanted the police department to contract for their services. To entice us, the company offered us a 30-day free trial, and so I tried it. Just by entering a very limited amount of information about a person, I found I could get back page after page of very personal, and frighteningly accurate, information.

24. If the abductor is an avid reader of certain magazines, check to see if a change of address has been entered. Also, check book clubs the abductor belongs to.

25. The abductor will often want important mail forwarded. Check with the post office for a forwarding address. If the abductor's mail is being sent to a friend or family member, that means this person likely knows the abductor's location. The threat of a lawsuit can often bring information.

26. Vehicles owned by the abductor will eventually have to have new license plates and registrations. Check with the Department of Motor Vehicles in the various states when the renewal is due.

27. Credit Bureaus keep extensive records on credit purchases of practically everyone in America, along with also keeping current addresses.

28. A good detective, when talking to a possible source of information, doesn't just try to get the information needed, but also tries to find other possible good sources of information. Often a source won't have the information you need, or only part of it, but will know where you can find more information.

29. Basically, be a pest. Don't let the police or others put you off. Insist on action, and go to the next level of supervision if no action is taken. The old saying about "the squeaky wheel always getting the grease" is 100 percent accurate when dealing with government agencies. We usually quickly take care of those who make the most noise and commotion, if only to get rid of them.

30. Go to www.ojjdp.ncjrs.org/search/topiclist.asp and click on "missing children" for even more information about searching for an abducted child.

31. As you can see by the length of this list, the number of possible sources of information about an abductor and an abducted child is limited only by the imagination and ingenuity of the left-behind parent. There will be other sources than those listed above, but finding these will take knowledge and insight into the nature and habits of the abductor, which the left-behind parent should have.

As might be imagined, searching for an abducted child can become a full-time job. Often, because of the need to care for other children, keep a job, pay bills, etc., a left-behind parent simply can't give the search the real effort it needs. In these cases, left-behind parents might want to consider hiring a private investigator. While this won't be cheap, a private investigator can often do things that parents and the police can't or won't do.

"We have access to databases the police don't," Tim Wilcox of International Investigators, Inc. told me. "A private investigator can give left-behind parents much more time and personal service than the police can, who are often so overburdened with cases they simply can't take that much time with any one case. If a child is taken to another state, we find the child and let the parents know, then coordinate the child's recovery with local authorities."

Tim Wilcox also added, "Private investigators have much more latitude than the police do. Short of breaking the law, we don't have to go by the same thick book of rules and regulations the police do. We can go into gray areas the police can't."[15]

Mr. Wilcox also endorses a program called Child Shield U.S.A. This program, which requires a $99 sign up fee and a $15 monthly renewal fee (the fee covers all eligible children under 18), offers its members a number of benefits. The program will provide a $50,000 reward for the safe return of your child, duplication and distribution of posters, and the services of a private investigator. This last benefit can be worth several thousand dollars. Interested parents can obtain more information about this program at 1-800-OK-Child or www.childshieldusa.com.

Okay, you, the police, or a private investigator have located the abductor and your child. You now have more decisions to make. What is the best way to get the child returned home safely and quickly? What must be done?

1. The very first thing left-behind parents need to do once they have located their abducted children, if not already done, is to retain an attorney with experience in child abduction return. Don't let attorneys assure you that they can handle it or that they'll be able to figure it out. This is a highly complex area of law, particularly cases involving international abduction. Ask for references of past abduction cases handled, and check them out. The International Academy of Matrimonial Lawyers, 727 Atlantic Ave., Boston, MA 02111-2891, 1-617-542-3881, www.iaml-usa.com, can give you a referral list of U.S. attorneys who handle child abduction cases.

    "When you ask another parent about an attorney and the response is something like, 'I guess he was all right, but...,' this is definitely not the right attorney for you," said left-behind parent Paul Marinkovich. "When the response is something like, 'Oh my gosh, you have to use this attorney because he is fantastic and takes these cases to heart,' then you have found the right one and are ready for your interview."[16]

2. Team HOPE, www.teamhope.org, is a group of parents who have gone through the experience of a child abduction. They can be a great source of information and support for left-behind parents. They can share information about how to make it through the nightmare of a child abduction, and what works best, and what doesn't work, when dealing with a child abduction recovery.

3. While many legal and other options exist for getting an abducted child returned, the best option, and the first thing left-behind parents should try, is negotiation with the abductor. Often, the abductors just wanted to show their power, or to hurt the other parents. Abductors many times, as it turns out, didn't really want to be a single parent to the abducted child. Consequently, if a left-behind parent acts civil and even a bit remorseful for causing the abductor so much grief (I say "act," because I'm certain the left-behind parent doesn't really feel that way), the abductor may turn the child over voluntarily. I realize that the left-behind parents are being forced to treat individuals nicely who they would probably like to strangle, but the abducted children's welfare should be their first concern.

Left-behind parents might also want to consider soliciting help from family and friends of the abductor. Abductors are likely to listen to counsel from these individuals, and it can be a way for the abductors to get out of the spot they have gotten themselves into: by claiming to be giving in to pressure from family and friends. In addition to this, Child Find of America, Inc., 1-800-A-WAY-OUT, offers mediation services at no cost, and can help negotiate a settlement between the abductor and the left-behind parent.

4. If negotiation doesn't work and a child has been taken to a country that has signed the Hague Convention, left-behind parents need to immediately file a Hague petition. Lengthy delays can cost left-behind parents custody of their children. Left-behind parents also need to contact the U.S. Department of State, Office of Children's Issues, at 1-888-407-4747. Officials from this office can visit the abducted child and report back on the child's condition. These officials may even be able to set up supervised visits for the left-behind parents. As we spoke about in a previous chapter, information on the Hague Convention can be found at www.incadat.com.

5. While there are a number of horror stories about the use of the Hague Convention, such as cases in which countries that have signed this treaty ignore its requirements, there are still a large number of success stories in using it, and it should be the first thing the parent of an internationally abducted child does if a negotiated return by the abducting parent can not be obtained. In one study of 22 cases of children internationally abducted and then returned, 19 had been returned through the use of the Hague Convention. As the study concluded, "These figures would support the view that Hague Convention proceedings are the usual, and most effective, way in which abducted children are returned to the State of habitual residence."[17]

A word of caution: If left-behind parents have filed criminal charges against the abductors, this may interfere with their use of the Hague Convention. Some countries will not return an abducted child if the abducting parent will be arrested if he or she accompanies the child. Also, criminal charges can possibly send the abductor into hiding, making it more difficult to locate the abductor and abducted child before the Hague Convention one-year expiration date.

In non-Hague Convention countries the rate of return is much, much less than that talked about above. For example, an article in *Newsday* about international child abductions said, "As one American Bar Association study concluded, 'Returns from some Islamic countries are considered practically impossible.'"[18]

6. If children have been abducted to a country that has not signed the Hague Convention, the left-behind parents must start legal proceedings within the court system of that country. While it is not impossible that the left-behind parents will prevail and have their children returned, the odds in these countries are usually stacked against them and for the abducting parents, since the abductors are many times citizens of that country. Starting these legal proceedings often means retaining an attorney in the country where the children are being held. The U.S. Department of State, Office of Children's Issues,

can advise left-behind parents of attorneys in the country who speak English and have experience in such matters. Left-behind parents can also contact the Family Law Division of the International Bar Association, 6950 N. Fairfax Dr., Arlington, VA 22213, 1-703-532-9300, www.ibanet.org, for a referral list of attorneys in foreign countries who are experienced in handling international abduction cases and who speak English.

7. Left-behind parents shouldn't expect, if they find their children in another country, that the U.S. government will be of any great help in getting the children returned. As an article in the *Foreign Service Journal* stated, "Many left-behind parents and members of the press have unrealistic expectations of what kind of assistance the government can provide. They often assume that U.S. government representatives abroad will advocate on behalf of left-behind American citizen parents in domestic custody disputes. Another commonly-held belief is that a U.S. consular officer can simply take custody of an American citizen child who has been abducted to another country and put him or her on a plane for home."[19] Unfortunately, the U.S. government will do none of these things. Actually, the left-behind parents of internationally abducted children are pretty much on their own, with the exception of information and advice, when it comes to help from the U.S. government.

8. A very informative Web site that outlines the child custody laws in various countries around the world can be accessed at http://travel.state.gov/family/abduction/country/country_486.html.

9. If, on the other hand, you find that your child has been taken to another community or state within the United States, have your attorney handle the paperwork, court filings, and the recovery efforts by the local police. While these local police may be reluctant, or even unwilling, to assist parents of abducted children, even though the parents are within their legal rights, most will assist if an attorney insists on it.

   In addition to this, most parents think that if their children are abducted and taken to another state, all they have to do is show up with their custody order in the state where the children are being held and the children will be handed over to them. Unfortunately, it's not as simple as that. At one time all states had passed the UCCJA (Uniform Child-Custody Jurisdiction Act), whose intent was to solve the problem of the courts of one state not recognizing custody orders made by the courts of another state. However, conflicting interpretations of UCCJA about which courts had jurisdiction to settle custody issues, the courts of the children's home state or the courts of the state the children had been abducted to, led to the creation in 1997 by the National Conference of Commissioners on Uniform State Laws of the Uniform Child-Custody Jurisdiction and Enforcement Act (UCCJEA), whose intent was to establish that the home state of the abducted children should have precedent in settling custody issues. The problem with this, however, is that all states have not as yet adopted UCCJEA. This is why it is so important to hire a competent attorney to handle the legal issues for you.

10. Another option for left-behind parents is the hiring of a company that specializes in the legal recovery of abducted children. One such company

is Dabbagh & Associates. "Dabbagh & Associates provides expert assistance to professionals as well as parents in putting into place recovery efforts, which include a broad range of approaches from mediation to complex strategies, utilizing numerous resources, agencies, and experts," Maureen Dabbagh told me. "Dabbagh & Associates understands the issue of international child abduction, and the complex nature of seeking remedy while dealing with multi-jurisdictional issues as well as, often times, conflicting laws and policies in those jurisdictions.

"However," Ms. Dabbagh also added, "this is not a 'snatch and grab' agency."[20]

As a person should do whenever hiring an agency such as this, ask for and check their references. This is a complex field and left-behind parents want to be certain they are getting their money's worth.

11. A number of transportation companies, including airlines, rail, and bus systems, offer assistance to parents in need who must travel to recover their abducted children. Readers wanting more information on this service should contact the National Center for Missing and Exploited Children at 1-800-843-5678 or www.missingkids.com.

So, if left-behind parents have tried all of the legal options and nothing is successful, what should these parents do? They could just simply write the child off and try to forget the child ever existed. Or they could just simply live the rest of their lives pining away for a child they will likely never see again. Or they could consider hiring a mercenary service such as the one we talked about in the anecdote above involving Joan Faber and her abducted son Adam. Left-behind parents should keep in mind, however, that if they do decide to do this they will likely be breaking the law in the country where their abducted child is being held, and that there is the real threat of physical danger.

"I always tell parents that 'only they can organize and manage the recovery of their child,'" Gus Zamora of Zamora & Associates told me, "and that if they are waiting for the law enforcement agencies to go and get the child, that will never happen in 99 percent of the cases. Law enforcement can only do so much. In the end, parents have to do what they have to do to get a child or children back, and most of the time this means taking great risk, both physically and financially."[21]

Still, if left-behind parents decide that this is the only option left, it is crucial to discuss and settle on any fees before beginning, and, most important, to ask for references and check them out. This is a field with a lot of good people, but also with a large helping of pretenders and con artists.

"This is a very sad business, and I actually do not know of anyone who I would refer any parent to for help, if I could not take the case myself," Gus Zamora said. "There are a lot of people out there who claim to be recovery agents, but in reality very few, if any, can actually prove any extended record of successful recoveries."

Gus Zamora then goes on to warn, "There are many 'con artists and false recovery agents' out there. These people prey on the left-behind parents, and tell them whatever they want to hear in order to get their money. Parents must verify credentials and demand references from anyone they plan on hiring. Parents must speak directly to other parents who have had their children recovered by the recovery agents. Otherwise, do not hire them!"[22]

Interestingly, in a study conducted for the U.S. Department of Justice, Office of Juvenile Justice and Delinquency Prevention, researchers found that 77 percent of the people who had hired mercenaries to retrieve their children (21 percent of the sample) said that these mercenaries had moderate to great knowledge of international parental abduction. This was the highest rating given to any group, which included attorneys, police officers, and judges.[23]

"The most important thing I have always felt and always tell my parents and potential clients," Gus Zamora told me, "is that 'they are not my client, that the child or children are my clients,' because in the end they are the ones who will be affected by my actions and their recovery from the parent who physically has them. I make it very clear that at any time or point in the recovery operation, if I find out that they lied to me, falsified any documents, or that their children would be better off with the parent who currently has them, that I will terminate the recovery. I consider the safety and well-being of the children above and beyond the desires of either parent."[24]

In addition to all of the information and advice given so far in this chapter, there are, for left-behind or potentially left-behind parents, a number of other good reference sources that can give additional information about child abduction, its prevention, and the recovery of an abducted child. These include the following:

1. *When Your Child Is Missing: A Family Survival Guide,* available at http:// ojjdp.ncjrs.org/PUBS/childismissing/contents.html.
2. *Early Identification of Risk Factors for Parental Abduction,* available at www.ncjrs.gov/html/ojjdp/2001_3_1/contents.html.
3. *Issues in Resolving Cases of International Child Abduction by Parents,* available at www.ncjrs.gov/pdffiles1/ojjdp/190105.pdf.
4. *Family Abduction: Prevention and Response,* available at www.missingkids .com/en_US/publications/NC75.pdf.
5. *Parental Kidnapping: Prevention and Remedies,* available at www.abanet .org/child/pkprevrem.pdf.
6. *A Family Resource Guide on International Parental Kidnapping,* available at www.ncjrs.gov/pdffiles1/ojjdp/215476.pdf.

For any left-behind parents without an Internet connection, I would advise them to go to the nearest public library with an Internet connection and have a librarian assist them. However, documents 1, 2, 3, and 6 can also be ordered by contacting the National Criminal Justice Reference Service at PO Box 6000, Rockville, MD 20849-6000, 1-800-851-3420; document 4 from the National Center for Missing and Exploited Children at 699 Prince St., Alexandria, VA 22314-3175, 1-800-843-5678; and document 5 from the American Bar Association at 321 N. Clark St., Chicago, IL 60610, 1-800-285-2221.

Finally, for those parents who have followed the advice in this chapter and recovered their abducted children, I have an additional note of warning. A very unfortunate side effect of child abduction is that even for those parents lucky enough to recover an abducted child safely, the problems are still not over. Often, the stress of the abduction and recovery will leave its mark on the children and the left-behind parents. As we will see in the next chapter, healing from the damaging effects of the stress and anxiety of a child abduction can often require a considerable amount of mental health therapy and treatment.

Helping Victims of Abduction Recover

In the early 1970s, Sarah Cecilie Finkelstein lived in Norway with her mother. Her father, who lived several hundred miles away, would pick her up on weekends and holidays. One day when Cecilie was four, her father picked her up and told Cecilie's mother that he was taking Cecilie to the park. However, instead her father took her to the airport and they boarded an airplane for New York. When Cecilie cried for her mother, her father told her that her mother didn't want her any longer and had decided to stay in Norway. Following this, Cecilie's father would become very upset if she told him that she missed her mother, eventually stifling any such complaints.

"I was given the silent treatment by my father if I talked about my mother, and soon learned not to mention the 'M' word again," Cecilie told me.[1]

In New York, Cecilie's father changed her name and began teaching her English. Soon, memories of her mother began to fade.

Suddenly though, after two years in New York, Cecilie's father told her that her mother had found them and had decided that she did want Cecilie back after all, and that she was going to make Cecilie move back to Norway. Her father painted a horrible picture of Cecilie's mother, and made Cecilie fear any reunion with her.

"I lived in a state of hyper-vigilance. 'You never know when she could come and snatch you' was something my father often said," Cecilie told me. "I was terrified of a woman I had forgotten. I didn't remember what she looked like, and I had almost no memory of being together with her. I had suppressed the good memories to avoid feeling the pain of losing her presence in my life."[2]

Soon, Cecilie and her father were on the run. "The next 14 years were spent living on Greyhound buses and traveling through three countries and 34 of the 50 states," Cecilie said. "I had to pretend to be a boy, dye my hair, and change identities, all to hide from a mother who just wanted to love me."

Cecilie's life on the run was hard. "It was a life of homelessness, of sleeping in a different place every few days or weeks, and telling lies to avoid being found," Cecilie recalled. "I had to remember which name to use where, and to beg for money and food at times."[3]

One day though, at age 13, Cecilie saw her own picture on a milk carton, and she realized that her mother must really love her to keep searching like that for her, and that perhaps everything her father had told her about her mother wasn't true. Cecilie struggled for several years with the decision of whether or not to call her mother. She didn't know what her mother's reaction would be and she feared that if she did call, her father would go to jail. Finally, however, at age 18, Cecilie at last called her mother and reestablished contact.

"I'll never forget her first words, tinged with relief, sadness, and pain, 'Are you okay?'" Cecilie recalls. "It touched me deeply. She didn't talk about her own feelings, or ask many questions. She was just happy that I was alive."[4]

But then, Cecilie also told me, "I had to deal with and accept the fact that my father had betrayed my trust in a deep way, and that he chose to take away from me the love of both parents. I tried to hang on to the belief that what he did might have been justified, because it hurt to believe otherwise."[5]

Although Cecilie's mother wanted to have a full blown reunion and immediately reestablish their relationship, it took Cecilie several years to work out her problems in dealing with what her father had told her all of those years, and the fact that she hadn't seen her mother for 14 years. Her father had convinced her that her mother was an evil woman who would hurt her, and it took awhile to get rid of those misconceptions.

"Over the next few years my mother and I established a relationship, but it took time" Cecilie said. "Looking back, the closer she tried to get the more I pushed her away. I can only imagine my mother's pain when I didn't include her in my life right away, but it was going to take time. I had too many feelings to go through first."[6]

Eventually, however, Cecilie and her mother did establish a solid relationship, and once more become mother and daughter. "When I was 18 I found my mother again, and my mother and I have a good relationship today, although there are ups and downs that come with having such a rocky history," Cecilie told me. "It was difficult to start from where we started from: shared pain and lost time, of knowing each other but not knowing each other, of having to do so much healing, and establishing so intimate a relationship in a context that was so unfamiliar. We had a lot of healing to do, but we made it. It is comforting to have accepted her, as it helps me to accept myself."[7]

Cecilie's mother added, "It was not easy for either of us at first. But we worked at it, and our relationship is now a warm and open one."[8]

Looking back on her life, Cecilie told me, "The pain doesn't end when a child is 'found'; there is so much aftershock to deal with. But healing can and does happen. I am healing more everyday. I have a beautiful family of my own and have moved forward with my life."[9]

Cecilie today, in addition to being married and having a child of her own, acts as an advocate for missing children. "Although things are going really well now, it took a long time to get my life together," Cecilie said. "There was so much to deal with, and I felt really alone. It would have been really helpful to be in contact with others who have been through a similar experience."[10]

* * * *

As can be seen from this anecdote, victims of child abduction have often been so thoroughly indoctrinated into the abductor's way of thinking that they many times have difficulty thinking in other terms, despite the fact they have finally come to the realization that the abductor has been lying to them, often for years. Abduction victims many times cannot just simply begin thinking differently. As in Cecilie's case, it can often take years before an abduction victim can break free from the mental control of the abductor.

Along with this effect on an abducted child's thinking processes, other detrimental effects that children may suffer because of an abduction can vary, depending on the length of the abduction, the severity of how it was carried out, and how much change the abduction brought to the victim's life. A few of the detrimental effects that psychologists, psychiatrists, and other professionals who deal with child abduction victims see include sleep disturbances (including nightmares), eating problems, depression, academic decline, anxiety, mood swings, uncontrollable crying, and feelings of insecurity.

While Cecilie worked out her problems for herself and finally managed to establish a warm, loving relationship with her left-behind mother, others simply can't do it for themselves, and must have professional help in order to heal. For some of these child abduction victims, as Cecilie spoke about in the last sentence of the anecdote above, group therapy is the best way to recover from the effects of an abduction. What these victims need is to hear from other victims about how they went through much of the same trauma, and then to listen to how they managed to recover from it. For other abduction victims though, individual therapy is necessary in order for them to fully recover from the effects of the abduction.

A good resource when looking for help in assisting an abducted child to recover is the organization Take Root, which can be reached at www.takeroot.org or 1-800-766-8674. This organization was founded by adults who had been abducted as children. Their CD *Kid Gloves* tells about how others have recovered from the effects of a child abduction, and the best approaches for adults to use when interacting with the victim of a child abduction.

Another good resource is a booklet from the National Center for Missing and Exploited Children, titled "Just in Case...Parental Guidelines in Finding Professional Help in Case Your Child Is Missing or the Victim of Sexual Exploitation." This booklet discusses what parents should look for when searching for a therapist to treat an abducted child, and where best to find one. This booklet can be downloaded from the Center's Web site at www.missingkids.com or a copy can be obtained by calling 1-800-843-5678.

Often, mental health experts find, the physical recovery of abducted children can be just as traumatic to the children as the abduction itself was. The police may have to break down a door, forcibly take the abductor into custody, and often the authorities give the abducted children to parents who have become strangers to them. To address this problem, a number of communities have found that using a team approach for the recovery of abducted children—a team that includes police officers, social workers, victims' advocates, and mental health professions—can greatly reduce the detrimental effects of a child abduction recovery, and make the child's transition back to a normal life much smoother.

The primary task of any such child abduction recovery team is to work with the family of an abducted child, and to insure that the reunification is carried out with the least amount of stress and disruption, allowing the healing to begin as quickly as possible. This team approach works so smoothly because while all members of the team have tasks to complete, they can also be assisted and advised by other members of the team about the best way, considering the abducted child's emotional and psychological interests, to accomplish these tasks.

Los Angeles is an example of a community that uses this team approach. The Los Angeles Interagency Council on Child Abuse and Neglect, which works with local law enforcement, mental health, and social service agencies, joined with the nonprofit agency Find the Children and created the "Child Abduction Task Force." This is a team that assists in the reunification of abducted children with their families, and, as described above, does it in a manner that allows the family to begin healing right away.

According to the Office of Juvenile Justice and Delinquency Prevention book *Recovery and Reunification of Missing Children: A Team Approach,* "Family behavior and coping styles prior to the abduction will often predict the ability of the family to cope with the abduction itself and the recovery and reunification of the child. Thus it is the responsibility of the professionals involved with the reunification to access the needs of the family and make every effort to help the family meet all of those needs in a sensitive, effective, efficient, and economical way."[11]

In addition, though, to the actual recovery of an abducted child, how the left-behind parent handles the reintegration of the abducted child into the family in the weeks and months after the recovery can also lessen or aggravate any effects the abduction may have had. The recovered child, for example, may not be able to totally get rid of the bad stories the abductor told about the left-behind parent, and so the child isn't sure how this parent really feels. And in many cases, the recovered child may not even remember the left-behind parent. Consequently, the child needs love and reassurance, and lots of it. The child may also feel partly to blame for the abduction, and needs to be reassured over and over that no blame is attached to him or her. In addition, the recovered child may have trouble adjusting to having brothers and sisters, who themselves may not even remember the recovered child. This all takes time, patience, and compassionate care.

According to a study of the effects of child abduction, "There appears to be consensus amongst these parents that the return of the child is not the end of the abduction process and, in many cases, marks the beginning of a new stage of management, far more taxing than anything that has come before."[12]

We talked in a previous chapter about the secondary victims of child abduction, who are most commonly the left-behind parents. Often, these individuals also need psychological and emotional help after abducted children have been returned to them. However, even more problems for these secondary victims arise because not only do the left-behind parents have their own psychological issues to deal with, they also have to deal with the psychological issues their recovered children may be experiencing. Consequently, in addition to seeking help for their own problems, they must also seek help for their children. But just as important, left-behind parents must weigh everything they say and do with the recovered children to be certain it will help cure, not aggravate, the psychological problems the children may be experiencing.

For many left-behind parents, it has been found, the best therapy, and the best way to know what to say and do to help recovered children heal, is talking with other parents who have had similar experiences. Comparing stories, and talking about how they have solved or are working through their problems, can be extremely helpful to left-behind parents recovering from a child abduction. Fortunately, there are many such groups of parents available. A few of these are listed as follows:

1. Team HOPE at www.teamhope.org or 1-866-305-HOPE.
2. Child Abduction Resource Center at www.globalmissing.com.
3. The National Center for Missing and Exploited Children at www.missingkids.com or 1-800-843-5678.

Another good resource that discusses how left-behind parents can deal with the stress and anxiety of the abduction, the search for, and the recovery of a child is a book we talked about in a previous chapter, *When Your Child Is Missing: A Family Survival Guide*. This book contains advice on how left-behind parents, even though going through a child abduction, can still maintain a normal lifestyle, emotionally, psychologically, and fiscally.

For those families, however, experiencing extreme difficulty in reintegrating after an abduction, there are professional programs available to assist them, such as The Rachel Foundation. This organization, located in Kerrville, Texas, about 65 miles northwest of San Antonio, assists families torn apart by child abduction and helps them to reunite and reintegrate. Families going through the program stay at the facility during the therapy, and then can receive offsite aftercare for a year afterward, or even longer if necessary. This organization uses experts from the fields of psychology, education, law, and social work, and has a very high success rate with families wanting to heal. The Rachel Foundation can be contacted at www.rachelfoundation.org or 1-830-864-4460. Their mailing address is PO Box 294810, Kerrville, Texas 78029.

However, while the recovery, return, and reintegration of an abducted child can be stressful, in a number of cases every year the missing child never returns because an abductor murders the child, often after a sexual assault. Dealing with the violent death of a child is probably the most stressful thing any parent could ever experience, but add to that the knowledge that the child was raped and possibly tortured before being murdered, and the event becomes almost too much for anyone to bear. To be able to recover from such an event and to have any semblance of a normal life afterward takes an enormous effort, especially when most parents experiencing such an event simply couldn't go on at all. Most of the parents who have recovered from such a traumatic event have done so by dedicating their lives to making sure other parents don't have to go through such an experience.

Erin Runnion, for example, the mother of murdered five-year-old Samantha Runnion, talked about in Chapter 8, suffered through six months of depression before finally starting a group called Samantha's PRIDE, a program of adult volunteers who escort young children to both school and extracurricular activities. This program has now spread to all 50 states.

Magdalen Bish had to live through the experience of someone kidnapping and murdering her 16-year-old daughter Molly. Following this horrific event, she started the Molly Bish Foundation, which gives child safety presentations at schools, and also distributes child identification kits.

After an abductor murdered Gay Smither's 12-year-old daughter Laura, she launched The Laura Recovery Center. This nonprofit group mobilizes citizen volunteers to assist the police in searching for missing children. The Laura Recovery Center has already assisted in over 1,000 searches.

"Most of the leading activists in this field are mothers whose children have been reported missing," said Barbara Smith, head of the Association of Missing and Exploited Children's Organizations. "Though their children may never be recovered, these women continue fighting against all odds and against all hope. They cope with their loss by making sure this never happens to other families like theirs."[13]

Not all abducted children advocates are women, however. John Walsh, following the abduction and murder of his son Adam in 1981, founded the Adam Walsh Child Resource Center, which eventually merged with the National Center for Missing and Exploited Children, which John and his wife Reve cofounded in 1984. Most readers though know John Walsh best as the host of the television show *America's Most Wanted*. This program has resulted in many child abduction recoveries and in numerous arrests of child abductors.

A child abduction is a tragic and psychologically damaging event no matter how it is carried out, how long it lasts, or how it is resolved. Fortunately, as seen in this chapter, for most victims, with enough resolve and self-determination, the effects of a child abduction can be overcome and a normal life resumed.

Some Final Thoughts about Child Abduction

Throughout this book we have examined many problems dealing with the crime of child abduction. We discussed the need for local police departments to take child abduction reports right away, the need for them to establish both training and written policies concerning child abduction, and the benefit to the public of these agencies forming specialized child abduction units. On a national level we talked about the need for a national standard for issuing Amber Alerts, the need to keep reliable national statistics on child abduction, the necessity of much more involvement by the federal government in resolving international child abductions, and the need to provide counseling and financial assistance to the parents of abducted children.

While all of these are important problems that must be resolved, there is another problem concerning child abduction that goes beyond these. There is another problem that, rather than just involving government agencies, instead involves every citizen in the United States. And consequently, every citizen in the United States must take part in solving it.

Few people, I think, would argue that when a pedophile, a criminal aiming for a ransom, a person wanting a baby in order to save a relationship, or someone simply out looking for a thrill abducts a child it is a crime, and these abductors need to be tracked down and punished. However, this consensus seems to blur a bit when the child abductor is a parent, by far the most common type of child abduction.

This consensus, though, should not blur. As shown many times in this book, parental child abduction is a serious crime. In only very, very few cases do parents abduct their children in order to protect them from sexual or physical abuse. Instead, in the very large majority of cases, parental child abduction occurs, not because of love and concern for the children, but because one parent wants to strike at the other, and in doing so uses the most potent and powerful weapon available: that person's children.

While doing this is against the law in every state, far too often parental child abduction isn't treated as the crime it actually is. It is instead much too often treated as a private family matter. Consequently, police departments don't want to get involved, prosecutors don't want to try the cases, and juries don't want to convict the abductors. This must change.

Child abduction, though not seen as such, is a crime not just against the custodial parent, but also against the abducted child. The child is torn away from familiar surroundings, away from friends, and away from the love of family members. A child abduction victim can suffer emotional and psychological scars that last a lifetime. Most parental child abductors, however, don't see this or even care. They are having their revenge, and that is all that counts.

This must change. Society must recognize parental child abduction for what it is, not just a crime against the other parent, but also a crime against an innocent child. Society must demand that these crimes stop, and that those who perpetrate them receive harsh punishment. Only through this can America's children be safe from the threat of abduction. Only through this can America's children be assured of the type of childhood they deserve.

Notes

CHAPTER 1

1. Erica Curless and Susan Drumheller, "Victims in CdA Homicide Were Bludgeoned," *SpokesmanReview.com,* May 20, 2005, www.spokesmanreview.com/sections/duncan/?ID=70581.

2. Ibid.

3. Nicholas K. Geranios, "Idaho Murder/Abduction Suspect Allegedly Staked Out Home," *Associated Press,* July 13, 2005, www.lineofduty.com.

4. "Suspect's Blog Showed Malicious Thoughts," *Associated Press,* July 7, 2005, www.msnbc.msn.com/id/8500603/.

5. "Idaho Suspect Has Violent History," *MSNBC.com,* July 6, 2005, www.msnbc.msn.com/id/8485031/.

6. David Crary, "Solid Data Scarce for Child Abductions," *Associated Press,* January 19, 2007, www.foxnews.com.

7. David Finkelhor, Heather Hammer, and Andrea J. Sedlak, "National Incidence Studies of Missing, Abducted, Runaway, and Thrownaway Children," U.S. Department of Justice, October 2002, www.ojjdp.ncjrs.org.

8. Kathy L. Reschke, "Keeping Children Safe from Abduction by Strangers," *Family Tapestries,* 2002, http://ohioline.osu.edu/flm02/FS17.html.

9. Finkelhor, Hammer, and Sedlak, "National Incidence Studies of Missing, Abducted, Runaway, and Thrownaway Children."

10. Katherine M. Brown et al., "Case Management for Missing Children Homicide Investigation," Office of the Attorney General, Olympia, WA, May 2006.

11. Press Release from the Washington State Attorney General's Office, July 28, 2006, www.atg.wa.gov/pressrelease.aspx?&id=4234.

12. Brown et al., "Case Management for Missing Children Homicide Investigation."

13. "Executive Summary—Case Management for Missing Children Homicide Investigation," U.S. Department of Justice, May 1997, www.ojjdp.ncjrs.org.

14. Barbara Simpson, "The Lost Boys of Missouri," *WorldNetDaily,* January 15, 2007, www.worldnetdaily.com/news/article.asp?ARTICLE_ID=53768.

15. Ibid.

16. Janet Chiancone, Linda Girdner, and Patricia Hoff, "Issues in Resolving Cases of International Child Abduction by Parents," *Juvenile Justice Bulletin*, U.S. Department of Justice, December 2001.

17. Susan Bartelstone, "How to Help Safely!" *The Safety Solutions Company*, January 2008, www.dearsafetysolutions.com.

18. Monique C. Boudreaux, Kenneth V. Lanning, and Wayne D. Lord, "Investigating Potential Child Abduction Cases," *FBI Law Enforcement Bulletin*, April 2001, 2.

CHAPTER 2

1. Liza Porteus, "Police: Suspect's Father, Friend 'Confessed' to Burying Missing Boy, But There's No Body," *Foxnews.com*, March 15, 2007, www.foxnews.com/story/0,2933,258710,00.html.

2. Ibid.

3. Jeff Brumley, "Grandmother Blames Failed Legal System in Boy's Death," *The Florida Times—Union*, March 20, 2007, A-1.

4. Chuck Hustmyre, "George Edenfield Says 'Devil' Made Him Kill Christopher Barrios," *Crime Library*, March 22, 2007, www.crimelibrary.com/news/original/0307/2202_barrios.html.

5. "Prosecutor: Slain Ga. Boy Was First Molested," *Associated Press*, March 22, 2007, www.msnbc.msn.com/id/17739868/.

6. "Molester, Parents Charged with Child's Murder," *Associated Press*, March 21, 2007, www.msnbc.msn.com/id/17722385/.

7. Finkelhor, Hammer, and Sedlak, "National Incidence Studies of Missing, Abducted, Runaway, and Thrownaway Children: Nonfamily Abducted Children: National Estimates and Characteristics."

8. Kenneth A. Hanfland, Robert Keppel, and Joseph Weis, "Case Management for Missing Children Homicide Cases," Office of the Attorney General, Olympia, WA, May 1997.

9. Boudreaux, Lanning, and Lord, "Investigating Potential Child Abduction Cases."

10. *Diagnostic and Statistical Manual of Mental Disorders* (Washington, DC: American Psychiatric Association, 2000).

11. Ernest E. Allen, "Keeping Children Safe: Rhetoric and Reality," *Juvenile Justice Journal* 5, no. 1 May 1998.

12. John Reitmeyer and Elsie Young, "Suspects' Use of Social Sites Raises Concerns," *NorthJersey.com*, October 5, 2007, www.northjersey.com.

13. Brown et al., "Case Management for Missing Children Homicide Investigation."

14. Gene Johnson, "Tacoma Police Look at Abduction Suspect for Other Disappearances," *Associated Press*, July 13, 2007, www.columbian.com/printArticle.cfm?story=167608.

15. Brian Alexander, "Missing Tacoma Girl's Body Found," *The Seattle Times*, July 13, 2007, A-1.

16. Torsten Ove, "Web Cops Tighten Net on Sex Offenders," *Rocky Mountain News*, July 17, 2006, www.rockymountainnews.com/drmn/tech/article/0,2777,DRMN_23910_4848932,00.html.

17. Boudreaux, Lanning, and Lord, "Investigating Potential Child Abduction Cases," 8.

18. Christina Almedeida, "Two Teenage Girls Kidnapped in Calif. Are Found Safe," *Associated Press,* August 1, 2002, www.boston.com/news/daily/01/calif _abductions.htm.

19. "CNN Larry King Live," *CNN.com,* August 1, 2002, http://transcripts.cnn .com/TRANSCRIPTS/0208/01/lkl.00.html.

20. Ibid.

CHAPTER 3

1. "Official: Nurse Imposter Snatches Ill Newborn," *CNN.com,* March 10, 2007, www.cnn.com/2007/US/03/10/newborn.kidnapped/index.html.

2. Ibid.

3. "Baby's Abductor Fell Victim to Obsession," *Associated Press,* March 18, 2007, www.msnbc.msn.com/id/17680125.

4. Betsy Blaney, "Missing Baby Found, Alleged Abductor Held," *Associated Press,* June 6, 2006, www.boston.com.

5. "Missing 5-Day-Old Girl Found in Texas," *CNN.com,* June 5, 2006, www.cnn.com/2006/US/06/05/missing.baby.

6. Blaney, "Missing Baby Found, Alleged Abductor Held."

7. Susan Candiotti, "Accused Texas Baby Snatcher Arraigned," *CNN.com,* August 15, 2002, www.cnn.com/2002/LAW/08/15/texas.abduction.arraignment/ index.html.

8. Interview by author, November 2, 2007.

9. Cynthia Leonor Garza, Mike Glenn, and Kevin Moran, "Taser Used on Dad Leaving Houston Hospital with Baby," *Houston Chronicle,* April 16, 2007, www.chron.com.

10. "Dad Abducts 2-Hour-Old Baby from Hospital," *CBS 2—KCAL 9,* March 6, 2007, http://cbs2.com/.

11. Susan Donaldson James, "Baby Abductors: Typically Manipulative, Clever and Even Kind," *ABC News,* March 13, 2007, http://abcnews.go.com/print?id=2946697.

12. Larry G. Ankrom and Cynthia J. Lent, "Cradle Robbers: A Study of the Infant Abductor," *FBI Law Enforcement Bulletin,* September 1995, 17.

13. Interview by author, November 2, 2007.

14. James, "Baby Abductors: Typically Manipulative, Clever and Even Kind."

15. National Center for Missing and Exploited Children, Abduction report made available to law enforcement personnel, 2001.

16. Lisa Kathleen Strohman, "Stranger Infant Abductions: Offense Characteristics, Victim Selection, and Offender Motivation of Female Offenders" (Ph.D. Thesis, submitted to Drexel University, May 2005), 42.

17. Ankrom and Lent, "Cradle Robbers: A Study of the Infant Abductor," 20.

18. Cathy Nahirny and Ann Scofield, "Keeping the Youngest Patients Safe," *Minority Nurse.com,* August 2, 2005, www.minoritynurse.com/features/health/ 08-02-05f.html.

19. National Center for Missing and Exploited Children, Abduction report made available to law enforcement personnel, 2001.

20. Ann Wolbert Burgess and Kenneth V. Lanning, "An Analysis of Infant Abductions," The National Center for Missing and Exploited Children, 1995, www.missingkids.com.

21. Nahirny and Scofield, "Keeping the Youngest Patients Safe."

22. Ann Wolbert Burgess and Kenneth V. Lanning, "An Analysis of Infant Abductions, Second Edition," The National Center for Missing and Exploited Children, July 2003.

23. Interview by author, November 2, 2007.

24. Burgess and Lanning, "An Analysis of Infant Abductions, Second Edition."

Chapter 4

1. Paul Nelson, "It's Been Five Years Since Elizabeth Smart Was Abducted," *KSL.com,* June 5, 2007, www.ksl.com/index.php?nid=481&sid=1308694.

2. "Elizabeth Smart Found Alive Nine Months After Vanishing from Utah Home," *CourtTVNews,* March 12, 2003, www.courttv.com/news/2003/0312/smart_ap.html.

3. Jane Clayson, "Was Elizabeth's Cousin Next?" *CBS News,* March 14, 2003, www.cbsnews.com/stories/2003/03/15/national/printable544135.shtml.

4. "Then & Now: Elizabeth Smart," *CNN.com,* November 4, 2005, www.cnn.com/2005/US/11/04/cnn25.smart.tan/.

5. "Elizabeth Smart Found Alive," *CNN.com,* March 12, 2003, www.cnn.com/2003/US/West/03/12/smart.kidnapping.

6. Marion Hixon, "Elizabeth Smart Will 'Never Be the Same,'" *People,* July 28, 2006, www.people.com/people/article/0,26334,1220083,00.html.

7. "Elizabeth Smart Talks about Her 9-Month Kidnapping," *NBCSandiego.com,* May 5, 2006, www.nbcsandiego.com/news/9169424/detail.html?rss=dgo&psp =news.

8. "Missing Children Are Found Unharmed," *Associated Press,* July 1, 2003, www.sptimes.com/2003/07/01/news_pf/State/Missing_children_are_.shtml.

9. "Grandmother Reunited with Abducted Children," *CNN.com,* July 1, 2003, www.cnn.com/2003/US/South/07/01/amber.alert/index.html.

10. "Two Children Taken by Bipolar Mother Found Safe," *CNN.com,* July 1, 2003, http://transcripts.cnn.com/TRANSCRIPTS/0307/01/ltm.10.html.

11. "Medical Encyclopedia," National Institute of Health, July 28, 2007, www.nlm.nih.gov/medlineplus/ency/article/001553.htm.

12. Martha-Elin Blomquist et al., "Early Identification of Risk Factors for Parental Abduction," U.S. Department of Justice, March 2001, www.ncjrs.gov/html/ojjdp/2001_3_1/contents.html.

13. "Police Using Hallucination Machine as Training Tool," *Associated Press,* March 25, 2006.

Chapter 5

1. Liza Porteus, "Washington Mom Pleads with Ex-Husband to Return Abducted Kids," *FoxNews.com,* March 29, 2007, www.foxnews.com/printer_friendly _story/0,3566,262340,00.html.

2. Alicia Acuna, Kevin McCarthy, and Liza Porteus, "Colorado Cops Arrest Washington Dad Who Abducted Kids," *FoxNews.com,* March 29, 2007, www.foxnews.com/printer_friendly_story/0,3566,262487,00.html.

3. "Mother of Abducted Kids Sentenced," *ABC7News.com,* July 19, 2003, http://abclocal.go.com/kgo/story?section=News&id=1899320&ft=print.

4. "Biological Mother Arrested in Kidnapping of Her Adopted Baby," *CNN.com,* July 22, 2007, www.cnn.com/2007/US/07/22/baby.kidnapped.ap/index.html.

5. Ibid.

6. "Kidnapped Baby Ends Up at Home of Aunt's Friend," *Associated Press,* July 23, 2007, www.journalnow.com.

7. Ryan Wolf, "Father Charged with Kidnapping Today," *KGBT4,* January 10, 2007, www.team4news.com/global/story.asp?s=5909273&ClientType=Printable.

8. Finkelhor, Hammer, and Sedlak, "National Incidence Studies of Missing, Abducted, Runaway, and Thrownaway Children."

9. "History of Troubles Preceded Plane Crash," *Indianapolis Star,* March 8, 2007, B-4.

10. Rob Schneider, "Pilot in Fatal Crash Called Bitter, Caring," *Indianapolis Star,* March 7, 2007, A-1.

11. David Finkelhor, Gerald Hotaling, and Andrea Sedlak, "Missing, Abducted, Runaway, and Thrownaway Children in America, First Report: Numbers and Characteristics," U.S. Department of Justice, 1990.

12. Geoffrey L. Greif and Robecca L. Hegar, *When Parents Kidnap: The Families Behind the Headlines* (New York, The Free Press, 1993), 147.

13. Finkelhor, Hotaling, and Sedlak, "Missing, Abducted, Runaway, and Thrownaway Children in America. First Report: Numbers and Characteristics."

14. Toba Gladstone, Barry Nurcombe, and Neil Senior, "Child Snatching: A Case Report," *Journal of the American Academy of Child Psychiatry,* 1982, 579–83.

15. Dorothy Huntington, "Parental Kidnapping: A New Form of Child Abuse," in *Investigation and Prosecution of Parental Abduction* (Alexandria, VA: American Prosecutors Research Institute, 1995).

16. Nancy Faulkner, "Parental Child Abduction Is Child Abuse," Paper presented to the United Nations Convention on Child Rights, June 9, 1999.

17. Jenni Thompson, "The Secret Truth about Child Abduction," *San Francisco Chronicle,* March 11, 2004, B-9.

18. Blomquist et al., "Early Identification of Risk Factors for Parental Abduction."

19. Greif and Hegar, *When Parents Kidnap: The Families Behind the Headlines.*

20. William Rigler and Howard L. Wieder, "The Epidemic of Parental Child-Snatching: An Overview," 2001, http://travel.state.gov/family/abduction/resources/resources_545.html.

CHAPTER 6

1. Eckhard Schneider and Ingrid Sischy, *Jeff Koons* (Koln, Germany: Taschen, 2007).

2. Thomas Maier, "Far from Heaven," *Newsday.com,* July 16, 2003, www.newsday.com.

3. Ibid.

4. Amy Worden, "Feds: Foreign Courts Soft on Parental Abductions," *APBnews .com*, September 13, 2000, http://news.findlaw.com/apbnews/s/20000913/ apbabduction.html.

5. Barbara J. Greig, "Helping to Reunite Families: The Office of Children's Issues," *Foreign Service Journal*, April 2003, 59.

6. Chiancone, Girdner, and Hoff, "Issues in Resolving Cases of International Child Abduction by Parents."

7. "The Hague Convention on the Civil Aspects of International Child Abduction," May 2007, http://patriot.net/~crouch/haguetext.html.

8. Chiancone, Girdner, and Hoff, "Issues in Resolving Cases of International Child Abduction by Parents."

9. "The Hague Convention on the Civil Aspects of International Child Abduction."

10. Maura Harty, "International Parental Child Abduction Prevention Act," Testimony before Congressional Committee, July 9, 2003, www.state.gov/r/pa/ ei/othertstmy/32994.htm.

11. Timothy W. Maier, "State Abandons Kidnapped Kids," *Insight on the News*, June 14, 1999.

12. Ibid.

13. Kate O'Beirne, "Without Their Daughters: The Outrage of Child Abduction and U.S. Complacency," *National Review*, May 20, 2002.

14. George Gedda, "Abducted Children: Should State Do More?" *Foreign Service Journal*, November 2000, www.afsa.org/fsj/Nov00/geddanov.cfm.

15. Kirsten Brown, "Frustrated Fathers of Abducted Children Turn to Public for Support," *Japan Children's Rights Network*, December 15, 2006, www.crnjapan.com /articles/2006/en/20061215-fatherspublicsupport.html.

16. Ibid.

17. "International Child Abduction," U.S. State Department, January 2007, http://travel.state.gov/family/abduction/abduction_580.html.

18. Ibid.

19. Gedda, "Abducted Children: Should State Do More?"

20. O'Beirne, "Without Their Daughters: The Outrage of Child Abduction and U.S. Complacency."

21. "Specific Action Plan Needed to Improve Response to Parental Child Abductions," U.S. General Accounting Office, March 2000, 8.

22. "Federal Response to International Child Abductions," U.S. General Accounting Office, October 14, 1999, 1–2.

23. "Specific Action Plan Needed to Improve Response to Parental Child Abductions," 7.

24. Ibid, 19–21.

25. www.icps.20m.com/custom4.html.

26. Nigel Lowe, "International Forum on Parental Child Abduction: Hague Convention Action Agenda," Report from Conference held September 15–16, 1998.

27. Thomas Maier, "Coming to America," *Newsday.com*, July 18, 2003, www.newsday.com.

28. Testimony of Ernie Allen before the Senate Subcommittee on Criminal Justice Oversight, October 27, 1999.

CHAPTER 7

1. "Philly Family Rejoices over Girl's Return," *CNN.com*, July 24, 2002, http:// archives.cnn.com/2002/US/07/24/philadelphia.girl/index.html.

2. "Kidnapped Philadelphia Girl Breaks Free," *CNN.com*, July 23, 2002, http:// archives.cnn.com/2002/US/07/23/philadelphia.girl/index.html.

3. "Seven-Year-Old Philadelphia Girl Escapes Abduction," *Jet*, August 12, 2002.

4. Mitch Stacy, "Pin for Torn Jacket Was Teen's Salvation," *Washingtonpost.com*, February 27, 2007, www.washingtonpost.com.

5. "Man Arrested in Abduction of Florida Boy, 13," *CNN.com*, March 7, 2007, www.cnn.com/2007/US/03/07/florida.abduction/index.html.

6. Stacy, "Pin for Torn Jacket Was Teen's Salvation."

7. Tim Mitchell, "Father's Child Abduction Trial Gets Underway," *The News-Gazette*, October 13, 2006, A-1.

8. Matt Buedel, "Peoria Girls Caught Up in Custody Battle Found with Religious Sect in Belize," *Peoria Journal Star*, May 2, 2006, A-1.

9. Mitchell, "Father's Child Abduction Trial Gets Underway."

10. "French Commandos Storm Cult Compound, Free 12-Year-Old," *Associated Press*, August 6, 2007, www.foxnews.com/printer_friendly_story/ 0,3566,292266,00.html.

11. Suellen E. Dean and Ralph Greer, Jr., "We Are Not Ruling Out Anything," *Spartanburg Herald-Journal*, October 29, 1994, www.tcleplcx.nct/shj/smith/ ninedays/hunt.html.

12. Rachel Pergament, "The Investigation," *Crime Library*, August 2007, www.crimelibrary.com/notorious_murders/famous/smith/invest_7.html.

13. Rachel Pergament, "The Big Lie," *Crime Library*, August 2007, www .crimelibrary.com/notorious_murders/famous/smith/lie_6.html.

14. Rick Bragg, "Insanity Plea Expected in Boys' Drownings," *New York Times*, November 9, 1994, www.nytimes.com.

15. "Bronx Mother Charged with Murder after Lying about Infant Abduction," *NY1*, April 30, 2007, www.ny1.com/ny1/content/index.jsp?stid=12&aid=65742.

16. Amy Argetsinger and Katherine Shaver, "Police: Father Staged Carjacking, Killed Son," *Washington Post*, September 10, 1999, A-1.

17. Ruben Castaneda, "Mom Turns Own Tragedy into Career of Advocacy," *Washington Post*, July 5, 2006, B-1.

CHAPTER 8

1. Terry McCarthy, "The Playtime Killer," *Time*, July 21, 2002, www.time.com/ time/printout/0,8816,322651,00.html.

2. "Sheriff '100 Percent Certain' Avila Killed Calif. Girl," *NBC4.tv*, July 19, 2002, www.knbc.com/sh/news/stories/nat-news-156702220020719-070714 .html.

3. McCarthy, "The Playtime Killer."

4. "Sheriff to Killer: 'We Are Coming after You,'" *CNN.com*, July 17, 2002, http://archives.cnn.com/2002/US/07/17/girl.abducted/index.html.

5. "Charles Feldman: Police Fear Sexual Predator," *CNN.com*, July 18, 2002, http://archives.cnn.com/2002/US/07/18/feldman.otsc/index.html.

6. "Sheriff to Killer: 'We Are Coming after You.'"

7. "Sheriff: '100 Percent Certain' Suspect Killed Samantha," *CNN.com,* July 19, 2002, http://archives.cnn.com/2002/US/07/19/girl.abducted/index.html.

8. Ibid.

9. "Thousands Attend Funeral of Samantha Runnion," *Associated Press,* July 25, 2002, www.foxnews.com/printer_friendly_story/0,3566,58680,00.html.

10. "Samantha's Mom: 'Little Room for Anger,'" *CNN.com,* July 26, 2002, http://archives.cnn.com/2002/US/07/26/lkl.erin.runnion/index.html.

11. "'Personal Goodbye' for Runnion Family," *CBS News,* July 26, 2002, www.cbsnews.com/stories/2002/07/16/national/printable515287.shtml.

12. "Avila's Old Lawyer Says He's Rethinking Career," *CNN.com,* July 26, 2002, http://archives.cnn.com/2002/LAW/07/26/avila.acquittal.reax/index.html.

13. "Man Charged with Murder in Samantha Case," *CNN.com,* July 22, 2002, http://archives.cnn.com/2002/US/07/22/girl.abducted/index.html.

14. John Hall, "Avila Guilty of Killing Samantha Runnion," *NC Times,* April 28, 2005, A-1.

15. Gwendolyn Driscoll, "Avila Jury Foreman Speaks," *Orange County Register,* May 16, 2005, www.ocregister.com/ocr/sections/breaking_news/article_517302.php.

16. Jeremiah Marquez, "Judge Formally Sentences Samantha Runnion's Killer to Death," *Associated Press,* July 22, 2005, www.northcountytimes.com.

17. Marilyn Freeman, "International Child Abduction—the Effects," The Reunite Research Unit, May 2006.

18. "Death for Man Who Murdered Runnion," *CBS News,* July 22, 2005, www.cbsnews.com/stories/2005/07/22/national/printable711061.shtml.

19. McCarthy, "The Playtime Killer."

20. "Thousands Attend Funeral of Samantha Runnion."

21. "Cops: Killer Left His 'Calling Card,'" *FoxNews.com,* July 18, 2002, www.foxnews.com/printer_friendly_story/0,3566,57900,00.html.

22. "Next for Avila: Death or Life in Prison?" *NC Times,* April 29, 2005, A-1.

23. Driscoll, "Avila Jury Foreman Speaks."

24. Barbara Simpson, "Get 'em and Burn 'em!" *KSFO 560,* July 22, 2002, www.worldnetdaily.com/news/article.asp?ARTICLE_ID=28360.

25. Dennis Klass, *Parental Grief: Solace and Resolution* (New York: Springer, 1988).

26. Freeman, "International Child Abduction—the Effects."

27. Sue Andriola, "The Impact of Child Abduction," *Journal of Employee Assistance,* December 2004.

28. C. Crofton, Roxane Silver, and Camille Wortman, "The Role of Coping in Support Provision: The Self-Presentational Dilemma of Victims of Life Crises," in *Social Support: An Interactional View,* eds. Gregory R. Pierce, Barbara R. Sarason, and Irwin G. Sarason (New York: Wiley & Sons, 1990), 397–426.

29. Ann Wolbert Burgess, "Infant Abduction: A Family Crisis," *Nursing Spectrum,* 2000, 294.

30. Rex Forehand et al., "Child Abduction: Parent and Child Functioning Following Return," *Clinical Pediatrics* 28, no. 7 (1989): 311–16.

31. Lenore C. Terr, "Child Snatching: A New Epidemic of an Ancient Malady," *Journal of Pediatrics* 103 (1983): 151–56.

32. www.nimh.nih.gov.
33. Burgess and Lanning, "An Analysis of Infant Abductions, Second Edition."
34. "Thousands Attend Funeral of Samantha Runnion."

CHAPTER 9

1. "Boy Tries to Reconnect with Old Life after 4 Years," *CNN.com,* January 15, 2007, www.cnn.com/2007/US/01/15/missouri.boys/index.html.
2. "DA: Suspect Confessed to Snatching Boy, 13," *CNN.com,* January 18, 2007, www.cnn.com/2007/LAW/01/18/devlin.hearing/index.html.
3. "Families Revel in Sons' Safe Return," *MSNBC.com,* January 13, 2007, www.msnbc.msn.com/id/16607683/.
4. Libby Sander and Susan Saulny, "Soul-Searching by Missouri Suspect's Neighbors," *New York Times,* January 21, 2007, www.nytimes.com.
5. Christopher Leonard, "Life Term in Teenage Mo. Boy's Abduction," *Associated Press,* October 8, 2007, www.kansascity.com/449/.
6. Jim Salter, "Boy Might Have Given Clues to His Abduction," *Indianapolis Star,* January 16, 2007, A-2.
7. Arian Campos-Flores and Ellen Harris, "What Made the Captive Missouri Boy Stay?" *Newsweek,* January 17, 2007.
8. Elizabethe Holland, "Questions Linger after Boys' Rescue," *St. Louis Post-Dispatch,* January 15, 2007, A-1.
9. Andrea Faville, "Hidden in Plain Sight," *Newsweek,* January 29, 2007.
10. Campos-Flores and Harris, "What Made the Captive Missouri Boy Stay?"
11. Darla Bishop, "Ease Up on Abducted Boy," *The Sheboygan Press,* January 23, 2007, B-3.
12. "Case of Missing Boys Stands Out," *USA Today,* January 13, 2007, www.usatoday.com.
13. Campos-Flores and Harris, "What Made the Captive Missouri Boy Stay?"
14. Sharon Cohen, "In Mo., Shawn Comes Home a Different Boy," *Associated Press,* January 18, 2007.
15. "Police: Kidnapping Suspect Was 'Brazen,'" *MSNBC.com,* January 13, 2007, www.msnbc.msn.com/id/16612257/.
16. "Insight," *CNN.com,* January 16, 2007, http://transcripts.cnn.com/TRANSCRIPTS/0701/16/i_ins.01.html.
17. Ibid.
18. "Mo. Kidnap Suspect Eyed in Another Case," *MSNBC.com,* January 17, 2007, www.msnbc.msn.com/id/16674715/GT1=8921.
19. Cheryl Wittenauer, "Teen's Parents Suspect Abuse," *Indianapolis Star,* January 19, 2007, A-3.
20. Faville, "Hidden in Plain Sight."
21. "Kidnapper: Boy Persuaded Me Not to Kill Him," *MSNBC.com,* October 9, 2007, www.msnbc.msn.com/id/21206715/?GT1=10450.
22. "Devlin Faces Child Porn Charges," *MSNBC.com,* March 1, 2007, www.msnbc.msn.com/id/17404404/.
23. "Parents: Abducted Mo. Boy Ready to Help Others," *MSNBC.com,* January 19, 2007, www.msnbc.msn.com/id/16690284/.

24. Arian Campos-Flores and Evan Thomas, "The Saga of Kidnapped Missouri Boys," *Newsweek*, January 29, 2007.

25. Arian Campos-Flores, "Crime: Living with Evil," *Newsweek*, January 29, 2007.

26. "Parents: Abducted Mo. Boy Ready to Help Others."

27. Ibid.

28. "Shawn Hornbeck Makes Appearance at Foundation's Fundraiser," *4kmov.com*, July 20, 2007, www.kmov.com.

29. Donald Dewey, "The Stockholm Syndrome," *Scandinavian Review*, Spring 2007.

30. "Hearst: Elizabeth May Face Future Trauma," *CNN.com*, March 13, 2003, www.cnn.com/2003/US/West/03/13/life.after.kidnapping.

31. Elizabethe Holland, "A Child Abductee's Journey Back," *St. Louis Post-Dispatch*, January 20, 2007.

32. "Translation of Natascha Kampusch's Letter," *TimesOnLine*, August 28, 2006, www.timesonline.co.uk/tol/news/world/europe/article621640.ece?print=yes.

33. Ibid.

34. "New Details Arise on Captive Austrian Girl's Life," *Associated Press*, August 29, 2006, www.msnbc.msn.com/id/14555654/.

35. "Slow Climb Back to Normal Life for Austria's Kidnapping Survivor," *San Francisco Chronicle*, August 30, 2006, www.sfgate.com/cgi-bin/blogs/sfgate/category?blogid=15&cat=889.

36. V. Dion Haynes and Vincent J. Schodolski, "Captive Girl's Actions Hint at Brainwashing," *Chicago Tribune*, March 15, 2003, A-1.

37. Joseph M. Carver, "Love and Stockholm Syndrome: The Mystery of Loving an Abuser," *Counselling Resource*, August 23, 2007, http://counsellingresource.com/quizzes/stockholm/index.html.

CHAPTER 10

1. Anthony Bruno, "A Bunch of Cracked-Out Individuals," *Crime Library*, April 2007, www.crimelibrary.com/serial_killers/predators/jessica_lunsford/4.html.

2. "Jessica Lunsford," *America's Most Wanted*, March 19, 2005, www.amw.com/missing_children/recovered.cfm?id=30448.

3. Ibid.

4. Mabel Perez, "Couey Found Guilty," *Ocala Star-Banner*, March 8, 2007, A-1.

5. Stephen E. Steidel, ed., *Missing and Abducted Children: A Law Enforcement Guide to Case Investigation and Program Management* (Alexandria, VA: The National Center for Missing and Exploited Children, 2000).

6. "NISMART Bulletin: National Estimates of Missing Children: An Overview," U.S. Department of Justice, October 2002, www.ncjrs.gov/html/ojjdp/nismart/01/ns4.html.

7. Janet L. Chiancone et al., "The Criminal Justice System's Response to Parental Abduction," U.S. Department of Justice, December 2001, www.ncjrs.gov.

8. Ernie Allen, "The Kid Is with a Parent, How Bad Can it Be?" The National Center for Missing and Exploited Children, 1991.

9. Chiancone et al., "The Criminal Justice System's Response to Parental Abduction."

10. Ibid.

11. Ibid.

12. Marlene L. Dalley and Jenna Ruscoe, "The Abduction of Children by Strangers in Canada: Nature and Scope," Royal Canadian Mounted Police, December 1, 2003, www.ourmissingchildren.gc.ca/omc/publications/002/abduction_e.htm.

13. James O. Beasley and Kristen R. Beyer, "Nonfamily Child Abductors Who Murder Their Victims," *Journal of Interpersonal Violence* 18, no. 10 (2003): 1167–88.

14. Kenneth V. Lanning, "Child Molesters Who Abduct: Summary of the Case in Point Series," The National Center for Missing and Exploited Children, 1995, 17–36.

15. Brown et al., "Case Management for Missing Children Homicide Investigation."

16. David Finkelhor, Gerald T. Hotaling, and Peggy S. Plass, "Police Response to Family Abduction Episodes," *Crime and Delinquency* 41, no. 2 (1995): 205–17.

17. Chiancone, Girdner, and Hoff, "Issues in Resolving Cases of International Child Abduction by Parents."

18. Ibid.

19. Sean Webby, "Child Abduction Unit among Best in State," *Oakland Tribune*, November 30, 2006, B-1.

20. Ibid.

21. "Alert CBP Officer Prevents Child Abduction," *Custom and Border Protection TODAY*, May 2004, www.cbp.gov/xp/CustomsToday/2004/May/kidnap.xml.

22. Patricia M. Hoff, *Family Abduction—Prevention and Response* (Alexandria, VA: The National Center for Missing and Exploited Children, 2002), 119.

23. Boudreaux, Lanning, and Lord, "Investigating Potential Child Abduction Cases."

CHAPTER 11

1. "Body of Missing Fla. 11-Year-Old Found," *Court TV News*, February 6, 2004, www.courttv.com/news/2004/0206/abduction_ap.html.

2. "Fla. Mechanic Faces Death Penalty in Girl's Car-Wash Abduction, Murder," *Court TV News*, November 7, 2005, www.courttv.com/trials/brucia/110705_background_ctv.html.

3. "Officials Await Enhanced Images of Girl Whose Abduction from Car Wash Was Videotaped," *Court TV News*, February 4, 2004, www.courttv.com/news/2004/0204/abduction_ap.html.

4. Charles Montaldo, "Joseph Smith Guilty of Carlie Brucia's Murder," *About: Crime/Punishment*, November 17, 2005, http://crime.about.com/b/a/220030.htm.

5. John Springer, "Carlie Brucia's Killer Sentenced to Death," *Court TV News*, March 15, 2006, www.courttv.com/trials/brucia/031506_sentencing_ctv.html.

6. Cybele K. Daley, Speech to Child Abduction Response Team Training Conference, San Diego, CA, January 26, 2006, www.ojp.usdoj.gov/aag/speeches/CART.htm.

7. "Department of Justice Holds First Training Session on Child Abduction Response Teams," U.S. Department of Justice Press Release, January 26, 2006, www.ojp.usdoj.gov/newsroom/pressreleases/2006/OJJDP06033.htm.

8. "Introducing the Child Abduction Rapid Deployment (CARD) Teams," FBI Press Release, June 2006, www.fbi.gov/card/.

9. "When Kids Go Missing," FBI Press Release, June 16, 2006, www.fbi.gov/page2/june06/card_teams061606.htm.

10. Chiancone et al., "The Criminal Justice System's Response to Parental Abduction."

11. Blake Nicholson, "Child Abduction Response Teams Forming in N.D.," *Bismarck Tribune*, April 15, 2007, A-1.

12. David Krajicek, "Eight Minutes in Texas," *Crime Library*, September 2007, www.crimelibrary.com/notorious_murders/famous/amber_hagerman/1_index.html.

13. Jeff Mosier, "After 10 Years, Anguish over Amber's Abduction Still Fresh," *The Dallas Morning News*, January 13, 2006, A-1.

14. David Krajicek, "Sad Tableau," *Crime Library*, September 2007, www.crimelibrary.com/notorious_murders/famous/amber_hagerman/2.html.

15. David Krajicek, "Dead-End Probe," *Crime Library*, September 2007, www.crimelibrary.com/notorious_murders/famous/amber_hagerman/4.html.

16. Steve Pickett, "Lead Amber Hagerman Investigator Retiring," *CBS 11/TXA 21*, February 28, 2007, http://cbs11tv.com/seenon/local_story_059191246.html.

17. Mosier, "After 10 Years, Anguish over Amber's Abduction Still Fresh."

18. "Department of Justice Commemorates National Amber Alert Awareness Day," U.S. Department of Justice Press Release, January 12, 2007, www.earthtimes.org/articles/printpressstory.php?news=43767.

19. Press Release from the National Center for Missing and Exploited Children, January 23, 2007, www.missingkids.com.

20. David Krajicek, "Pressure on Police," *Crime Library*, September 2007, www.crimelibrary.com/notorious_murders/famous/amber_hagerman/8.html.

21. David Krajicek, "An Old Bugaboo," *Crime Library*, September 2007, www.crimelibrary.com/notorious_murders/famous/amber_hagerman/7.html.

22. David Krajicek, "Playing Favorites?" *Crime Library*, September 2007, www.crimelibrary.com/notorious_murders/famous/amber_hagerman/10.html.

23. Krajicek, "Pressure on Police."

24. "Amber Alert FAQs," *CBC News*, August 1, 2006, www.cbc.ca/news/background/missingchildren/amberalert.html.

25. David Krajicek, "Bittersweet Thing," *Crime Library*, September 2007, www.crimelibrary.com/notorious_murders/famous/amber_hagerman/11.html.

26. Kevin Bonsor, "How Amber Alert Works," *How Stuff Works*, September 2007, http://people.howstuffworks.com/amber-alert.htm/printable.

27. Freeman, "International Child Abduction—the Effects."

28. Maier, "State Abandons Kidnapped Kids."

29. Thomas Maier, "Pressure Points," *Newsday.com*, July 17, 2003, www.newsday.com.

30. "Specific Action Plan Needed to Improve Response to Parental Child Abductions."

31. "Federal Response to International Child Abductions."

32. Chiancone, Girdner, and Hoff, "Issues in Resolving Cases of International Child Abduction by Parents."

33. Blomquist et al., "Early Identification of Risk Factors for Parental Abduction."

CHAPTER 12

1. "B.C. Children Escape Abductors after Home Invasion Goes Wrong," *CBC News,* May 8, 2006, www.cbc.ca/canada/story/2006/05/08/burnabyinvasion 05082006.html.

2. "Children's Rescuer Asked, 'What Are You Doing in the Trunk?'" *CBC News,* May 9, 2006, www.cbc.ca/canada/story/2006/05/09/abduction05092006.html ?ref=rss.

3. Robert L. Snow, *The Complete Guide to Personal and Home Safety* (Cambridge, MA: Perseus Publishing, 2002), 47.

4. George Derringer, "'radKids' Course to Teach Kids How to Escape Abduction, Violence," *Swampscott Reporter,* May 20, 2004, www.radkids.org/articles/ 2004052001/.

5. "Girl Abducted, Later Found Walking Alone," *MSNBC.com,* January 27, 2007, www.msnbc.msn.com/id/16838496/.

6. Aisha Sultan, "Abductions Spur Big Turnout for Kiddie IDs," *St. Louis Post-Dispatch,* January 21, 2007, B-1.

7. Interview by author, November 6, 2007.

8. Blomquist et al., "Early Identification of Risk Factors for Parental Abduction."

9. Jon Leyden, "Security Bracelet Foils Child Abduction," *The Register,* July 21, 2005, www.theregister.co.uk/2005/07/21/child_abduction_foiled/.

10. "Keeping Tabs on Babies," *Harris County Hospital District,* April 7, 2007, www.hchdonline.com/about/news/0704/babies.htm.

11. Thomas Maier, "Far from Home," *Newsday.com,* July 13, 2003, www .newsday.com.

12. Interview by author, November 1, 2006.

13. Maier, "Far from Home."

14. "Daring Recovery Just after 9-11," *Zamora.NL,* September 2007, www .zamora.nl/.

15. Interview by author, November 1, 2007.

16. *A Family Resource Guide on International Parental Kidnapping* (Washington, DC: U.S. Government Printing Office, February 2002), 61.

17. "The Outcomes for Children Returned Following an Abduction," *Reunite International Child Abduction Centre,* September 2003, www.reunite.org.

18. Maier, "Pressure Points."

19. Barbara J. Greig, "What We're Doing Now about Child Abduction," *Foreign Service Journal,* November 2000, www.afsa.org/fsj/nov00/greignov.cfm.

20. Interview by author, November 1, 2007.

21. Interview by author, November 1, 2007.

22. Ibid.

23. Chiancone, Girdner, and Hoff, "Issues in Resolving Cases of International Child Abduction by Parents."

24. Interview by author, November 1, 2007.

CHAPTER 13

1. Interview by author, November 2, 2007.

2. Ibid.

3. Cecilie Finkelstein, "My Message to Separating Parents," *Equal Justice,* February 2001, www.equaljustice.ca/cgi-bin/forum.cgi/noframes/read/14456.

4. Cecilie Finkelstein, "Cecilie's Story," *The Link,* 2001, www.parent international.com/.

5. Interview by author, November 2, 2007.

6. Cecilie Finkelstein, "Cecilie," *Take Root,* 2005, www.takeroot.org/missing _side/cecilie_01.php.

7. Interview by author, November 2, 2007.

8. Finkelstein, "Cecilie's Story."

9. Interview by author, November 2, 2007.

10. Finkelstein, "Cecilie's Story."

11. Kathryn M. Turman, *Recovery and Reunification of Missing Children: A Team Approach* (Alexandria, VA: The National Center for Missing and Exploited Children, 1995), 8.

12. Freeman, "International Child Abduction—the Effects."

13. Molly M. Ginty, "Grieving Mothers Become Anti-Abduction Crusaders," *WeNews,* July 26, 2004, www.womensenews.org/article.cfm/dyn/aid/1924/ context/archive.

Bibliography

Acuna, Alicia, Kevin McCarthy, and Liza Porteus. "Colorado Cops Arrest Washington Dad Who Abducted Kids." *FoxNews.com*, March 29, 2007, www.foxnews.com/printer_friendly_story/0,3566,262487,00.html.

"Alert CBP Officer Prevents Child Abduction." *Custom and Border Protection TODAY*, May 2004, www.cbp.gov/xp/CustomsToday/2004/May/kidnap.xml.

Alexander, Brian. "Missing Tacoma Girl's Body Found." *The Seattle Times*, July 13, 2007, A-1.

Allen, Ernest E. "Keeping Children Safe: Rhetoric and Reality." *Juvenile Justice Journal* 1, no. 1 (May 1998).

———. "The Kid Is with a Parent, How Bad Can It Be?" The National Center for Missing and Exploited Children, 1991.

Almedeida, Christina. "Two Teenage Girls Kidnapped in Calif. Are Found Safe." *Associated Press*, August 1, 2002, www.boston.com/news/daily/01/calif_abductions.htm.

"Amber Alerts FAQs." *CBC News*, August 1, 2006, www.cbc.ca/news/background/missingchildren/amberalert.html.

Andriola, Sue. "The Impact of Child Abduction." *Journal of Employee Assistance*, December 2004.

Ankrom, Larry G., and Cynthia J. Lent. "Cradle Robbers: A Study of the Infant Abductor." *FBI Law Enforcement Bulletin*, September 1995, 17.

Argetsinger, Amy, and Katherine Shaver. "Police: Father Staged Carjacking, Killed Son." *Washington Post*, September 10, 1999, A-1.

"Avila's Old Lawyer Says He's Rethinking Career." *CNN.com*, July 26, 2002, http://archives.cnn.com/2002/LAW/07/26/avila.acquittal.reax/index.html.

"Baby's Abductor Fell Victim to Obsession." *Associated Press*, March 18, 2007, www.msnbc.msn.com/id/17680125.

Bartelstone, Susan. "How to Help Safely!" *The Safety Solutions Company*, January 2008, www.dearsafetysolutions.com.

"B.C. Children Escape Abductors after Home Invasion Goes Wrong." *CBC News*, May 8, 2006, www.cbc.ca/canada/story/2006/05/08/burnabyinvasion05082006.html.

Beasley, James O., and Kristen R. Beyer. "Nonfamily Child Abductors Who Murder Their Victims." *Journal of Interpersonal Violence* 18, no. 10 (2003): 1167–88.

"Biological Mother Arrested in Kidnapping of Her Adopted Baby." *CNN.com*, July 22, 2007, www.cnn.com/2007/US/07/22/baby.kidnapped.ap/index.html.

Bishop, Darla. "Ease Up on Abducted Boy." *The Sheboygan Press,* January 23, 2007, B-3.

Blaney, Betsy. "Missing Baby Found, Alleged Abductor Held." *Associated Press,* June 6, 2006, www.boston.com.

Blomquist, Martha-Elin, Linda K. Girdner, Janet R. Johnson, and Inger Sagatun-Edwards. "Early Identification of Risk Facts for Parental Abduction." U.S. Department of Justice, March 2001, www.ncjrs.gov/html/ojjdp/2001_3_1/contents.html.

"Body of Missing Fla. 11-Year-Old Found." *Court TV News,* February 6, 2004, www.courttv.com/news/2004/0206/abduction_ap.html.

Bonsor, Kevin. "How Amber Alert Works." *How Stuff Works,* September 2007, http://people.howstuffworks.com/amber-alert.htm/printable.

Boudreaux, Monique C., Kenneth V. Lanning, and Wayne D. Lord. "Investigating Potential Child Abduction Cases." *FBI Law Enforcement Bulletin,* April 2001, 2, 8.

"Boy Tries to Reconnect with Old Life after 4 Years." *CNN.com,* January 15, 2007, www.cnn.com/2007/US/01/15/missouri.boys/index.html.

Bragg, Rick. "Insanity Plea Expected in Boy's Drownings." *The New York Times,* November 9, 1994, www.nytimes.com.

"Bronx Mother Charged with Murder after Lying about Infant Abduction." *NY1,* April 30, 2007, www.ny1.com/ny1/content/index.jsp?stid=12&aid=65742.

Brown, Katherine M., Robert D. Keppel, Marvin E. Skeen, and Joseph G. Weis. "Case Management for Missing Children Homicide Investigations." Office of the Attorney General, Olympia, WA, May 2006.

Brown, Kirsten. "Frustrated Fathers of Abducted Children Turn to Public for Support." *Japan Children's Rights Network,* December 15, 2006, www.crnjapan.com/articles/2006/en/20061215-fatherspublicsupport.html.

Brumley, Jeff. "Grandmother Blames Failed Legal System in Boy's Death." *The Florida Times-Union,* March 20, 2007, A-1.

Bruno, Anthony. "A Bunch of Cracked-Out Individuals." *Crime Library,* April 2007, www.crimelibrary.com/serial_killers/predators/jessica_lunsford/4.html.

Buedel, Matt. "Peoria Girls Caught Up in Custody Battle Found with Religious Sect in Belize." *Peoria Journal Star,* May 2, 2006, A-1.

Burgess, Ann Wolbert. "Infant Abduction: A Family Crisis." *Nursing Spectrum,* 2000, 294.

Burgess, Ann Wolbert, and Kenneth V. Lanning. "An Analysis of Infant Abductions." The National Center for Missing and Exploited Children, 1995, www.missingkids.com.

———. "An Analysis of Infant Abductions, Second Edition." The National Center for Missing and Exploited Children, July 2003, www.missingkids.com.

Campos-Flores, Arian. "Crime: Living with Evil." *Newsweek,* January 29, 2007.

———. "The Saga of the Kidnapped Missouri Boys." *Newsweek,* January 29, 2007.

Campos-Flores, Arian, and Ellen Harris. "What Made the Captive Boy Stay?" *Newsweek,* January 17, 2007.

Candiotti, Susan. "Accused Texas Baby Snatcher Arraigned." *CNN.com*, August 15, 2002, www.cnn.com/2002/LAW/08/15/texas.abduction.arraignment/ index.html.

Carver, Joseph M. "Love and Stockholm Syndrome: The Mystery of Loving an Abuser." *Counselling Resource*, August 23, 2007, http://counsellingresource .com/quizzes/stockholm/index.html.

"Case of Missing Boys Stands Out." *USA Today*, January 13, 2007, www .usatoday.com.

Castaneda, Ruben. "Mom Turns Own Tragedy into Career of Advocacy." *Washington Post*, July 5, 2006, B-1.

"Charles Feldman: Police Fear Sexual Predator." *CNN.com*, July 18, 2002, http:// archives.cnn.com/2002/US/07/18/feldman.otsc/index.html.

Chiancone, Janet L., Linda Girdner, and Patricia Hoff. "Issues in Resolving Cases of International Child Abduction by Parents." *Juvenile Justice Bulletin*, U.S. Department of Justice, December 2001.

Chiancone, Janet L., Frances Gragg, Kathi L. Grasso, Joseph F. Ryan, Dana Shultz, and Andrea J. Sedlak. "The Criminal Justice System's Response to Parental Abduction." U.S. Department of Justice, December 2001, www.ncjrs.gov.

"Children's Rescuer Asked, 'What Are You Doing in the Trunk?'" *CBC News*, May 9, 2006, www.cbc.ca/canada/story/2006/05/09/abduction05092006.html ?ref=rss.

Clayson, Jane. "Was Elizabeth's Cousin Next?" *CBS News*, March 14, 2003, www.cbsnews.com/stories/2003/03/15/national/printable544135.shtml.

"CNN Larry King Live." *CNN.com*, August 1, 2002, http://transcripts.cnn.com/ TRANSCRIPTS/0208/01/lkl.00.html.

Cohen, Sharon. "In Mo., Shawn Comes Home a Different Boy." *Associated Press*, January 18, 2007.

"Cops: Killer Left His 'Calling Card.'" *FoxNews.com*, July 18, 2002, www.foxnews .com/printer_friendly_story/0,3566,57900,00.html.

Crary, David. "Solid Data Scarce for Child Abductions." *Associated Press*, January 19, 2007, www.foxnews.com.

Crofton, C., Roxane Silver, and Camille Wortman. "The Role of Coping in Support Provision: The Self-Presentational Dilemma of Victims of Life Crises." In *Social Support: An Interactional View*, edited by Gregory R. Pierce, Barbara R. Sarason, and Irwin G. Sarason, 397–426. New York: Wiley & Sons, 1990 .

Curless, Erica, and Susan Drumheller. "Victims in CdA Homicide Were Bludgeoned." *SpokesmanReview.com*, May 20, 2005, www.spokesmanreview.com/ sections/duncan/?ID=70581.

"DA: Suspect Confessed to Snatching Boy, 13." *CNN.com*, January 18, 2007, www.cnn.com/2007/LAW/01/18/devlin.hearing/index.html.

"Dad Abducts 2-Hour-Old Baby from Hospital." *CBS 2—KCAL 9*, March 6, 2007, http://cbs2.com/.

Daley, Cybele K. Speech to Child Abduction Response Team Training Conference, San Diego, CA, January 26, 2006, www.ojp.usdoj.gov/aag/speeches/ CART.htm.

Dalley, Marlene L., and Jenna Ruscoe. "The Abduction of Children by Strangers in Canada: Nature and Scope." Royal Canadian Mounted Police, December 1, 2003, www.ourmissingchildren.gc.ca/omc/publications/002/abduction_e.htm.

"Daring Recovery Just after 9-11." *Zamora.NL,* September 2007, www.zamora.nl/.

Dean, Suellen E., and Ralph Greer, Jr. "We Are Not Ruling Out Anything." *Spartanburg Herald-Journal,* October 29, 1994, www.teleplex.net/shj/smith/ninedays/hunt.html.

"Death for Man Who Murdered Runnion." *CBS News,* July 22, 2005, www.cbsnews.com/stories/2005/07/22/national/printable711061.shtml.

"Department of Justice Commemorates National Amber Alert Awareness Day." U.S. Department of Justice Press Release, January 12, 2007, www.earthtimes.org/articles/printpressstory.php?news=43767.

"Department of Justice Holds First Training Session on Child Abduction Response Teams." U.S. Department of Justice Press Release, January 26, 2006, www.ojp.usdoj.gov/newsroom/pressreleases/2006/OJJDP06033.htm.

Derringer, George. "'radKids' Course to Teach Kids How to Escape Abduction, Violence." *Swampscott Reporter,* May 20, 2004, www.radkids.org/articles/2004052001.

"Devlin Faces Child Porn Charges." *MSNBC.com,* March 1, 2007, www.msnbc.msn.com/id/17404404/.

Dewey, Donald. "The Stockholm Syndrome." *Scandinavian Review,* Spring 2007.

Diagnostic and Statistical Manual of Mental Disorders. Washington, DC: American Psychiatric Association, 2000.

Driscoll, Gwendolyn. "Avila Jury Foreman Speaks." *Orange County Register,* May 16, 2005, www.ocregister.com/ocr/sections/breaking_news/article_517302.php.

"Elizabeth Smart Found Alive." *CNN.com,* March 12, 2003, www.cnn.com/2003/US/West/03/12/smart.kidnapping.

"Elizabeth Smart Found Alive Nine Months after Vanishing from Utah Home." *CourtTVNews,* March 12, 2003, www.courttv.com/news/2003/0312/smart_ap.html.

"Elizabeth Smart Talks about Her 9-Month Kidnapping." *NBCSandiego.com,* May 5, 2006, www.nbcsandiego.com/news/9169424/detail.html?rss=dgo&psp=news.

"Executive Summary—Case Management for Missing Children Homicide Investigation." U.S. Department of Justice, May 1997, www.ojjdp.ncjrs.org.

"Families Revel in Sons' Safe Return." *MSNBC.com,* January 13, 2007, www.msnbc.msn.com/id/16607683/.

A Family Resource Guide on International Parental Kidnapping. Washington, DC: U.S. Government Printing Office, February 2002, 61.

Faulkner, Nancy. "Parental Child Abduction Is Child Abuse." Paper presented to the United Nations Convention on Child Rights, June 9, 1999.

Faville, Andrea. "Hidden in Plain Sight." *Newsweek,* January 21, 2007.

"Federal Response to International Child Abductions." U.S. General Accounting Office, October 14, 1999, 1–2.

Finkelhor, David, Heather Hammer, and Andrea J. Sedlak. *National Incidence Studies of Missing, Abducted, Runaway, and Thrownaway Children.* U.S. Department of Justice, October 2002, www.ojjdp.ncjrs.org.

Finkelhor, David, Gerald T. Hotaling, and Peggy S. Plass. "Police Response to Family Abduction Episodes." *Crime and Delinquency,* 1995, 205–17.

Finkelhor, David, Gerald T. Hotaling, and Andrea J. Sedlak. "Missing, Abducted, Runaway, and Thrownaway Children in America, First Report: Numbers and Characteristics." U.S. Department of Justice, 1990.

Finkelstein, Cecilie. "Cecilie." *Take Root,* 2005, www.takeroot.org/missing_side/cecilie_01.php.

———. "Cecilie's Story." *The Link,* 2001, www.parentinternational.com/link/issue1.htm (accessed October 4, 2007).

———. "My Message to Separating Parents." *Equal Justice,* February 2001, www.equaljustice.ca/cgi-bin/forum.cgi/noframes/read/14456.

"Fla. Mechanic Faces Death Penalty in Girl's Car-Wash Abduction, Murder." *Court TV News,* November 7, 2005, www.courttv.com/trials/brucia/110705_background_ctv.html.

Forehand, Rex, Nicholas Long, Elizabeth Parrish, and Carolyn Zogg. "Child Abduction: Parent and Child Functioning Following Return." *Clinical Pediatrics* 28, no. 7 (1989): 311–16.

Freeman, Marilyn. "International Child Abduction—the Effects." The Reunite Research Unit, May 2006.

"French Commandos Storm Cult Compound, Free 12-Year-Old." *Associated Press,* August 6, 2007, www.foxnews.com/printer_friendly_story/0,3566,292266,00.html.

Garza, Cynthia Leonor, Michael Glenn, and Kevin Moran. "Taser Used on Dad Leaving Houston Hospital with Baby." *Houston Chronicle,* April 16, 2007, www.chron.com.

Gedda, George. "Abducted Children: Should State Do More?" *Foreign Service Journal,* November 2000, www.afsa.org/fsj/Nov00/geddanov.cfm.

Geranios, Nicholas K. "Idaho Murder/Abduction Suspect Allegedly Staked Out Home." *Associated Press,* July 13, 2005, www.lineofduty.com.

Ginty, Molly M. "Grieving Mothers Become Anti-abduction Crusaders." *WeNews,* July 26, 2004, www.womensenews.org/article.cfm/dyn/aid/1924/context/archive.

"Girl Abducted, Later Found Walking Alone." *MSNBC.com,* January 27, 2007, www.msnbc.msn.com/id/16838496/.

Gladstone, Toba, Barry Nurcombe, and Neil Senior. "Child Snatching: A Case Report." *Journal of the American Academy of Child Psychiatry,* 1982, 579–83.

"Grandmother Reunited with Abducted Children." *CNN.com,* July 1, 2003, www.cnn.com/2003/US/South/07/01/amber.alert/index.html.

Greif, Geoffrey L., and Rebecca L. Hegar. *When Parents Kidnap: The Families Behind the Headlines.* New York: The Free Press, 1993, 147.

Greig, Barbara J. "Helping to Reunite Families: The Office of Children's Issues." *Foreign Service Journal,* April 2003, 59.

———. "What We're Doing Now about Child Abduction." *Foreign Service Journal,* November 2000, www.afsa.org/fsj/nov00/greignov.cfm.

"The Hague Convention on the Civil Aspects of International Child Abduction," May 2007, http://patriot.net/~crouch/haguetext.html.

Hall, John. "Avila Guilty of Killing Samantha Runnion." *NC Times,* April 28, 2005, A-1.

Hanfland, Kenneth A., Robert D. Keppel, and Joseph G. Weis. "Case Management for Missing Children Homicide Cases." Office of the Attorney General, Olympia, WA, May 1997.

Harty, Maura. "International Parental Child Abduction Prevention Act." Testimony before Congressional Committee, July 9, 2003, www.state.gov/r/pa/ei/othertstmy/32994.htm.

Haynes, V. Dion, and Vincent J. Schodolski. "Captive Girl's Actions Hint at Brainwashing." *Chicago Tribune*, March 15, 2003, A-1.

"Hearst: Elizabeth May Face Future Trauma." *CNN.com*, March 13, 2003, www.cnn.com/2003/US/West/03/13/life.after.kidnapping.

"History of Troubles Preceded Plane Crash." *Indianapolis Star*, March 8, 2007, B-4.

Hixon, Marion. "Elizabeth Smart Will 'Never Be the Same.'" *People*, July 28, 2006, www.people.com/people/article/0,26334,1220083,00.html.

Hoff, Patricia M. *Family Abduction—Prevention and Response*. Alexandria, VA: The National Center for Missing and Exploited Children, 2002, 119.

Holland, Elizabethe. "A Child Abductee's Journey Back." *St. Louis Post-Dispatch*, January 20, 2007, A-1.

———. "Questions Linger after Boys' Rescue." *St. Louis Post-Dispatch*, January 15, 2007, A-1.

Huntington, Dorothy. "Parental Kidnapping: A New Form of Child Abuse." In *Investigation and Prosecution of Parental Abduction*. Alexandria, VA: American Prosecutors Research Institute, 1995.

Hustmyre, Chuck. "George Edenfield Says 'Devil' Made Him Kill Christopher Barrios." *Crime Library*, March 22, 2007, www.crimelibrary.com/news/original/0307/2202_barrios.html.

"Idaho Suspect Has Violent History." *MSNBC.com*, July 6, 2005, www.msnbc.msn.com/id/8485031/.

"Insight." *CNN.com*, January 16, 2007, http://transcripts.cnn.com/TRANSCRIPTS/0701/16/i_ins.01.html.

"International Child Abduction." U.S. State Department, January 2007, http://travel.state.gov/family/abduction/abduction_580.html.

"Introducing the Child Abduction Rapid Deployment (CARD) Teams." FBI Press Release, June 2006, www.fbi.gov/card/.

James, Susan Donaldson. "Baby Abductors: Typically Manipulative, Clever, and Even Kind." *ABC News*, March 13, 2007, http://abcnews.go.com/print?id=2946697.

"Jessica Lunsford." *America's Most Wanted*, March 19, 2005, www.amw.com/missing_children/recovered.cfm?id=30448.

Johnson, Gene. "Tacoma Police Look at Abduction Suspect for Other Disappearances." *Associated Press*, July 13, 2007, www.columbian.com/printArticle.cfm?story=167608.

"Keeping Tabs on Babies." *Harris County Hospital District*, April 7, 2007, www.hchdonline.com/about/news/0704/babies.htm.

"Kidnapped Baby Ends Up at Home of Aunt's Friend." *Associated Press*, July 23, 2007, www.journalnow.com.

"Kidnapped Philadelphia Girl Breaks Free." *CNN.com*, July 23, 2002, http://archives.cnn.com/2002/US/07/23/philadelphia.girl/index.html.

"Kidnapper: Boy Persuaded Me Not to Kill Him." *MSNBC.com*, October 9, 2007, www.msnbc.msn.com/id/21206715/?GT1=10450.

Klass, Dennis. *Parental Grief: Solace and Resolution*. New York: Springer, 1988.

Krajicek, David. "Bittersweet Thing." *Crime Library*, September 2007, www
.crimelibrary.com/notorious_murders/famous/amber_hagerman/11.html.
———. "Dead-End Probe." *Crime Library*, September 2007, www.crimelibrary.com/
notorious_murders/famous/amber_hagerman/4.html.
———. "Eight Minutes in Texas." *Crime Library*, September 2007, www
.crimelibrary.com/notorious_murders/famous/amber_hagerman/1_index
.html.
———. "An Old Bugaboo." *Crime Library*, September 2007, www.crimelibrary
.com/notorious_murders/ famous/amber_hagerman/7.html.
———. "Playing Favorites?" *Crime Library*, September 2007, www.crimelibrary
.com/notorious_murders/famous/amber_hagerman/10.html.
———. "Pressure on Police." *Crime Library*, September 2007, www.crimelibrary
.com/notorious_murders/famous/amber_hagerman/8.html.
———. "Sad Tableau." *Crime Library*, September 2007, www.crimelibrary.com/
notorious_murders/famous/amber_hagerman/2.html.
Lanning, Kenneth V. "Child Molesters Who Abduct: Summary of the Case in
Point Series." The National Center for Missing and Exploited Children, 1995,
17–36.
Leonard, Christopher. "Life Term in Teenage Mo. Boy's Abduction." *Associated Press*,
October 8, 2007, www.kansascity.com/449/v-print/story/307877.html.
Leyden, Jon. "Security Bracelet Foils Child Abduction." *The Register*, July 21, 2005,
www.theregister.co.uk/2005/07/21/child_abduction_foiled/.
Lowe, Nigel. "International Forum on Parental Child Abduction: Hague Convention
Action Agenda." Report from Conference held September 15–16, 1998.
Maier, Thomas. "Coming to America." *Newsday.com*, July 18, 2003, www
.newsday.com.
———. "Far from Home." *Newsday.com*, July 13, 2003, www.newsday.com.
———. "Far from Heaven." *Newsday.com*, July 16, 2003, www.newsday.com.
———. "Pressure Points." *Newsday.com*, July 17, 2003, www.newsday.com.
Maier, Timothy W. "State Abandons Kidnapped Kids." *Insight on the News*, June 14,
1999.
"Man Arrested in Abduction of Florida Boy, 13." *CNN.com*, March 7, 2007,
www.cnn.com/2007/US/03/07/florida.abduction/index.html.
"Man Charged with Murder in Samantha Case." *CNN.com*, July 22, 2002, http://
archives.cnn.com/2002/US/07/22/girl.abducted/index.html.
Marquez, Jeremiah. "Judge Formally Sentences Samantha Runnion's Killer to
Death." *Associated Press*, July 22, 2005, www.northcountytimes.com.
McCarthy, Terry. "The Playtime Killer." *Time*, July 21, 2002, www.time.com/time/
printout/0,8816,322651,00.html.
"Medical Encyclopedia." National Institute of Health, July 28, 2007, www.nlm
.nih.gov/medlineplus/ency/article/001553.htm.
*Missing and Abducted Children: A Law Enforcement Guide to Case Investigation and
Program Management*. Alexandria, VA: The National Center for Missing and
Exploited Children, 2000.
"Missing Children Are Found Unharmed." *Associated Press*, July 1, 2003,
www.sptimes.com/2003/07/01/news_pf/State/Missing_children_are_.shtml.
"Missing 5-Day-Old Girl Found in Texas." *CNN.com*, June 5, 2006, www.cnn.com/
2006/US/06/05/missing.baby.

Mitchell, Tim. "Father's Child Abduction Trial Gets Underway." *The News-Gazette*, October 13, 2006, A-1.

"Mo. Kidnap Suspect Eyed in Another Case." *MSNBC.com*, January 17, 2007, www.msnbc.msn.com/id/16674715/GT1=8921.

"Molester, Parents Charged with Murder." *Associated Press*, March 21, 2007, www.msnbc.msn.com/id/17722385/.

Montaldo, Charles. "Joseph Smith Guilty of Carlie Brucia's Murder." *About: Crime and Punishment*, November 17, 2005, http://crime.about.com/b/a/220030.htm.

Mosier, Jeff. "After 10 Years, Anguish over Amber's Abduction Still Fresh." *The Dallas Morning News*, January 13, 2006, A-1.

"Mother of Abducted Kids Sentenced." *ABC7News.com*, July 19, 2003, http://abclocalgo.com/kgo/story?section=News&id=1899320&ft=print.

Nahirny, Cathy, and Ann Schofield. "Keeping the Youngest Patients Safe." *Minority Nurse.com*, August 2, 2005, www.minoritynurse.com/features/health/08-02-05f.html.

National Center for Missing and Exploited Children. Abduction report made available to law enforcement personnel, 2001.

Nelson, Paul. "It's Been Five Years Since Elizabeth Smart Was Abducted." *KSL.com*, June 5, 2007, www.ksl.com/index.php?nid=481&sid=1308694.

"New Details Arise on Captive Austrian Girl's Life." *Associated Press*, August 29, 2006, www.msnbc.msn.com/id/14555654/.

"Next for Avila: Death or Life in Prison?" *NC Times*, April 29, 2005, A-1.

Nicholson, Blake. "Child Abduction Response Teams Forming in N.D." *Bismarck Tribune*, April 15, 2007, A-1.

"NISMART Bulletin: National Estimates of Missing Children: An Overview." U.S. Department of Justice, October 2002, www.ncjrs.gov/html/ojjdp/nismart/01/ns4.html.

O'Beirne, Kate. "Without Their Daughters: The Outrage of Child Abduction and U.S. Complacency." *National Review*, May 20, 2002.

"Official: Nurse Imposter Snatches Ill Newborn." *CNN.com*, March 10, 2007, www.cnn.com/2007/US/03/10/newborn.kidnapped/index.html.

"Officials Await Enhanced Images of Girl Whose Abduction from Car Wash Was Videotaped." *Court TV News*, February 4, 2004, www.courttv.com/news/2004/0204/abduction_ap.html.

"The Outcomes for Children Returned Following an Abduction." *Reunite International Child Abduction Centre*, September 2003, www.reunite.org.

Ove, Torsten. "Web Cops Tighten Net on Sex Offenders." *Rocky Mountain News*, July 17, 2006, www.rockymountainnews.com/drmn/tech/article/0,2777,DRMN_23910_4848932,00.html.

"Parents: Abducted Mo. Boy Ready to Help Others." *MSNBC.com*, January 19, 2007, www.msnbc.msn.com/id/16690284/.

Perez, Mabel. "Couey Found Guilty." *Ocala Star-Banner*, March 8, 2007, A-1.

Pergament, Rachel. "The Big Lie." *Crime Library*, August 2007, www.crimelibrary.com/notorious_murders/famous/smith/lie_6.html.

———. "The Investigation." *Crime Library*, August 2007, www.crimelibrary.com/notorious_murders/famous/smith/invest_7.html.

"'Personal Goodbye' for Runnion Family." *CBS News*, July 26, 2002, www.cbsnews.com/stories/2002/07/16/national/printable515287.shtml.

"Philly Family Rejoices over Girl's Return." *CNN.com,* July 24, 2002, http://archives.cnn.com/2002/US/07/24/philadelphia.girl/index.html.

Pickett, Steve. "Lead Amber Hagerman Investigator Retiring." *CBS 11/TXA 21,* February 28, 2007, http://cbs11tv.com/seenon/local_story_059191246.html.

"Police: Kidnapping Suspect Was 'Brazen.'" *MSNBC.com,* January 13, 2007, www.msnbc.msn.com/id/16612257/.

"Police Using Hallucination Machine as Training Tool." *Associated Press,* March 25, 2006.

Porteus, Liza. "Police: Suspect's Father, Friend 'Confessed' to Burying Missing Boy, But There's No Body." *FoxNews.com,* March 15, 2007, www.foxnews.com/story/0,2933,258710,00.html.

———. "Washington Mom Pleads with Ex-Husband to Return Abducted Kids." *FoxNews.com,* March 29, 2007, www.foxnews.com/printer_friendly_story/0,3566,262340,00.html.

Press Release from the National Center for Missing and Exploited Children, January 23, 2007, www.missingkids.com.

"Prosecutor: Men Molested, Killed Ga. Boy." *Associated Press,* March 22, 2007, www.msnbc.msn.com/id/17739868/.

Reitmeyer, John, and Elsie Young. "Suspects' Use of Social Sites Raises Concerns." *NorthJersey.com,* October 5, 2007, www.northjersey.com.

Reschke, Kathy L. "Keeping Children Safe from Abduction by Strangers." *Family Tapestries,* 2002, http://ohioline.osu.edu/flm02/FS17.html.

Rigler, William, and Harold L. Wieder. "The Epidemic of Parental Child-Snatching: An Overview," 2001, http://travel.state.gov/family/abduction/resources/resources_545.html.

Salter, Jim. "Boy Might Have Given Clues to His Abduction." *Indianapolis Star,* January 16, 2007, A-2.

"Samantha's Mom: 'Little Room for Anger.'" *CNN.com,* July 26, 2002, http://archives.cnn.com/2002/US/07/26/lkl.erin.runnion/index.html.

Sander, Libby, and Susan Saulny. "Soul-Searching by Missouri Suspect's Neighbors." *The New York Times,* January 21, 2007, www.nytimes.com.

Schneider, Eckhard, and Ingrid Sischy. *Jeff Koons.* Koln, Germany: Taschen, 2007.

Schneider, Rob. "Pilot in Fatal Crash Called Bitter, Caring." *Indianapolis Star,* March 7, 2007, A-1.

"Seven-Year-Old Philadelphia Girl Escapes Abduction." *Jet,* August 12, 2002.

"Shawn Hornbeck Makes Appearance at Foundation's Fundraiser." *4kmov.com,* July 20, 2007, www.kmov.com.

"Sheriff to Killer: 'We Are Coming after You.'" *CNN.com,* July 17, 2002, http://archives.cnn.com/2002/US/07/17/girl.abducted/index.html.

"Sheriff '100 Percent Certain' Avila Killed Calif. Girl." *NBC4.tv,* July 19, 2002, www.knbc.com/sh/news/stories/nat-news-156702220020719-070714.html.

"Sheriff: '100 Percent Certain' Suspect Killed Samantha." *CNN.com,* July 19, 2002, http://archives.cnn.com/2002/US/07/19/girl.abducted/index.html.

Simpson, Barbara. "Get 'em and Burn 'em!" *KSFO 560,* July 22, 2002, www.worldnetdaily.com/news/article.asp?ARTICLE_ID=28360.

———. "The Lost Boys of Missouri." *WorldNetDaily,* January 15, 2007, www.worldnetdaily.com/news/article.asp?ARTICLE_ID=53768.

"Slow Climb Back to Normal Life for Austrian Kidnapping Survivor." *San Francisco Chronicle,* August 30, 2006, www.sfgate.com/cgi-bin/blogs/sfgate/category ?blogid=15&cat=889.

"Suspect's Blog Showed Malicious Thoughts," *Associated Press,* July 7, 2005, www.msnbc.msn.com/id/8500603/.

Snow, Robert L. *The Complete Guide to Personal and Home Safety.* Cambridge, MA: Perseus Publishing, 2002, 47.

"Specific Action Plan Needed to Improve Response to Parental Child Abductions." U.S. General Accounting Office, March 2000, 8.

Springer, John. "Carlie Brucia's Killer Sentenced to Death." *Court TV News,* March 15, 2006, www.courttv.com/trials/brucia/031506_sentencing_ctv.html.

Stacy, Mitch. "Pin for Torn Jacket Was Teen's Salvation." *Washingtonpost.com,* February 27, 2007, www.washingtonpost.com.

Strohman, Lisa Kathleen. "Stranger Infant Abductions: Offense Characteristics, Victim Selection, and Offender Motivation of Female Offenders," Ph.D. Thesis submitted to Drexel University, May 2005, 42.

Sultan, Aisha. "Abductions Spur Big Turnout for Kiddie IDs." *St. Louis Post-Dispatch,* January 21, 2007, B-1.

Terr, Lenore C. "Child Snatching: A New Epidemic of an Ancient Malady." *Journal of Pediatrics* 103 (1983): 151–56.

Testimony of Ernie Allen before the Senate Subcommittee on Criminal Justice Oversight, October 27, 1999.

"Then and Now: Elizabeth Smart." *CNN.com,* November 4, 2005, www.cnn.com/ 2005/US/11/04/cnn25.smart.tan/.

Thompson, Jenni. "The Secret Truth about Child Abduction." *San Francisco Chronicle,* March 11, 2004, B-9.

"Thousands Attend Funeral of Samantha Runnion." *Associated Press,* July 25, 2002, www.foxnews.com/printer_friendly_story/0,3566,58680,00.html.

"Translation of Natascha Kampusch's Letter." *TimesOnLine,* August 28, 2006, www.timesonline.co.uk/tol/news/world/europe/article621640.ece?print=yes.

Turman, Kathryn M. *Recovery and Reunification of Missing Children: A Team Approach.* Alexandria, VA: The National Center for Missing and Exploited Children, 1995, 8.

"Two Children Taken by Bipolar Mother Found Safe." *CNN.com,* July 1, 2003, http://transcripts.cnn.com/TRANSCRIPTS/0307/01/ltm.10.html.

Webby, Sean. "Child Abduction Unit among Best in State." *Oakland Tribune,* November 30, 2006, B-1.

"When Kids Go Missing." FBI Press Release, June 16, 2006, www.fbi.gov/page2/ june06/card_tcams061606.htm.

Wittenauer, Cheryl. "Teen's Parents Suspect Abuse." *Indianapolis Star,* January 19, 2007, A-3.

Wolf, Ryan. "Father Charged with Kidnapping Today." *KGBT4,* January 10, 2007, www.team4news.com/global/story.asp?s=5909273&ClientType=Printable.

Worden, Amy. "Feds: Foreign Courts Soft on Parental Abductions." *APBNews.com,* September 13, 2000, http://news.findlaw.com/apbnews/s/20000913/ apbabduction.html.

www.icps.20m.com/custom4.html.

www.nimh.nih.gov.

Index

About the Author

ROBERT L. SNOW is a retired Commander of the Homicide Branch in the Indianapolis Police Department. He is the author of many books including *Deadly Cults, Murder 101, Sex Crimes Investigation, Technology and Law Enforcement,* and others. He has published more than 100 articles and short stories in such national magazines as *Playboy, Reader's Digest,* the *National Enquirer, Police Magazine,* and others.

DATE DUE

FEB 23		
FEB 2 2 2010		
FEB 0 7 2012		

Demco